More praise for *The Road to Dawn*

"*The Road to Dawn* tells the story of a courageous man who pursued the common good in spite of painful wounds, discouraging setbacks, and personal flaws. Josiah's winsome character and role within the broader abolitionist context keep us turning the page, as does Jared Brock's fine storytelling about this American storyteller. And these stories remind us that we have much to learn from those who embody the message of justice and mercy, whatever their flaws or fortune may be."

—Timothy B. Tyson, Senior Research Scholar at the Center for Documentary Studies at Duke University, author of *The Blood of Emmett Till* and *Blood Done Sign My Name*

"Finally, a biography worthy of the man. *The Road to Dawn* elevates Josiah Henson to his rightful place among important international liberators and frees him from the grip of 'Uncle Tom.' Black history, when properly told will transform your life and your thinking."

—Cheryl Janifer LaRoche, PhD author of *Free Black Communities and the Underground Railroad*

"*The Road to Dawn* expertly casts Josiah Henson's heroic struggle for emancipation against the backdrop of a national fight for freedom, and in doing so, re-introduces a vital character to American history."

—Jamie Glavic, National Underground Railroad Freedom Center

"*The Road to Dawn* is a deeply moving and inspirational biography of a little-known Underground Railroad hero. Jared Brock does a fabulous job of bringing Josiah Henson to life. A must-read for *everyone*."

—Janice Wilson, Charles County NAACP President

"Josiah Henson comes to life in Jared Brock's ground-breaking biography on one of the most famous figures of the nineteenth century. *The Road to Dawn* will ensure that Henson's story is never lost again."

—Michael Nardolilli, Executive Director, Montgomery Parks Foundation

"Jared Brock's remarkable *The Road to Dawn* is an important antidote to the sanitized (and very white) version of American emancipation and reconstruction. While the life of Josiah Henson was the inspiration for *Uncle Tom's Cabin*, it was very much more than that. Henson was a liberator, leader, thinker, organizer, and prophet, and we should ask why he was displaced from his proper place in the history of abolition. Brock gives us a key to a crucial component of antislavery's usable past, the unvarnished lessons that will help guide today's efforts to bring slavery to an end."

—Kevin Bales CMG, Pulitzer Prize–nominee and Professor of Contemporary Slavery at the University of Nottingham's School of Politics and International Relations

"Harriet Tubman [and] Frederick Douglass are well known figures in the abolition of slavery. Josiah Henson was less known. Here was a man who had spent more than 40 years in slavery but promised to use his freedom well. He delivered on that promise. Jared A. Brock takes us through the life of a hero of the abolitionist era who overcame unspeakable pain and adversity to make an impact on his home country. A must read."

—Ameenah Gurib-Fakim, President of the Republic of Mauritius

"Authoritatively researched and meticulous in its detail, *The Road to Dawn* captures the fierce determination and undeniable presence of one of Canada's extraordinary pioneers for freedom and social justice. Jared Brock's passionate narration enhances Josiah Henson's rightful place as a figure of national historic significance."

—Steven Cook, Curator, Uncle Tom's Cabin Historic Site

"Jared Brock brings to life the struggles and perseverance of a man almost forgotten in history. This well-researched book documents the life of Josiah Henson, whose experiences in Maryland, his escape to Canada, and his work on the Underground Railroad reveal a man of incredible fortitude and determination." —Maryland Senator Thomas M. Middleton

"*The Road to Dawn* re-introduces the world to a man whose life story fueled the abolition movement in 19th-century America. In doing so, Jared Brock issues a clarion call to readers to stand for the oppressed, right now as never before. His timing couldn't be better."

—Julia A. King, Professor of Anthropology at
St. Mary's College of Maryland

"Josiah Henson suffered more than forty years at the hands of unbelievable cruelty and violence, yet went on to impact the world in profoundly important ways. As a personal survivor of modern day slavery, I heartily endorse *The Road to Dawn*'s inspirational message of hope, justice, and reconciliation."

—Toshia Shaw, Purple W.I.N.G.S

"Josiah Henson's riveting life story challenges us to fight injustice and never despair. Thanks to *The Road to Dawn*, a local hero has finally re-appeared on the international stage."

—Maryland Senator William C. Smith, Jr.

"I learned additional history of the fight for freedom by reading Jared Brock's book, *The Road to Dawn*. I now know that Josiah Henson was a courageous trail blazer and a pioneer for our people seeking freedom in a new world into which they were enslaved."

—Gerald A. Stansbury, Maryland State Conference
NAACP President

"*The Road to Dawn* is an engaging and accessible biography of Josiah Henson, a forgotten hero of abolitionist history whose freedom narrative inspired Stowe's internationally famous antislavery novel *Uncle Tom's Cabin*. Brock has brought to light the powerful experiences which shaped Henson's life and fight for freedom."

—Beth Burgess, Harriet Beecher Stowe Center

"The story of Josiah Henson is beyond fascinating . . . a must read in the telling of slave history, American history, and the interconnectedness of American, Canadian, and British links to slavery and freedom. Henson's story is beyond the savagery of an institution that sought to maim, suppress, and even destroy a people, but about resistance, triumph and recovery. *The Road to Dawn* is able to capture that story through Josiah Henson's trials, tribulations, and ultimate triumph from slavery to freedom. More importantly, *The Road to Dawn* separates myth from fact, the myth of 'Uncle Tom' and the reality of Josiah Henson and all that he accomplished, in slavery and in freedom. His story is worthy of being told."

—Mamie E. Locke, Professor of Political
Science at Hampton University

THE ROAD
TO DAWN

THE ROAD
TO DAWN

Josiah Henson and the Story
That Sparked the Civil War

Jared A. Brock

PublicAffairs
New York

PublicAffairs
Hachette Book Group
1290 Avenue of the Americas, New York, NY 10104
www.publicaffairsbooks.com
@Public_Affairs

Printed in the United States of America
First Edition: May 2018
Published by PublicAffairs, an imprint of Perseus Books, LLC, a subsidiary of Hachette Book Group, Inc. The PublicAffairs name and logo is a trademark of the Hachette Book Group.

The Hachette Speakers Bureau provides a wide range of authors for speaking events. To find out more, go to www.hachettespeakersbureau.com or call (866) 376-6591. The publisher is not responsible for websites (or their content) that are not owned by the publisher.

PRINT BOOK INTERIOR DESIGN BY LINDA MARK.

Library of Congress Cataloging-in-Publication Data

Names: Brock, Jared, author.
Title: The road to dawn : Josiah Henson and the story that sparked the Civil War / Jared Brock.
Other titles: Josiah Henson and the story that sparked the Civil War
Description: New York, NY : PublicAffairs, Hachette Book Group, [2018] | Includes bibliographical references and index.
Identifiers: LCCN 2017056511 (print) | LCCN 2018007706 (ebook) | ISBN 9781541773936 (e-book) | ISBN 9781541773929 (hardcover)
Subjects: LCSH: Henson, Josiah, 1789-1883. | Slaves—United States—Biography. | African Americans—Biography. | Fugitive slaves—United States—Biography. | Fugitive slaves—Canada—Biography. | Blacks—Canada—Biography. | Clergy—Canada—Biography.
Classification: LCC E444.H526 (ebook) | LCC E444.H526 B76 2018 (print) | DDC 306.3/62092 [B] —dc23
LC record available at https://lccn.loc.gov/2017056511

ISBNs: 978-1-5417-7392-9 (hardcover), 978-1-5417-7393-6 (ebook)

LSC-C

10 9 8 7 6 5 4 3 2 1

Dedicated to all those who desire freedom

CONTENTS

Illustrations appear between pages 140 and 141.

When we get a little farther away from the conflict, some brave and truth-loving man, with all the facts before him . . . will gather from here and there the scattered fragments . . . and give to those who shall come after us an impartial history of this the grandest moral conflict of the century.

—FREDERICK DOUGLASS

AUTHOR'S NOTE

IN FEBRUARY 2014, I WAS PERUSING A BOOKSHOP IN FLORIDA when I came across a copy of *Uncle Tom's Cabin* by Harriet Beecher Stowe. My wife, Michelle, had been wanting the novel for a while, so I purchased a copy and stuffed it in her Christmas stocking. She read it and was moved by it, and I decided to do a little more research.

I knew that Stowe's novel had often been credited with influencing the debate at the heart of the Civil War. But I was surprised to discover that her novel was based on the life of a real man, named Josiah Henson. *Did this man's story spark the Civil War?*

When I found out Josiah's cabin was just a few short hours from my own home, I had to visit. We drove to Dresden, Ontario, on a blazing hot summer day, and Michelle read me Josiah's humble little memoir on the return ride.

We learned that the prime minister of Great Britain had thrown a surprise banquet in his honor, and that Earl Grey had offered him a job. The archbishop of Canterbury had wept after hearing his story. This man had been feted by queens and presidents, and he had won a medal at the first World's Fair in London. He had rescued 118 slaves, including his own brother, and helped build a five-hundred-person freeman settlement, Dawn, that was known as one of the final stops on the Underground Railroad. *How had I never heard of Josiah Henson?*

I spent the next few years of my life immersed in Josiah's story, and the result is in your hands. I traveled to multiple countries, visited libraries and museums, interviewed dozens of experts, pored over thousands of documents, and produced a documentary wherein I retraced Father Henson's three-thousand-mile journey from Maryland to Washington to New Orleans to Kentucky to Canada. I have shared meals with his descendants, visited his gravesite, and I have begun taking steps to start a foundation to ensure his legacy is never lost again.

This is the story of a man who spent more than forty years in slavery, vowed to use his freedom well, and made good on that promise. As with every slave narrative, there are gaps in the story that we may never be able to fill with anything more than speculation. And because Josiah never learned to write, and his story was filtered through the perspectives of those who recorded his story, some of the intimate details of his vocation and family life remain a mystery.

Our story's hero was, of course, complicated and flawed. Yet he still deserves a place in the pantheon amid Frederick Douglass, Harriet Tubman, Solomon Northup, and others. This is a man whose life in microcosm represents both the history and the fate of America. It is my great privilege and pleasure to introduce you to one of our greatest lost figures, the Reverend Josiah Henson.

Jared A. Brock
Guelph, Ontario

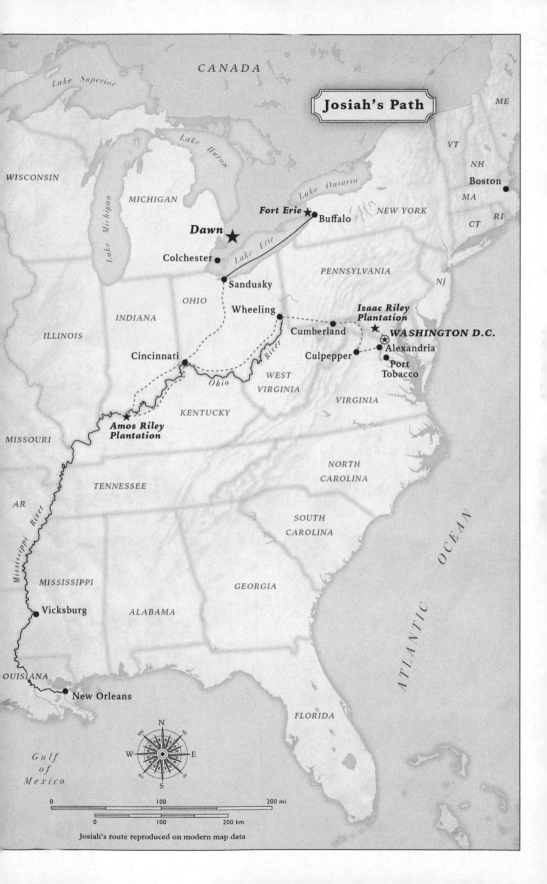

ONE

PORT TOBACCO

Slavery is founded in the selfishness of man's nature.

—ABRAHAM LINCOLN

A YOUNG WOMAN NAMED CELIA STRUGGLED, ALONE, IN A FIELD far removed and hidden from the others. The woman was small, perhaps eighty or ninety pounds, with sinewy arms and strong hands. The wooden hoe rubbed her palms raw as she dug and dragged the instrument through the dirt and mud. She had been working all day, and her stomach ached with hunger.

The white overseer, who had sent her to this far field, appeared suddenly. Celia immediately knew what was coming and tried to run, but the man was too fast and too powerful.

Mason was in a distant field when he heard his wife's screams. He dropped his hoe and sprinted through the rows of tobacco and corn, their sharp edges cutting like razors. As he ran, he lifted his hands to shield his eyes.

The assault on his wife had been brutal. He charged the rapist and began to beat him. Celia begged her husband to stop hitting the overseer, knowing the punishment that awaited any slave who hit a white man. The overseer, too, begged for the blows to cease, promising not to tell the owner what the slave had done.

Mason relented, and looked at the injured man. His shirt was a tattered mess and stained with blood. His nose stood at a crooked angle, and his eyes were already swollen tight and black.

Mason turned and ran as fast as his legs could carry him.

⁂

"A NIGGER HAS STRUCK A WHITE MAN!"[1]

The word went out and had the whole county talking. No one asked what incited the incident. It didn't matter; the law was on the overseer's side. They were in Maryland, which, like other slave states, provided generous means of legal revenge for slave owners—and whites in general—who had been attacked by a slave.

Mason hid in the woods for days. He ventured out at night in search of food, but the overseer's guards kept such strict surveillance that his efforts were thwarted. His supplies dwindled until he was starved out.

The day for punishment arrived. Whites from across Charles County made up the majority of the audience, though slaves from the neighboring plantations were forced to witness the scene. The overseer dragged Mason forward and tied him to the whipping post with an iron chain. He tore off the black man's shirt.

A well-dressed white man, Mason's owner, stepped forward. Francis Newman had been born around 1759 to a wealthy family from Devon, England, but had fled to America after getting caught in a scandal with a mistress. He had quickly remarried in the New World and had prospered financially. Newman eventually owned over a thousand acres across several plots, along with the La Grange estate, a large, well-built red-brick house about a mile from Port Tobacco. He purchased the house in November 1798 from Dr. James Craik, George Washington's personal physician, who later became chief surgeon for the Continental Army.[2]

By 1798, Newman owned twenty-four slaves. Seven of them were healthy individuals between the ages of twelve and fifty, and therefore taxable. The other seventeen were either children or they were elderly, sick, or disabled. He rented still more slaves. But Newman was a cold, hard man who mistreated his enslaved workers, purchased and rented alike.[3]

The illiterate white audience was furious that Newman hadn't immediately sold Mason south. Some of them believed Newman himself deserved to be lynched for not administering the "justice" they so craved. But Newman was a businessman. He knew a slave like Mason was far too valuable to be executed. No one kills a cow for trampling carrots. He would teach all his slaves a lesson this day.

Newman nodded to a heavyset man with a leather bullwhip in hand.

The burly blacksmith, Mr. Hewes, took his position a few feet away from his victim. The overseer pulled the rope until Mason's arms were raised taut above his head. The slave shook with fear and braced in preparation.

The first lash fell. Mason howled with pain. The leather cord cut deep, its bulbous end leaving a hard bruise, while its lengthy feathered edged left a searing red stripe across Mason's back.

Flogging was commonplace on Maryland plantations. Some people earned a good living from punishing errant slaves, and blacksmith Hewes profited greatly from his well-honed side-craft.

Crack. Snap.

The blacksmith's powerful arms worked the barbed whip with a steady cadence. The stripe gouged deeper and deeper into the slave's flesh. Blood ran from his back. Mason's cries could be heard a mile into the tobacco fields.

Ten. Twenty. Thirty. Forty. Fifty lashes.

Blacksmith Hewes paused at fifty strokes. Several men stepped forward to check Mason's vitals, knowing the slave was valuable property that mustn't be damaged. They agreed he was strong enough to handle the whole hundred.

Francis Newman wasn't the only slave owner in the area who severely chastised his slaves. A farmer five miles south of Port Tobacco named

Samuel Cox once whipped a slave named Jack Scroogins to death. When he began, the enslaved man had on a new cotton shirt; by the time Cox finished three hours later, all that remained were the collar and wristbands.[4]

Again and again the whip cracked against Mason's lacerated back. The slave's cries grew fainter, until a faint groan was the only response to the final stripes.

Upon reaching the hundredth lash, blacksmith Hewes wiped beads of perspiration from his forehead. He laid down the whip, grabbed Mason's head, and held it against the whipping post. The overseer picked up a hammer and nailed Mason's right ear to the beam.

The blacksmith produced a long, sharp knife and, with a swift slice, left the bleeding appendage affixed to the pole.

Mason screamed as blood splattered from the open wound. A loud cheer went up from the whites in the crowd. A black woman fainted. The overseer's cheer was loudest of all. "That's what he gets for striking a white man!"

⁓

MASON HOWLED AS HE STUMBLED THROUGH THE DOORS OF THE wooden slave shack. He caught sight of Celia and collapsed on the dirt floor in a heap of agony. His head was bleeding badly and his back was a ragged pulp of bloody furrows that ran so deep the white of bone was exposed.

Other slaves rushed into the squalid hovel with water and bandages. Celia's six children stood by as their mother carefully dabbed the bloody gashes. Mason thrashed in pain as healing salve was applied to his cuts. Upon inspection of the head wound, Celia saw that his right ear had been cut off too close to his scalp for stitching. One of the slaves heated a clothing iron on the fire—cauterization was the only way to save him from deadly infection. After the blazing brand was pressed hard against Mason's head, he curled up in the fetal position and begged for death.

It was Josiah Henson's first memory.

BIRTH OF A LEGEND

Josiah's story begins in Port Tobacco, Maryland, a thriving town with fifty homes, a hotel, and a courthouse. Tobacco farmers could load goods at Warehouse Landing in Port Tobacco, float them five miles down the Port Tobacco River to the Potomac, and from there north to the markets of Washington.

Josiah claimed he was born on Monday, June 15, 1789, in Charles County, Maryland, on a farm belonging to Mr. Francis Newman. This date seems oddly specific, as a slave's birthday was rarely recorded, and certainly not celebrated. The year 1789 may simply have been a printing typo that remained uncorrected in subsequent editions of the autobiography. In fact, research suggests Josiah may have been off by as many as ten years.

Enslaved people simply didn't know, or weren't allowed to know, their date of birth. Slave owners discouraged the recording of the birthdates of slaves, because one of the most effective tools of slave oppression was ignorance. A slave with knowledge of the wider world is a slave who can cause problems. A slave with a memory of the past and a vision of the future is dangerous. A slave who can say, "I was born on a particular day" is a slave who possesses self-knowledge.

We don't know for sure what Josiah's parents' names were. Josiah's mother's name was likely Celia, and his father may have been named Mason. New purchasers often changed the names of their slaves in an effort to confound any attempt on their part to reunite at a later date. During Reconstruction, freed blacks, searching for each other, placed thousands of advertisements in newspapers that were read from church pulpits.

> *My mother, known in Mississippi as Susan, was*
> *moved to Alabama and I think called Sarah.*

When Josiah entered the world, American domestic policy was changing rapidly. By the time he died, slavery would be illegal, but he was born into the brutal world of the transatlantic slave trade. Maryland wasn't the worst place to be a slave, however. All the slaves knew—the northern owners made certain they knew—that down South, in the steamy and forbidding regions of Louisiana, Alabama, and Georgia, slaves faced cruelty far worse than in the northern slave states. No northern slave wanted to be sold down South. The stories were gruesome: skin flayed from flesh, bodies branded with red-hot irons, whip blisters burst and rubbed with turpentine, tongues torn out, slaves fed alive to mosquitoes and alligators.[5] One rumored instrument of torture was the thumbscrew, a device allowing an owner or overseer to force a slave's thumb between two flat metal pieces fitted with ridges or spikes, which then crushed the victim's thumb when screwed tight together. Slave trader turned Christian hymn writer John Newton wrote of the pain of the enslaved in his journals: "I have seen them agonizing for hours, I believe for days together, under the torture of the thumbscrews; a dreadful engine, which, if the screw be turned by an unrelenting hand, can give intolerable anguish."[6] It was a simple, affordable, and convenient device for punishing slaves in a barbarically torturous manner, and the very stories were enough to make a northern slave shudder. A life of misery in Maryland seemed better than the horrors that awaited any slave down South.

Slavery in the Deep South was undoubtedly horrific, but conditions were still often far worse on plantations in the Caribbean and South America, which frequently implemented a "work to death" policy. The Church of England's Codrington plantation in Barbados relied on a steady stream of new slaves from Africa because slaves died so frequently from sickness and overwork. It was reported that four in ten slaves bought by the plantation in 1740 were dead within three years.

As for the six free states (Pennsylvania, Connecticut, Rhode Island, New Hampshire, Massachusetts, and Maine), or the free territories of the Northwest, a slave's chances of getting to one of these places were almost as good as his or her chances of sprouting wings. Those who attempted escape and were caught—even in a free state—were beaten and sold down the river into the hungry jaws of the barbaric South.

From the day of his torture on, Josiah's father was a changed man. He had been a good-humored and lighthearted fellow who had played the banjo at corn huskings and all-night parties, but, as Josiah put it, "the milk of human kindness turned to poison in his heart."[7] Cruelty and injustice—sanctioned by American law—had curdled his character. He refused to work. He became morose, stubborn, brooding, and disobedient. Francis Newman threatened to sell him down South, but Mason was unmoved. Once his wounds had healed, he was sent to Newman's son in the South.

Josiah never saw his father again.

SLAVERY HAS EXISTED SINCE AT LEAST THE BEGINNING OF RECORDED history. The first civilizations in Sumeria held slaves, along with ancient China, Egypt, Iran, and many others. When the Romans and other powers made conquests, they often took captives to be used as slave labor.

The institution of slavery in the United States began shortly after the arrival of the Europeans, and it lasted for more than three hundred years. But American slavery was cruelly worse than the slavery practiced in other countries at the time. In Europe, people could become slaves as a result of debt or crime, but could eventually earn their freedom by paying their debts. Even in these scenarios, neither the slaves nor their children were considered the property of their debtors. In America, people could be purchased as slaves and held like any other form of property.

In the early stages of the transatlantic slave trade, African leaders would trade war captives or criminals to Europeans who were traveling to the United States. In return, the African leaders would receive alcohol, firearms, and other items. Naturally, the number of criminals very quickly diminished, but the European demand for slaves did not.

The early slave trade was driven almost entirely by economics. As European nations colonized America, a labor force was needed to work the vast plantations. Slaves provided a lifetime source of free labor that replaced itself with offspring. The profit margins were massive compared to those in Europe, and suddenly the New World was rich with cash crops such as rice and tobacco.

Slavery soon became an arms race between the warring African tribes. If they didn't capture and sell other Africans in exchange for guns, nearby groups might do the same to them. Additionally, European merchant ships bound for the Americas would first stop in West Africa to raid villages for slaves. Africans were kidnapped from their homes, transported across the Atlantic Ocean, and sold into slavery for generations to come.

The only certain way to escape slavery was death. When some slaves realized the misery that lay ahead, they took their own lives.

There are many accounts of slaves refusing to eat and starving to death. Others hanged themselves. Captain Thomas Phillips of a slave ship called the *Hannibal* recalled twelve slaves drowning themselves to escape what they judged would be a worse fate. Slaves would cut their wrists in an attempt to bleed themselves to death, and in one case, a slave twice attempted to slit his own throat with his fingernails. After his hands were tied, he resisted food until he starved to death ten days later.[8]

Between 1525 and 1866, almost 500,000 Africans arrived in North America. In total, over 12 million Africans were shipped to the New World, with almost 2 million dying during their treacherous trip across the Middle Passage. Insurance companies—such as Lloyd's of London—only compensated investors for slaves who drowned at sea, so captains often threw the sick or dying into the ocean. However, in one particularly egregious case, a captain named Luke Collingwood threw more than 130 enslaved Africans overboard simply because the ship was running low on drinking water.[9] In this case, the chief justice, Lord Mansfield, ruled that the insurance company shouldn't have to pay, saying it "was the same as if horses had been thrown overboard."*

---

* Incredibly, America was not the biggest offender when it came to the transatlantic slave trade. The Portuguese imported upward of 6 million slaves to Brazil, with approximately 700,000 dying en route. Brazil reluctantly became the last Western nation to abolish slavery on May 13, 1888.[10]

By the time Josiah was born, slavery in the New World was a brutal institution that was fully integrated into American life. The system became so deeply ingrained that slaveholders simply didn't see a problem with turning a profit from enslaving, abusing, torturing, or even killing their fellow man.

❧

ALTHOUGH JOSIAH WAS BORN ON FRANCIS NEWMAN'S PROPERTY, and fathered by Newman's slave, he legally belonged to his mother's master, Dr. Josiah McPherson. It was common practice for slave owners to rent their workers to others, especially during periods like springtime and harvest, and the doctor had rented Celia to Newman.

Josiah considered McPherson a kind man, and that kindness toward the family may have been unwittingly fostered by the little boy himself. Josiah was the last child born to his mother, but the first slave child ever born to the doctor's household. Josiah quickly became the man's special pet.

Dr. McPherson took a liking to the little lad. He gave him his own first name, and he also gave the boy a last name, Henson, in honor of his own uncle, who had been an officer in the Revolutionary War.

In 1664, the Maryland Assembly ruled that children of enslaved mothers should also be held in slavery for life. This was a break from English common law, which held that the social status of a child was derived from his or her father. In Maryland and other slave states after 1664, no matter who impregnated her, a slave woman's offspring was the property of her owner. This seemingly subtle change had a devastating effect, making slave-breeding a simple, efficient, and profitable business.

Josiah's mother believed her prayers had been answered when word of Mason's torture reached her owner. Josiah McPherson immediately recalled Celia and her six children to his property, never again renting her to another slave owner.

The slave grapevine brought Celia no news of Mason, however. In the meantime, like many slaves, she dreamed of freedom and even of escape. But for the slaves on Dr. McPherson's farm, the impulse to escape was blunted by their belief that living as a slave on some other plantation could be far worse. Even little Josiah had heard things, awful things. He shuddered when he thought of what his absent father could be enduring. By contrast, the doctor never allowed his slaves to be struck by anyone.

Two years passed. The workload was lighter, the conditions less harsh, and the constant threat of violence no longer lingered over Josiah's mother as it had on Francis Newman's plantation. But that would all change when the good doctor suddenly died.

∽≈∾

ALTHOUGH DR. MCPHERSON HAD MAINTAINED A REPUTATION FOR "goodness of heart and an almost saint-like benevolence," his drunkenness had steadily gained ground in his life, and it eventually brought about his death.[11] One night, McPherson went out drinking and fell off his horse while crossing a stream on his way home. Being too drunk to stagger across, he drowned in less than a foot of water.

A few days later, a fellow slave pointed out the spot to little Josiah. "There's the place where massa got drownded at," the man said.[12]

The funeral had barely concluded when McPherson's heirs started squabbling about the inheritance. They eventually agreed to break up the property and divide the proceeds among themselves.

THE SOUL AUCTION

Dr. McPherson's estate was inventoried and appraised on April 9, 1805. It contained five enslaved persons, including Josiah, who was nicknamed "Sye" and estimated to be nine years old, along with Josiah's brother John, age twelve, and a woman who was likely Josiah's mother, Celia, age fifty. Josiah was valued at $30*—and both he and his mother were listed as "infirm."

---

* Calculating the modern equivalent of two-hundred-year-old currency values is a challenge far above my pay grade. I'm grateful for MeasuringWorth.com, which provides the

The administrators of McPherson's estate, Elisabeth B. McPherson and Josiah Hanson, petitioned the Charles County Orphan's Court the following day, claiming McPherson's debts could only be cleared if they were allowed to sell all his property. The court gave them permission to sell everything, provided they advertised for at least three weeks in order to attract the highest number of potential buyers.

The greedy heirs of the deceased doctor were callous to their property's condition and oblivious to the heartbreak they were about to inflict on them. For weeks, while the details were being worked out, the slaves were frantic at the thought of being sent down South and split from their families.

The practice of separating families was strategic as well as practical. Rending family ties, separating mother from child, brother from sister, husband from wife, and sending them to live among strangers was disorienting and made slaves less trusting of their peers, and therefore more dependent on the master for their survival and well-being. For the massive slave system to work, the slaves needed to be kept ignorant, in a state of anxiety, and fearful of the cost of rebellion or escape.

In 1845, forty slaves who tried to make their way to Canada were discovered by a volunteer slave patrol in Rockville, Maryland. The volunteers surrounded them and opened fire. One runaway was hit in the neck with a musket ball, while another was shot in the back. A third had his arm shattered, and a fourth had his cheek blown away. Others were shot in the face and left to die slow and painful deaths. One of the volunteers lamented that not all the slaves had resisted, which deprived him of "the pleasure of shooting them all down."[13] The fugitives were arrested and marched through Washington in ox chains. Those who survived their wounds were sold south to Louisiana. The very thought of such a fate was enough to break most slaves.

---

various ways to calculate relative value. The price put on Josiah, $30, for example, as a real commodity, would be equivalent to $634 today. But the labor value of that commodity would be $9,210, in terms of unskilled wages, or $20,400, in terms of production worker compensation. In terms of income value as a commodity, it would be $19,000.

The separation of family was one of the slave trade's most vicious features. Occasionally a buyer would take a sibling set or a mother and child, but rarely did a seller try to keep a family together if he could make more money by selling them separately. In 1857, Pierce Butler sold 429 of his slaves in order to pay off his debts. It is thought to be the largest sale of humans in US history. An acquaintance of Butler's who was familiar with the sale, Sidney George Fisher, wrote that "families will not be separated, that is to say, husbands and wives, parents and young children. But brothers and sisters of mature age, parents and children of mature age, all other relations and the ties of home and long association will be violently severed." The sale, which took place in Georgia, lasted two days. It was not recorded how many families were broken up in the process.[14]

On the day of the McPherson auction in Maryland, a crowd surrounded the stand to inspect the huddled group of slaves, along with the doctor's furniture and medical instruments. The purchasers felt the slaves' muscles and checked their teeth as they would livestock. They ran strength and agility tests while the auctioneer looked on with bored impatience. Once the inspection was complete, the slaves were put on display, one by one. Men clamored to place their bids.

꩜

AS THE SALE OF JOSIAH AND HIS FAMILY PROCEEDED, SLAVES FROM various other estates and plantations in the area were sold and separated by their owners. Through their grief and mourning, victims sang parting hymns:

> *My brethren, farewell; I do you now tell,*
> *I'm sorry to leave you, I love you so well. . . .*
>
> *Strange friends I shall find; I hope they'll prove kind;*
> *Neither people nor place shall alter my mind:*
> *Wherever I'll be, I'll still pray for thee,*
> *And, O, my dear brethren, do you pray for me.*[15]

Dr. McPherson's slaves were placed on the auction block one at a time and sold to the highest bidders, who would scatter them to various parts of the country. Josiah later said he watched silently as his siblings were torn from his mother's arms. He tried to scream when his brother John was taken away, but his throat felt like it was swollen shut.

Celia held her youngest child's hand in paralyzed grief. As the sale proceeded, Josiah's own fate came to him with dreadful clarity. Then his mother's lot was called. She was torn from Josiah and pushed onto the stage.[16]

A young man in the crowd eyed the weeping woman. He was mid-sized and stocky, a blacksmith by trade. He wore an open shirt that revealed his hairy chest, and black boots with heavy riding heels. Isaac Riley, of Rockville, Maryland, wasn't interested in producing new slaves, so it didn't matter if the aging woman was fertile or barren. She looked sturdy enough to bear the hardship of his rough plantation. Perhaps he could get her for a good price. He raised his heavy cane and placed the first bid.

Isaac Riley eventually succeeded, and Josiah's mother became his property.

The auctioneer's assistant grabbed Josiah's hand and yanked him onto the stage. The little boy searched the crowd for any sign of his mother or siblings, but they had all been taken away. All he saw were strange white faces, and beyond them the black faces of slaves who had accompanied their masters to the auction. In the front row sat a tavern keeper named Adam Robb.

Adam Robb was from Ayr, Scotland, and had emigrated to America around 1776.[17] His pub was called the Fountain Inn. He also owned a line of stagecoaches and trafficked in children on the side. Young slaves were a profitable commodity: over the space of five or six years, for little more than the cost of water and slave-raised food, he could grow a slave from a small boy to a prime working hand. He could then sell the slave at auction and get five or ten times his return on investment. Of course, if the child died, the investment was lost, but the loss was never much.

Montgomery County, Maryland, had a long and storied tradition of child trafficking. A tax assessment from 1804 indicates that 32 percent of the slaves in the district were under the age of eight. Of the 1,202 people held in slavery in Montgomery County's District Four, nearly half were under fourteen.[18] As Adam Robb's business flourished, he expanded into moneylending, often accepting slaves as collateral.*

The auctioneer pointed out the size of Josiah's head and suggested that he might grow into a large man like his older brother. Then he opened the bidding. Adam Robb's hand shot into the air.

Josiah's mother, overwhelmed by the thought of parting forever from all her children, broke free from her new overseer and pushed through the crowd to the spot where Isaac Riley stood. She begged him to bid on her youngest. Isaac eyed her with disgust as she took hold of his jacket. Again she begged. Her new owner slapped her face, and the sobbing woman fell at his feet and clung desperately to his knees. Isaac struggled to release his legs and punched her in the head. She tumbled to the dirt. The blacksmith kicked her savagely in the stomach. She cried for help, but none came. He kicked her again with his heavy boots. Josiah's mother moaned as she crawled out of reach.

"Oh, Lord Jesus," she sobbed. "How long, how long shall I suffer this way?"[19]

Adam Robb laughed as the auctioneer's hammer fell. The little boy was sold to a stranger.

---

* On one loan, Adam Robb accepted a four-year-old named Cronin and a two-year-old named Nora as security. If the debtor defaulted, the children would be his.

TWO

THE WOUNDED LEADER

Slavery is a weed that grows on every soil.

—EDMUND BURKE

THE TAVERN KEEPER, ADAM ROBB, TOOK JOSIAH TO HIS HOME near the Montgomery County courthouse, about forty miles away. He brought the boy to the slave quarters, where more than three dozen other slaves of all ages and conditions lived in squalor.

Josiah recognized no one. He went to a corner and lay down in the dirt. He coughed and shivered in the dark room.

Josiah's sickly body lay for days, almost dead, in a pile of rags on the dirt floor. The other slaves, who left at sunrise, took no notice. He was left alone all day, begging for water, crying for his mother. Occasionally a slave would give him a bit of cornbread or a piece of salt herring, but as the weeks passed he became so weak that he couldn't move.

Josiah didn't realize that his sickness would be his salvation.

After a few weeks, Adam Robb arranged a meeting with Isaac Riley, whose blacksmith shop was about five miles away. He offered to sell Josiah to Isaac for a song. Isaac worried that "the little nigger would die."[1] Adam struck a deal with the callous blacksmith. If the boy died, he owed him nothing. If he lived, Isaac would owe Adam some horse shoeing. It was an offer Isaac couldn't refuse.

Soon after, Josiah was taken to Isaac Riley's plantation, where he was reunited with his overjoyed mother.

⁂

THE OLD RILEY FARM WAS LOCATED AT WHAT IS NOW 11420 OLD Georgetown Road in Rockville, Maryland—just twelve miles from the nation's capital. Originally it was part of a 3,697-acre parcel of land. Isaac Riley, along with his brother George, who was a farmer and county commissioner, owned several farms in the area. They often bought, sold, and transferred pieces between themselves and other family members. Land on the fringes was regularly sold and resold in order to settle debts or expand operations. The Georgetown Road farmhouse was the Riley brothers' headquarters for the whole plantation operation.

Isaac Riley's main farm plot started as 282.5 acres, and was often recorded at 260 acres, but the numbers varied wildly. Isaac would sell or buy back pieces of the property with stunning regularity, either owing a debt or losing a bet.

Isaac Riley was a harsh man, and his slaves suffered the full force of his stress, anxiety, fear, and anger. He typically owned around fifteen or twenty slaves, including some children, but the numbers varied based on his financial situation. Slaves were simply property that could be bought, sold, inherited, gambled, or used as collateral for a debt. They could even be used as prizes in a raffle draw, with the seller hoping to capitalize on America's gambling mania by earning more money from ticket sales than he could at a typical slave auction. George Washington himself once helped organize a raffle of fifty-five slaves, including "a fine breeding woman named Pat, lame of one side, with child."[2]

Maryland played a huge role in the story of slavery, perhaps because of its close proximity to the nation's capital. Though it is generally considered a southern slave state, its climate was more like the rest of the mid-Atlantic, with colder winters and shorter growing seasons. Along with these differences came different labor systems, with far smaller plantations and fewer workers than in the massive operations of the Deep South.

⟳⟲

JOSIAH'S MOTHER MANAGED TO NURSE HER BOY BACK TO HEALTH, and he settled into life on the farm. He was pressed into service carrying buckets of water to the men in the fields. Having recovered his stamina, he proved himself capable of carrying out the task.

Despite Isaac's cruelty, Josiah faithfully served him. After carrying water, he learned to pull weeds from between the rows of tobacco. As he grew taller he was charged with looking after his master's riding horse and helping him sell the plantation's products at the nearby markets in Washington. Then a hoe was placed in his hands, and he was required to do the work of a man. By adolescence he could do the job as well as any of the older slaves.

Isaac Riley drove his slaves like dogs. They raised a little tobacco and a lot of potatoes. The slaves hoed endless rows of potatoes, working a withering number of hours at the weary, monotonous job under the cold eye of the overseer.

Though Josiah probably had it better than some of the other slaves on Isaac's farm, because of his strength and skill, his life was not in any way idyllic. Isaac's slaves had little opportunity for relaxation and were given the scantiest means of sustenance. If they were allowed possessions, it was only utilitarian items, such as cooking utensils. Their clothing was often made of tow cloth, the itchy fiber left over from the production of linen. The white men used the same fabric to clean their gun barrels, or as rags or kindling for their fires. Josiah and the other children wore nothing but a frock that reached to their knees. The adults received a pair of trousers or a sack dress, depending on their gender, and a pair of used shoes once per year. That was it, except for a winter overcoat and a wool hat for the males every two or three years.

The slaves on Isaac's plantation slept in single-room log huts on the dirt floor. Plank flooring would have been considered a luxury. Each room slept ten or twelve people, but the huts did not protect them from damp-ness and cold. They didn't have beds or furniture. Their mattresses were nothing more than a mix of straw and old rags, piled in layers and boxed in with boards. A single blanket was the only protection from the air and the cold earth. But even so, Josiah managed to find a comfortable way of sleeping—on a piece of wood, his head resting on an old jacket, with his feet toasting before the smoldering fire.

The wind howled, the rain and snow entered freely through the cracks, and the earth soaked in the wetness until the floor was as muddy as a barn. Here the children were born and the sick tended. In this hovel, Josiah was fed by day and penned at night.

The slaves labored from sunrise until noon without rest. Breakfast was at noon, and supper was eaten in the dark when the day's work was through. Both meals consisted of cornmeal and salt herring. In the sum-mer, they got a little buttermilk and whatever vegetables each slave had managed to raise on the little piece of land assigned to him.

Food was both a luxury and a weapon. In the life of a plantation slave, food was the primary source of personal enjoyment. The astute slave owner knew this, and therefore used the quality and quantity of food granted to the slaves as an effective tool of indoctrination and suppres-sion. The trick was to allow the slaves just enough food to keep their spirits up and maintain their strength for the hard work of the fields, but never so much as to make them satisfied or complacent. To a man who is constantly hungry, the promise of an extra morsel to eat is an incentive nearly as powerful as the desire to avoid the lash or the branding iron.

LITERACY LOST

Josiah was thirteen years old when he nearly lost his life a second time.

In Maryland in 1802, the school the local white children attended was generally several miles away from any given plantation. A slave boy was typically called upon to drive his master's children in a wagon to school each morning and to retrieve them in the afternoon.

One neighboring slave boy, named William, was a bright and clever lad. Josiah later recalled, "He learned to read and to spell by hearing his master's boys talk about their lessons while they were riding to and from school."[3] Josiah was quite impressed to hear a fellow slave read. William told Josiah that if he would buy a Webster's spelling book from a nearby store, he would teach him to read and write.

"I had already made some ink out of charcoal, and had cut a goose quill so that it looked like my master's pen, and I had begun to make scratches on odd bits of paper I had picked up in the market," Josiah later recalled.[4] He had noticed that all the butter he sold at the markets was stamped with Isaac Riley's initials, "I. R." They were the first letters he ever wrote.

Josiah soon figured out that if he took some of the apples that had fallen from the trees in the orchard and sold them, he would be able to get the money to buy his single school supply. A few days later, he was the proud owner of a Webster's spelling book, which he carefully tucked inside his hat. Letters and words seemed like magical things to Josiah. While his body was the prisoner of his cruel owner, and subject to endless pain and humiliation, his mind could be liberated by books.

But his attempt to enter this new world was cut short. Early that morning, as Isaac waited impatiently for Josiah to harness his horse, the animal bolted, and Josiah ran to catch him. The boy's hat fell off, and the book dropped to the ground.

Josiah rushed back to the book, but Isaac beat him to it and placed a heavy heel on the pages.

"What's that?" Isaac demanded.

"A spelling book," Josiah replied.

"Whose is it?"

"Mine."

Isaac glared at the teenager.

"Where did you get it?"

"Bought it, sir, when I went to market."

"How much was it?"

"Eleven cents."

"Where did you get the money?"

"I sold some apples out of our orchard."

"Our orchard?!" Isaac erupted. "I'll teach you to get apples from *our* orchard for such a vile purpose, so you'll remember it. Give me that book."

Josiah bent to pick it up, and as he saw Isaac's big cane coming down, he dodged to the side. The cane made only a glancing blow.

"Pick up that book!" Isaac ordered.[5]

Josiah was obliged to follow the command. As he stooped again to retrieve the book, Isaac struck Josiah across the head. He continued to beat him until the boy's eyes were swollen and he fell unconscious.

Celia found Josiah sometime later, and weeks passed before the boy recovered. When his master first saw him return to work, he sneered, "So you want to be a fine gentleman? Remember if you meddle with a book again I'll knock your brains out."[6] Josiah would not open another book for almost thirty years. He bore a scar across the back of his head for the rest of his life.

Many slaves wanted to learn to read, write, and do arithmetic. This was illegal in most states, but some learned anyway. It wasn't illegal for slaves in Maryland to learn to read and write, but whites were discouraged from teaching them. Sometimes slaves learned from each other or from free blacks. In Baltimore in the 1820s, a nineteen-year-old free black man named William Watkins ran a school for any black person who was allowed to attend.[7]

Frederick Douglass believed that the ability to read and write was the first step toward freedom. He wrote, "Education means emancipation; it means light and liberty."[8] Sustaining the institution of slavery required the dehumanization of slaves, but both slaves and their owners were real people with real feelings, and personal attitudes toward individual slaves varied considerably. Many owners were like Francis Newman and Isaac Riley—hard men who saw their slaves as deserving no better treatment than animals. Others believed in the humanity of their slaves and sought to somehow balance the harsh reality of slavery with an acknowledgment that slaves were sentient beings with human souls.

But the slave owners of Montgomery County were in agreement, and Josiah remembered their collective verdict, which was repeated throughout the neighborhood: "We will not have our niggers spoiled by that rascal."[9]

For the crime of teaching another slave to read, little William was sold south to Georgia.

⸙

DESPITE THE INHUMANE LIVING CONDITIONS ON ISAAC RILEY's plantation, Josiah grew to be an uncommonly robust and vigorous teenager. By age fifteen, very few could compete with him at work or sports. He was the tallest hand among Isaac's twenty slaves. Much to his master's annoyance, Josiah was even taller than Isaac himself. He could do any job on the farm, and he could run faster, wrestle better, and jump higher than any other slave around. He admitted to being a prideful young man, but if he had a slight sense of superiority, it was because of his abilities.

Josiah's life was hard, but despite being boxed in by circumstances, his joyful exuberance overcame them all. The slavery system did its best to make Josiah wretched, yet, alongside the hardships of dirty cabins, frozen feet, backbreaking toil under the blazing sun, and frequent beatings, happy moments appeared—Christmas parties, extra meat on holidays, midnight visits to apple orchards, the discovery of stray chickens, which could be covertly broiled, and the discovery of ways to escape hard labor.

Josiah soon obtained great influence with his companions by offering favors and helping them whenever he could. He became something of a Robin Hood, stealing more food than Isaac had allotted, and sharing it with his friends. Enslaved people created moral workarounds for their stealing habits, with one theory being that property couldn't steal property. Josiah certainly subscribed to that idea and considered the stolen goods as partial payment for his extra labor.

Josiah worked many extra hours in order to show his master what he could accomplish or to win a kind word or extract a benevolent deed from his callous heart. He convinced others to work extra hours, too. Despite his efforts, the master usually remained indifferent, or worse, coolly recalculated his slave's resale value.

⁓⁓⁓

MARCH 2, 1807, WAS NOT A GOOD DAY FOR THE RILEY BROTHERS. The newspaper reported that the US Congress had just passed a law prohibiting the importation of slaves. Starting next year, no new slaves would legally be brought to America from Africa or elsewhere. In the free states and in Congress, approval of the institution of slavery was steadily eroding, and this new law was yet another step toward restricting it.

Slavery had once been accepted everywhere in the colonies. A century earlier, in each of the thirteen colonies that joined to become the United States of America, slavery had been legal. Massachusetts—long regarded as a bastion of liberal thought—was the first colony in New England where men had owned slaves, and it continued to be a center of the slave trade throughout the seventeenth and eighteenth centuries.

The movement against slavery had started during the American Revolution, when all thirteen colonies had banned the international slave trade—Great Britain was the biggest practitioner of slavery and had earned huge profits from it. The expressions of equality evoked by the Declaration of Independence had inspired many black Americans to aid in the revolutionary cause and given them hope that emancipation might someday become a reality. Others joined the British Army, encouraged by the prospect of freedom in exchange for military service.

After the war, the slave trade continued in Georgia and South Carolina. In the North, the states of Pennsylvania, New Hampshire, Massachusetts, Connecticut, and Rhode Island adopted policies to gradually abolish slavery. The independent republic of Vermont abolished slavery in 1777. By 1804, New York and New Jersey had abolished the practice or set measures in place to gradually reduce it.

Congress passed the Slave Trade Act, which prohibited American ships from being used in the slave trade, in 1794. The act, in other words, limited the trade to foreign ships.

Four years later, Congress passed an act that imposed a penalty of $300 per slave on persons convicted of importing slaves illegally. In the Slave Trade Act of 1800, it outlawed investment in the trade by US citizens as well as the employment of US citizens on foreign vessels involved in the trade.

Then, on December 2, 1806, in his Sixth Annual Message to Congress, President Thomas Jefferson denounced the international slave trade for its "violations of human rights" and called for its criminalization on the first day that was possible, which, according to provisions already existing in the US Constitution, was January 1, 1808. He said: "I congratulate you, fellow-citizens, on the approach of the period at which you may interpose your authority constitutionally, to withdraw the citizens of the United States from all further participation in those violations of human rights which have been so long continued on the unoffending inhabitants of Africa, and which the morality, the reputation, and the best interests of our country, have long been eager to proscribe."[10]

The House and the Senate passed a bill called "An Act to Prohibit the Importation of Slaves Into Any Port or Place Within the Jurisdiction of the United States, From and After the First Day of January, in the Year of Our Lord, One Thousand Eight Hundred and Eight."

In a baffling paradox of liberty, on March 2, 1807—despite owning six hundred slaves of his own—Jefferson signed the bill into law. Though he would continue to own slaves for the rest of his life, the transatlantic slave trade was now basically over.*

This was bad news for farmers like George and Isaac Riley. Without the possibility of further imports, the price of slaves would increase, putting a squeeze on profit margins. But if slaves couldn't be imported, they could be bred. Men like Adam Robb would breed them like cattle. Child traffickers would actually profit from the new law.

A mass exodus was about to occur. The soil in the northern United States was being rapidly depleted of its nutrients, while the South was heading into a cotton boom. With slave prices rising, breeding slaves and

---

* After the death of his wife, Jefferson began a relationship with Sally Hemings, one of his slaves. It is believed Jefferson fathered six children with her, four of whom survived to adulthood. He allowed two to escape and freed the other two in his will at death.

selling them south could be a viable business model. Some slaves in the North, aware of their impending sale, considered escaping to Canada.

The Fugitive Slave Act of 1793 guaranteed slaveholders the right to recover their escaped property. The act, formally titled "An Act Respecting Fugitives from Justice, and Persons Escaping from the Service of Their Masters," created the legal mechanism for the task.

The law prescribed no statute of limitations: escaped slaves could be pursued for the remainder of their lives.

An enslaved woman named Oney Judge had been one of Martha Washington's chambermaids. She was forced to serve the Washington family in Virginia and in Philadelphia while George Washington was in office.

On May 21, 1796, Oney escaped to New Hampshire. She later had a child there. George Washington, forced to act discreetly to avoid controversy in Philadelphia, which had a strong Quaker abolitionist community, made two attempts to seize her. Later, Washington's nephew requested she return. None of the efforts were successful.

In the 1840s, the Reverend Benjamin Chase interviewed Oney, and on January 1, 1847, he published an account of the interview in a letter to the editor in the abolitionist newspaper *The Liberator*. He explained how, legally, Martha Washington's descendants could make a claim. Oney and her child were still at risk for being arrested as fugitives, even though fifty years had elapsed since her escape. Martha Washington's descendants had inherited them, just as they had inherited her furniture and jewelry.

"This woman is yet a slave," wrote Rev. Chase. "If Washington could have got her and her child, they were constitutionally his; and if Mrs. Washington's heirs were now to claim her, and take her before Judge Woodbury, and prove their title, he would be bound, upon his oath, to deliver her up to them."[11]

Isaac and George's brother, Amos Riley, owned a large piece of property in Kentucky on the Ohio River near modern-day Owensboro. Like the Mason-Dixon Line between Maryland and Pennsylvania, the Ohio River served as the western division between free and slave states. Amos Riley's slaves were just *six hundred yards* from freedom.

In 1802, Ohio became a state. Slavery had been abolished by its original constitution, but at the same time, with slave state Kentucky across the river, Ohio had tried to stifle black immigration. Ohio enacted Black Laws in 1804 and 1807 that compelled every black person entering the state to produce a court paper as proof that he or she was free, and to post a bond of $500 guaranteeing good behavior.

Fortunately for free blacks and escaped slaves entering Ohio, the Black Laws were widely ignored.

❧

ALTHOUGH THE LIFE OF A MALE SLAVE WAS BRUTAL, THE CONDITION of a female slave was arguably even worse. Women were forced to perform hard labor alongside men while bearing the unique burdens of their sex—menstruation, childbirth, and breastfeeding. In addition, they were frequent victims of sexual violence and rape at the hands of slave owners, overseers, and male slaves. Women often bore the double sorrow of slavery by day and rape by night.

A former male slave, W. L. Bost, who was interviewed in 1937 as part of the Slave Narrative project conducted by the Works Progress Administration, talked about the abuse many women suffered.[12] "Plenty of the colored women have children by the white men," he said. "She know bettern than to not do what he say. Then [the men] take them very same children what have they own blood and make slaves out of them. If the Missus find out she raise revolution. But she hardly find out. The white men not going to tell and the nigger women were always afraid to. So they jes go on hopin' that thing won't be that way always."*

---

* Although many women tried to resist or avoid sexual abuse, they were frequently punished for the lack of acquiescence. British-Dutch author John Gabriel Stedman once witnessed an eighteen-year-old girl receive two hundred lashes for refusing to have intercourse with an overseer. Stedman reported, "She was from her neck to her ancles [*sic*] literally dyed with blood." John Gabriel Stedman, *Narrative, of a Five Years' Expedition; Against the Revolted Negroes of Surinam: in Guiana, on the Wild Coast of South America; from the Year 1772, to 1777* (London: J. Johnson and J. Edwards, 1796), 325.

As a young man, Josiah learned to use his compassion and bravery for the benefit of the women he saw suffering intolerable miseries.

One of those women was Dinah. The young slave was as sharp and cunning as a fox, but she purposely acted like she was mentally handicapped in an attempt to lessen her burden. The Rileys weren't sure what to do with the girl. They whipped many of their slaves on a daily basis, but as religious folk, they didn't dare lash someone they thought was mentally deficient.

However, they didn't seem to have a problem with starving her. Josiah felt he needed to do something, though it was a risky proposition. Stealing a chicken was punishable by law with sixteen stripes at the public whipping post. It was twenty stripes for a turkey, thirty for a pig, and thirty-nine for sheep. But slaves frequently took the risk. Their lives were little more than incessant toil, and it was simply impossible to live on the meager rations provided by their masters.

Isaac Riley had plenty of sheep and pigs, and Josiah picked the best swine from the litter. While another slave, named Sambo, stood watch, Josiah led the pig deep into the woods, where he quickly slaughtered and butchered the animal. He dug a fire pit to roast the meat, being careful to hide the light from all angles.

Josiah buried the carcass and returned to the cabins. He distributed the pieces of meat among the women and children. To such poor people it was immediate sustenance, a luxury, and medicine. Isaac's slaves soon became deeply loyal to Josiah. At the same time, Josiah and other slaves like him had to find ways to justify this theft of the master's goods.

Was it theft? Was it a sin? Looking back, Josiah asked himself if it was wrong to steal. "My conscience does not reproach me for it," he said. If anything, he counted it "among the best of my deeds."[13]

❧

AROUND THE SAME TIME OF HIS STEALTHY PIG-ROASTING, JOSIAH began to suspect that Isaac Riley's white overseer was cheating his master. Whether it was stealing money or animals is not entirely clear, but it was a delicate matter. If the overseer caught Josiah spying, or discovered that he knew his secret, the young slave's life could be in grave danger.

The key was to engineer a situation in which the master himself would catch the overseer in the act, but Josiah would still get the credit. Josiah managed this, and although we don't know the exact circumstances, apparently the plan succeeded, because Isaac fired the overseer and, much to Josiah's surprise, promoted the young slave to superintendent of the farms.

Josiah's pride got the best of him. Though he didn't have much choice in the matter, the fact that a white man trusted him made Josiah anxious to continue to please his master. He quickly went to work as the farm's overseer—or, as he was known to the local whites, "Riley's head nigger."[14] One of the first actions he took was to diversify the farm's crops. For years they had grown little more than tobacco and potatoes, but the soil was tired and the climate was changing. The South had become tobacco and cotton territory, and potatoes were a cheap commodity. Josiah planted corn and blooming rye and oats and barley. He planted fruit orchards, made cider and apple brandy, and increased Isaac's profits exponentially.

Josiah's fellow slaves benefited, too, in little ways. He did whatever he could to ease the burden placed on them. From a hay surplus, he provided thicker mattresses to ward off the cold from the muddy floor. He enlarged the patches on which the slaves grew their own vegetables. He continued to kill animals for meat and share them.

Josiah's ambition helped him master every type of farm work. But ambition in a slave only attracts more work. Once Josiah showed he could be responsible for the crops, Isaac began to drink and gamble and fight, rather than help run his farm. And even though Josiah was clearly profitable to him, Isaac was unwilling to reward his slave with kindness or even decent treatment.

FAITH FOUND

John McKenny lived in Georgetown, just a few miles from Isaac Riley's plantation. A good man—a baker by trade—he detested slavery and refused to hire slave labor from any of the hundreds of renters in the state. He worked with his own hands, along with whatever hired free labor he could afford.

McKenny occasionally served as a minister, preaching in a county where preachers were lacking at the time. One day in 1807, Celia learned that McKenny was to officiate the Sunday service at a church less than four miles from Isaac's plantation. She wanted her son to attend the service.

Josiah was about eighteen years old. Celia wanted her son to have a relationship with God, but even though she had made him memorize the Lord's Prayer, in his young adult life he'd shown little interest in faith. He had never heard a sermon or had a conversation really with anyone about religion, although his mother had tried to convey a sense of the general accountability on the part of every individual human to a Supreme Being.

"I want you to go and ask master to let you go down and hear Mr. McKenny preach," Celia said.[15]

Josiah answered that he didn't want to go, for fear that Isaac Riley would beat him just for asking. Isaac had beaten Josiah for all sorts of reasons and non-reasons, like being late, or being early, or being slow, or being fast, or simply because Isaac was drunk and angry at life and the world.

"Go and ask him," Celia pleaded.

Like many other young men, he ignored his mother. Celia leaned against a rail, dropped her head, and started crying silently.

Josiah sighed. "I will go, mother."

Josiah went up to the big house, where he saw Isaac on the front veranda. His back was turned. As Josiah approached, Isaac saw his shadow and whipped around.

"What do you want, Siah?" Isaac asked.

As Josiah came closer, he could smell whiskey on his master's breath.

"I want to ask you if I can go to the meeting," Josiah replied.

"Where?"

"Down at Newport Mill."

"Who's going to preach?"

"Mr. McKenny."

Isaac grunted. "What do you want to hear him preach for?"

Josiah scratched his chin. He didn't have an answer.

"What good will it do for you?"

Josiah didn't have an answer, which compounded Isaac's curiosity.

"Who put that into your head?"

Josiah didn't want to get his poor old mother in trouble, but she'd always told him to tell the truth.

"My mother."

"Ah," Isaac laughed. "I thought it was your mother. I suppose she wants to have you spoilt. When will you come back?"

"As soon as the meeting is over."

Isaac nodded.

Josiah walked the forest path to the meeting at Newport Mill. It was held in a house along a stream that powered a handful of grain mills. When Josiah approached the door, he was barred entry. As he later recalled, "They would not let niggers go into the meeting."

Josiah circled the building, then stood in the doorway and watched the baker preach. He had never heard a sermon before. McKenny preached with passion about the character of Jesus. What kind of man dies for his enemies? What kind of man sacrifices himself for others?

The baker spoke in terms that anyone could understand. He spoke of Jesus, and his love for mankind, of his death and resurrection. He insisted that Christ died "for every man." McKenny continually repeated the phrase throughout his sermon.

Josiah's mind flashed back to the moment he had been torn from his mother's arms. He saw her tears. He heard her crying. He remembered everything. Through her grief she had prayed, called out to God for deliverance from her suffering. And he remembered the prayer she'd prayed with him as a child each night.

> *Your kingdom come.*
> *Your will be done.*
> *On earth.*

McKenny opened his Bible and began thumbing toward the New Testament as he spoke. Josiah grew excited and leaned as close as he dared. The baker landed at Hebrews 2:9. He raised his hands and looked toward the ceiling. "Jesus Christ, the Son of God, tasted death for every man; for the high, for the low, for the rich, for the poor, the bond, the free, the negro in his chains, the man in gold and diamonds."

Every man.

It was the first Bible verse Josiah had ever heard, and the words almost knocked him over.

Every man?

Josiah's heart pounded in his chest. He turned around and sprinted through the woods.

❧

JOSIAH RAN THROUGH THE FOREST UNTIL HIS LUNGS FORCED HIM TO stop. He heaved for air. He had never heard such talk before.

Did Jesus Christ die for me?

He paced back and forth. *What would have compelled someone to die for a slave?*

Josiah kept repeating the preacher's phrases to the forest.

"The compassionate Saviour . . . loves *me*. He looks down in compassion from heaven on *me*. . . . He died to save *my* soul. . . ." Describing the moment later, Josiah said he had been "transported with delicious joy."

In that moment, a transformation occurred in Josiah Henson's heart. He became painfully aware not only of the spiritual dimension of the great sin of slavery, but also of the subtler faults in his own life. He perceived the shadowy darkness of his pride and ego, his arrogance and selfishness.

This was his spiritual awakening. As Josiah walked home, he resolved to learn more of this God. He would study religious matters. He would listen in the market. He would go to church. He would pray, even for his enemies. He knew that even Isaac Riley himself would give up his wicked ways if he met Jesus. Josiah resolved to share what he learned with others, especially with his destitute fellow slaves, and encourage them to follow the same path to inner freedom.

◈

BY THE TIME HE WAS TWENTY, JOSIAH WAS A RESPECTED PREACHER in his local slave community. But he had chosen a path that would prove difficult and fraught with conflict.

The Christian religion of the slaves was both visible and invisible, organized formally and arising spontaneously. Sunday worship in a local church building—during which slaves were lectured about obeying authority and not stealing—was sometimes followed by informal, and sometimes illicit, prayer meetings in the slave cabins or in the woods. Slaves forbidden by their masters to attend church risked floggings to attend their secret gatherings. Preachers who were licensed by the church and hired by the master were later emulated by slave preachers who were self-taught and often delivered a more subversive message.

Religious services—whether permitted by owners or conducted in secret—provided slaves with welcome respite from incessant labor. They offered companionship and some measure of hope. The slaves could, for a fleeting moment, forget their misery. Religion helped them overcome the weakness they felt as individuals, as they felt stronger and safer as a group protected under the eyes of God.

The church was not, of course, innocent of the sin of slavery. Take, for example, Christopher Codrington, born to one of the wealthiest plantation owners in Barbados. The young man attended All Souls College at Oxford before taking over the family's Caribbean sugarcane plantation. When Codrington died in 1710, his will (found in one of his boots) left £10,000 in slavery profits to his Christian alma mater in order to build a library. Codrington also bequeathed his nearly eight-hundred-acre plantation to the Society for the Propagation of the Gospel so they could start a missionary college. The Anglican Church happily became a slave owner for the next 123 years, branding its initial three hundred slaves on the chest with the word "Society" to remind people that they belonged to the Lord.[16]

Christianity undoubtedly acted as an opiate, keeping slaves content with the hope of a higher power and a better future. But it also provided slaves with a bedrock strength against the hardships of their unavoidable reality.

As Josiah began to preach, he struggled with the possibility that he was complicit in perpetuating the institution of slavery. Black preachers were often trained by white pastors who actively supported slavery and were deeply suspicious of insurrection. Under the supervision of the white ruling class, many black preachers joined their masters in urging slaves to be obedient and submissive, telling them to wait patiently for their reward in heaven. The preachers said these things because they didn't want to be flogged for inciting rebellion, or because whites rewarded them with money, relief from labor, or even manumission. The black preachers, whether slave or free, often truly believed they were giving good advice on how to avoid the master's lash. It was harm reduction, at the very least.

As Anderson Edwards, a slave preacher born in 1844, told the Slave Narratives project, "When I starts preachin' I couldn't read or write and had to preach what massa told me, and he say tell them niggers iffen they obeys the massa they goes to Heaven; but I knowed there's something better for them, but daren't tell them 'cept on the sly. That I done lots. I tells 'em iffen they keeps prayin, the Lord will set 'em free."[17]

In his dual position as both overseer and preacher, Josiah faced a painful dilemma: as overseer, his physical needs were being met more adequately than before, and he wasn't being beaten, but he was still the property of another man. He was an agent of that man's will, charged with keeping his fellow slaves in line. And he was preaching to them the gospel of Jesus, who urged patience and love for one's enemies. In every way, Josiah was becoming more and more a tool of the oppressive slave system. Was there another choice? Escape was out of the question. Rebellion would be suicide. Given the stark reality of the institutionalized and fully legal system of slavery, there was little a slave preacher like Josiah Henson could do except exhort his followers to keep praying until the Lord sent delivery. Someday, perhaps, Josiah himself would be that deliverer.

❧

It was a hot Saturday night in the summertime when Josiah found himself in his customary spot, waiting on the porch of a smoke-filled tavern while his master got drunk and played cards inside.

Because the Maryland planters were perfectly aware that they would not be able to find their own way home after a cockfight or game of cards, each one typically ordered a slave to accompany him. Josiah couldn't count the number of times he had held Isaac on his horse when he could not hold himself in the saddle, or had walked by his side in the darkness on the muddy route from the tavern to his house.

Just as importantly, these nineteenth-century "designated drivers" also served as bodyguards to pull their masters out of the inevitable drunken brawls that broke out. Violent quarrels and fights erupted frequently, and whenever they became especially dangerous—when glasses were thrown, daggers drawn, or pistols fired—it was each slave's duty to drag his master from the fray.

Josiah felt no reluctance about this part of the job. He was young, athletic, and not afraid to put these traits on display. He waded in quickly, elbowing his way among the whites to grab his master and drag him out, and then toss him on his horse like a bag of corn. Josiah prided himself on his physical superiority, and he was always eager to get in there and drag Isaac out while getting in a few pushes for good measure. It was the only time he could rough up a white man without fear of punishment. He also knew that the more Isaac depended on him, the more comfortable and secure his life would become.

One night at the card table, Bryce Litton stared across at Isaac Riley. All evening, Litton had been losing dollar after dollar of his hard-earned money to the sweaty blacksmith. Litton couldn't seem to catch a break. He suspected his opponent was cheating, as he was known to do, but he hadn't caught Isaac in the act.

Litton worked for George Riley, Isaac's brother. He didn't mind George, or their far wealthier brother, Amos, but he'd grown to despise Isaac. The wedge had grown wider when Isaac had promoted his slave—Josiah Henson—to the position of overseer. The way Litton saw it, men like Josiah stole much-needed jobs from men like Litton. With a plug of chewing tobacco jammed into his cheek, Litton stared at Isaac while he waited for his final card. Litton had Isaac dead to rights.

Isaac eyed his brother's overseer with disgust. Even among slaveholders, there was a certain code of honor. Litton, a tyrannical and barbarous man, deserved to be cheated.*

Litton laid out his cards. The other men groaned. They had all been beaten. Only Isaac remained unruffled. The blacksmith revealed his cards.

Bryce Litton exploded. *You cheating son of a bitch!* He dove across the table and lunged for Isaac's throat. The swarthy Isaac stood and started swinging. The other men, along with half the bar, quickly joined the fray.

Sitting on the front steps of the tavern, Josiah heard the shouting and crashing of fists and bodies and rushed inside to look after his charge. Isaac was lodged in a corner with a dozen men swinging at him. They were using fists, pots, chairs, and anything else that came in handy. The moment he saw his slave, Isaac drunkenly hallooed, "That's it, Sie! Pitch in! Show me fair play!"[18]

Josiah dove in, shoving, tripping, and doing his best to effect a rescue. He received many bruises to his head and shoulders, but he steadily managed to gain ground against the drunken lot. But perhaps, on this occasion, Josiah fought a little too violently. At the height of the scuffle, whether from a shove or the whiskey he'd drunk, Bryce Litton fell hard.

He immediately blamed Josiah, and screamed he'd have revenge.

---

* Alternately spelled Lytton. Josiah calls him Bryce Litton, though the man in question is likely Brice Reuben Letton, born March 9, 1782, in Rockville, Montgomery County.[19]

As Josiah forced the drunken Isaac out the door and into his wagon, Litton glared at him with an intensity the young overseer had never seen before.

⁓ℓℯ⁓

A week later, Isaac Riley sent Josiah on horseback to mail some letters at the post office a few miles away. Josiah took a short-cut through a lane that was separated by gates from the high road and bounded by a fence on each side. The lane passed through George Riley's farm.

As Josiah rode past, he noticed the overseer, Bryce Litton, in the adjoining field with three slaves. Josiah had all but forgotten Isaac's fight with Litton, as it was such a common occurrence.

But Litton had not forgotten.

On Josiah's return, half an hour later, Litton was sitting on the fence. Josiah rode past, totally oblivious to any trouble. Litton jumped off the fence, while two slaves sprang from the bushes. They blocked the path in front of Josiah. Then a third hopped the fence and blocked the path behind him. He was trapped.

The overseer grabbed his horse's bridle and commanded Josiah to alight.

Josiah saw no way of escape. He got off the horse on the opposite side from Bryce Litton.

Litton lifted a stick to hit him. The sudden movement frightened the horse, which bolted away from Josiah. He had no way to escape the four-man attack. Litton swung at Josiah with his stick. Josiah backed up to avoid the blow and was cornered by the fence.

Litton commanded his slaves to attack.

The three slaves, knowing Josiah's physical strength, were slow to obey.

Reluctantly they approached Josiah. They did their best, but as they brought themselves within his reach, the powerful young man knocked them down in a row. One tried to trip Josiah's feet when he was down. Josiah kicked the man with his heavy shoe and knocked out three of his front teeth. The man ran away howling.

Meanwhile, Bryce Litton used every available opportunity to beat Josiah's head with a stick. It wasn't heavy enough to knock him down, but soon Josiah was pouring blood.

"Won't you give up?" Litton screamed again and again.

Josiah continued to defend himself against the two remaining slaves and the abuser with the stick. After five minutes of struggle, Litton grew exasperated at his victim's stubborn defense. He seized a heavy fence post, over six feet long, and rushed at Josiah with rage. He raised the plank and struck the slave with his whole strength. Josiah raised his right arm to ward it off, but the bone snapped like a brittle pipe stem. Josiah collapsed in agony.

Litton pile-drove blows into Josiah's back.

The slaves begged their master to stop.

"Didn't you see the nigger strike me?" Litton screamed.

The men nodded yes, afraid of doing anything else.

Bryce Litton smashed the fence post again and again into Josiah's back, until both shoulder blades were shattered and blood gushed from the young man's mouth.

His vengeance satisfied, Litton stopped and said, "Remember what it was to strike a white man."[20]

⁓✥⁓

WHEN JOSIAH'S HORSE RETURNED WITHOUT HIS RIDER, AN ALARM had been raised at the house. Isaac Riley assembled a small party and set off to learn what the trouble was.

When Isaac found Josiah lying in a bloody heap by the fence, he swore with rage.

"You've been fighting, you mean nigger!"

Josiah, through tears and blood, explained what had happened.

The wagon ride back to Isaac's farm was pure and total agony. Josiah could feel and hear the pieces of his shoulder blades grating against each other.

No doctor or surgeon was called to remedy his injuries. No one had ever been called to help a slave at Isaac's estate, no matter the injury. Nor could Josiah remember the same being done on any estate in the neighborhood. Slave owners assumed the robust health produced by a life of outdoor labor made their slaves' wounds heal just like their cattle's.

Josiah was wracked with pain. Isaac's sister, Miss Patty, was the medicine woman of the plantation. Josiah later described her as a "powerful, big-boned woman, who flinched at no responsibility, from wrenching out teeth to setting bones."[21] Josiah had even seen her shoot an ox in the head. Miss Patty splintered Josiah's arm and back as best she knew how.

As he lay on his mattress of straw, Josiah could not help but think of his father. Mason, too, had received a brutal beating—a whipping—from a white man. He had been seriously injured, and for weeks he could not work. Eventually he had been shipped to another plantation in the Deep South.

Was his father still alive?

Josiah didn't know.

Was it possible that by some machination of fate, Josiah was destined to find his father in the cruelest way possible—by being yet another half-dead Negro slave to be shipped down the Mississippi River and into the dreaded cotton fields?

Josiah's newfound faith in Jesus gave him the courage to survive. He didn't need riches or comfort, only the strength to endure. Josiah simply resolved to "trust in God, and never despair."[22]

❦

AFTER JOSIAH'S BROKEN BODY HAD BEEN BROUGHT BACK TO THE farm, and seeing how severe his injuries were, Isaac Riley was enraged.

He mounted his horse and rode to the Montgomery County courthouse to file a complaint.

A judge was called, and Isaac sued Litton for abusing and maiming his slave. Isaac made a statement of the facts and presented Josiah and his heavily bandaged body as evidence.[23]

The judge asked Litton for his side of the story. Litton swore Josiah had "sassed" him, jumped off his horse, and attacked him. Josiah would have killed him, he said, if his slaves hadn't rescued him.

The judge nodded thoughtfully. Since no black man's testimony was admitted against a free white man's, the judge ruled in favor of the defendant. Litton was acquitted, and Isaac Riley was forced to pay the court costs.[*]

ᘓᘖᘗ

Until the passage of the Fourteenth Amendment on July 9, 1868, slave testimony was effectively banned from the American judiciary. A key rule, which applied directly to cases involving slaves, was that a witness had to take an oath before he would be admitted to testify. In the seventeenth century, a time when the belief in divine intervention in the affairs of men was deeply held, the rationale was that an oath ensured immediate divine retribution upon false swearing. By the nineteenth century, when such beliefs had become less literal and more abstract, the oath had become a way to warn the witness of a future penalty for false swearing.

But in order to take an oath, a person had to be a member of the great community of human souls. For many white Christians, anyone who was not of the Christian faith, and especially any heathen African,

---

[*] As soon as he exited the courthouse, Isaac Riley collared Bryce Litton. Litton flashed a devilish grin. Isaac smashed him across the mouth with his heavy fist. Litton raised his hands to shield his face, and Isaac used the opportunity to rain blows upon the man's midsection. Litton crumpled to the ground, and Isaac booted him repeatedly. The man's face and body began to bruise and swell, and his mouth dripped blood. Isaac had the satisfaction of calling the overseer a liar and a scoundrel, among other things. Bryce Litton sued for damages and won a heavy fine.

was a soulless creature for whom swearing an oath was meaningless, at best, and blasphemous, at worst.

Thomas R. R. Cobb, a Georgia lawyer who became a brigadier general in the Confederate Army, and who is best known for his 1858 treatise on the law of slavery, titled *An Inquiry into the Law of Negro Slavery in the United States of America*, made much of this principle. Only free men, he wrote, were worthy to take oaths, and the testimony of those in a "menial" or degraded social position must be excluded altogether. Cobb implied that the judicial system was only for the free.

Isaac felt that a legal system designed to favor free white men had been used against him, a free white man, because his star witness was a black slave. Five months later, he deemed Josiah strong enough to return to work and sent him off to plow a field. But a hard knock of the blade against a stone shattered his shoulder blades again, and the agony was even worse than before.

From that day onward, Josiah went through life mutilated and in pain. Practice, over time, enabled him to perform many routine farm chores with considerable efficiency, but he was never again able to raise his hands higher than his head.* He was forced to lean forward even to place his hat on his head, a constant reminder of the pain he had endured.

---

* Historian Robin Winks weakly suggests that Josiah's editors exaggerated his arm problems. However, there are at least four third-party sources that counter such a claim: (1) Josiah's March 9, 1829, manumission paper contains a detailed physical description of Josiah, in which the clerk of the court, Bruce Selby, notes that although he is "straight and well formed, both arms are stiff being occasioned by some injury in the elbow joints."[24] The manumission papers are at the Owensboro Museum of Science and History. (2) Henry Wadsworth Longfellow, upon meeting Josiah for the first time, noted, "Almost every negro has the rheumatism. This man had it. His right arm was crooked and stiff." See Henry Wadsworth Longfellow, *The Works of Henry Wadsworth Longfellow*, vol. 13 (Boston: Houghton Mifflin, 1891), 48. (3) A January 12, 1882, article in the *Hamilton Evening Times* specifically mentions Josiah's crippled arms. (4) A white Methodist Episcopal minister, Henry Bleby, meeting Josiah in Boston, observed that "he could not lift his hand to his head; and . . . when he had to put on or take off his hat he brought his head down to his hand. Both his arms appeared to be shorter than they should have been in proportion to his size, and he was stiff and awkward in the use of them." Henry Bleby, *Josiah: The Maimed Fugitive* (London: Wesleyan Conference Office, 1873), 49.

THREE

KENTUCKY BOUND

Knowledge makes a man unfit to be a slave.

—FREDERICK DOUGLASS

JOSIAH HENSON STARED AT THE BLACK GIRL WITH THE SOARING voice. He was captivated by her, totally entranced. The chapel and all the people in its pews disappeared as she hit the high notes.

> *There is a balm in Gilead,*
> *To make the wounded whole;*
> *There's power enough in heaven,*
> *To cure a sin-sick soul.*

Josiah learned that her name was Charlotte and that she belonged to the owners of a nearby plantation called Williamsburg. The neighboring family who owned her was known for piety and kindness, and Charlotte had been well-educated—for a slave, at least.

In 1811, at age twenty-two, Josiah married the young girl with the lovely singing voice.

While the details of Josiah and Charlotte's marriage are lost to history, it was common for slave marriages to include a simple ritual that involved "jumping the broom," where the couple jumped over a broomstick to symbolize their union. The details of this custom varied from plantation to plantation. In one tradition, the bride and groom were required to jump backward over a broom held a foot off the ground. If either partner failed to clear the obstacle, the other would be declared head of the house. On other plantations, the couple would place two brooms on the floor in front of each other and step across the brooms at the same time, joining hands to signal that they were married.

Of course, slave marriages had no legal grounding; nor did they protect the couple in any way from their slave owners. Slaves often married without the use of a minister—they simply requested permission from the master to move into a cabin together, and that cabin in most cases contained other enslaved workers. Couples who lived on different plantations were only allowed to visit when both masters consented.

It's unclear when, exactly, Isaac Riley purchased Charlotte and brought her to live with her husband, but Josiah knew from experience that even this bond could be quickly torn apart.

Josiah later wrote that he and his wife shared a deep and intimate bond. Before long, Charlotte was pregnant with their first child, and in the coming decades she would bear Josiah twelve children. Four boys and four girls would make it to adulthood—a good survival rate, considering the harshness of their lives.

Josiah continued to supply his fellow slaves with food superior to what slaves typically received on neighboring plantations. If he cheated Isaac in small matters, he reasoned, it was unquestionably for Isaac's personal benefit in the more important ones, such as hard cash. Josiah was meticulous with every dollar he received from the sale of the remaining goods that made it to market.

Eventually the sale of everything raised on the farm was entrusted to Josiah—the hay, oats, wheat, butter, apples, potatoes, and everything else that was in season. It had become evident that he could get better prices for his goods than anyone else Isaac could hire.

For the next fourteen years, Josiah was Isaac's jack-of-all-trades. Isaac nicknamed him "Man Friday," after Robinson Crusoe's faithful servant. Josiah supplied Isaac with anything and everything he needed. He didn't approve of Isaac's character, but Josiah saw it as his duty to be his faithful overseer, no matter what.

One thing Josiah's faith had given him was the ability to forgive. He forgave Isaac for the beatings and injuries he'd inflicted on him as a child. Josiah was proud of the character and reputation he'd earned through his hard work and perseverance.

Josiah clearly had a complicated and conflicted relationship with Isaac—today we might call it advanced codependency or even Stockholm syndrome. He longed to please God and his master, and many masters used theology as a way to keep men like Josiah in their place. For as long as Josiah could remember, Isaac had been the lord of his life, and one can imagine how easy it might be to cling to the notion that the abuses he suffered in Maryland under Isaac were relatively moderate compared to the extreme anguish of life in the Deep South. Josiah's situation had improved since his childhood, and he could hope that things would improve even more in the years to come.

For more than a decade, Josiah oversaw the operation of four farms. As the market man for the Riley brothers, he carried a pass that allowed him to travel the twelve miles to Washington and Georgetown to sell their produce.

While Isaac Riley spent his years in general depravity, Josiah set about improving himself. Though he never formally studied arithmetic, he became an ace with complicated fractions and even sizable calculations. He sold Isaac's butter to some of the most intelligent gentlemen in Washington, and in making these sales he had the opportunity to spend time in their presence.

Whenever these educated men conversed, Josiah listened attentively to how they spoke their phrases and sentences, and he soon learned to speak in a manner that disguised his lack of education. His pronunciation became better than that of most slaves, and even better than that of the poor whites of the district. He also gained a practical knowledge of law from hearing lawyers explain their cases. Later in life, after he became a compelling preacher and debater, Josiah said that, had he been a white man, he would have chosen law as his profession.

~⚬⚬⚬~

ENSLAVED PEOPLE WHO TRAVELED FROM ONE PLACE TO ANOTHER needed to carry a pass signed by their owner. Any black person caught without such a pass could be detained, arrested, and jailed as a runaway. Some owners wrote general passes allowing their slaves to "pass" and "repass." Isaac often gave Josiah travel passes to conduct business in Georgetown and Washington, and having a practical knowledge of his very limited rights kept Josiah out of serious trouble.

Because many slaves had spouses, children, and other relatives who were owned by different masters and lived on other properties, slaves often requested passes to travel and visit family, especially over the Christmas holiday. Some slaves who were attempting to flee used the passes to explain their presence on the road and delay the discovery of their escape. The officials assumed their travel was legitimate, since they had passes, and their masters would not be expecting them to return from their "family visit" until the holiday was over.*

In order for the system of passes to work most effectively, slave owners relied on a proven tool: ignorance. If enslaved people were kept illiterate, they had less ability to forge fake passes, alter what their passes allowed for, or create other mischief. One justification for the laws banning black literacy was to protect the integrity of this primitive surveillance and identification system. If black people could read and write, they had a

---

* In 1834, when Jarm Logue, a twenty-one-year-old slave in Davidson County, Tennessee, plotted a Christmas escape, he knew that travel passes and the cover of the holidays were essential for success: "Lord speed the day!—freedom begins with the holidays!" he later wrote in his 1859 autobiography, *The Rev. J. W. Loguen, as a Slave and as a Freeman: A Narrative of Real Life*, edited by Jennifer A. Williamson, New York State Series (Syracuse, NY: Syracuse University Press, 2016). He made it to Canada and to freedom. When his book was published and became well known, Sarah Logue, the wife of his former master, wrote to Jermain Loguen (as he now called himself) and demanded $1,000 in compensation under the Fugitive Slave Act. Loguen declined to pay.

much better chance of maneuvering around the system of control and monitoring—and therefore also of escaping slavery.

However, passes, and even papers stating that a black person was a free citizen, still could be forged or given to another slave. If a free paper simply said something like, "Samuel Scott, thirty years old, purchased his freedom on 6 April 1832," any male person who could conceivably pass for approximately thirty years old might be able to use the paper to convince semi- or even fully literate whites that he was a free man.

White authorities kept well abreast of such efforts. Governments and slave owners began using printing presses to create standardized forms for free papers. These forms contained empty fields for the entry of specific personal characteristics such as height, weight, skin color, eye color, hair texture, body shape, and scars or deformities (like Josiah's shoulders and right arm). The personal physical traits noted on the forms made it much more difficult for slaves to transfer or reappropriate the papers.

The slave system and the Fugitive Slave Acts also led to the proliferation of wanted ads in newspapers that described escaped slaves in detail. These posters weren't just for the general public to keep an eye on. They were also closely watched by the local slave patrols.

First appearing in South Carolina in 1704, informal slave patrols started as a way to break up illicit slave meetings in which slaves planned revolts and uprisings. These meetings often occurred on holidays. As the population of black slaves grew, so did the necessity of finding a growing number of runaways, and slave patrols were formed throughout the South and given official sanction. They were permitted to question and search black travelers and subject them to other forms of harassment. Slaves found to be without passes were returned to their owners, and the punishments for runaway slaves were severe. But the slave patrols did not just harass travelers and return runaways—they also began visiting slave quarters and conducting searches there. They broke up slave gatherings in an effort to stop uprisings before they could occur. Slave patrollers used whips and guns as they carried out their brutal campaign of control over slaves—people who, like Josiah in his encounter with Litton, had no legal protection.

AN UNLIKELY FRIENDSHIP

When war broke out on June 18, 1812, with the British colonies in what is now Canada, Isaac Riley joined the Extra Battalion of the Maryland Militia. According to a pension document filed decades later, he served as a private in Captain Thomas Getting's company.[1] Men like Isaac had good reason to fight. Slaves were escaping north to the Canadian colonies. Wouldn't it be better if the whole continent became part of the United States?

The War of 1812 started in part because of Britain's economic sanctions against its former colonies, which virtually crippled American trade. The Americans hoped to gain some land and cut off Britain's supply lines to its agitators. They fought to a stalemate against the feisty Canadian colonials and their British counterparts, led by warriors such as Major General Isaac Brock and Shawnee leader Tecumseh, in and around the Niagara region. The war lasted for more than two and a half years, and almost 20,000 men lost their lives before both sides agreed to return to the status quo.

After the war, Isaac Riley returned to Maryland, where his older brother, George, died shortly thereafter. Isaac served as George's executor, tasked with caring for George's widow and three daughters. He continued to run the plantation with the help of his sister Patty and his slaves, and with Josiah as his market man and overseer.

At the age of forty-four, Isaac finally took a wife. In December 1818, he married eighteen-year-old Matilda Middleton. Matilda owned two slaves prior to her marriage, likely received from the estate of her grandfather William O'Neale. She also had some land, but it was embroiled for years in a series of legal battles. Their first child arrived the following year, and they would eventually have five children in total, four girls and a boy. Isaac now had almost twenty slaves, including several enslaved children.

Matilda had a thirteen-year-old brother, Francis Middleton, whom everyone called Frank. The Middleton parents must have died, because Isaac Riley was appointed Frank's guardian. It was his legal duty to maintain the boy's inherited estate until he reached the age of maturity, and, unsurprisingly, he would do an incredibly poor job of it.

Mrs. Riley's thriftiness was extreme, and it certainly added no additional comfort to the slaves' way of life, let alone her brother's. Matilda believed she owed her brother nothing. As mistress of the household, she controlled his food rations, believing every morsel he consumed was a debt to be repaid. Isaac Riley was no help to Frank. His sympathies lay with his new wife—and in getting his hands on as much of Frank's inheritance as possible.

The half-starved boy quickly became miserable. He often came to Josiah with tears in his eyes, complaining of hunger. Josiah gained a friend for life by sharing with Frank, giving him food he grew for his own family. Soon Frank was a regular in Josiah's cabin, where he played with his two young sons and ate whatever they could provide.

This friendship would prove helpful to Josiah in later years. Frank grew up to become one of the wealthiest men in Washington—and one of Isaac Riley's greatest enemies. But as it turned out, Frank wasn't the only family member with a bone to pick with Isaac Riley.

FORCED WEST

In time, even Matilda Riley's relentless attempts to control the family's spending were no match for her husband's continued extravagance, and Josiah's master fell into dire economic straits.

It started because George Riley's widow, Mary Richards, remarried. Her new husband, Arnold Thomas Windsor, became guardian of George's three daughters. Though Isaac controlled George's plantation and its several farms, Windsor knew Isaac Riley was a dishonest manager, and he had solid legal footing to demand that he liquidate part of the estate to financially provide for his nieces. On January 22, 1825, Arnold T. Windsor filed his first lawsuit against Isaac Riley.[2]

Isaac rode to the Montgomery County courthouse day after day in search of a favorable resolution, and every day his affairs grew more desperate. Night after night, he would come into Josiah's cabin to tell him his problems, and to pass the evenings moaning at his misfortune. Even though Isaac had been a hard tyrant, Josiah pitied the man in his present distress. Some nights, Isaac was dreadfully dejected; others, he became crazy with drink and rage. He cursed his brother-in-law and asked for Josiah's advice and assistance. Josiah comforted Isaac as best he could. Isaac had confidence in Josiah's loyalty and judgment, and partly through pride, partly through the love of God, Josiah took a genuine interest in his owner's problems. Isaac had resisted his brother-in-law's onslaught for years, but now his hand was being forced by the court.

On the night of January 22, long after Josiah had fallen asleep, Isaac came into the slave cabin. Josiah woke up, astonished at the sight of his master sitting alone, moodily warming himself by the fire. Josiah watched as Isaac began to groan and wring his hands.

"Sick, massa?" Josiah asked.[3]

Isaac made no reply, but kept on moaning.

"Can't I help you any way?" Josiah spoke tenderly, his heart full of compassion at the man's wretched appearance.

"Oh, Sie! I'm ruined, ruined, ruined!" Isaac wailed.

Although Josiah was not surprised, he was concerned. "How so?"

"They've got judgment against me, and in less than two weeks every nigger I've got will be put up and sold."

While Isaac burst into a storm of curses at his brother-in-law, only one word rang in Josiah's ears.

Sold.

Josiah sat silently, powerless to utter a word, feeling pity for Isaac and terror about his own family's future.

"And now, Sie," Isaac continued, "there's only one way I can save anything. You can do it. Won't you, won't you?"

Isaac stood and threw his arms around Josiah. The slave was stunned at this desperate outpouring of emotion. Misery had seemingly leveled the playing field.

"If I can do it . . . I will," Josiah said. "What is it?"

Isaac ignored the question.

"Won't you, won't you?" Isaac cried. "I raised you, Sie. I made you overseer. I know I have abused you, Sie, but I didn't mean it."

Josiah asked again what the task was, but Isaac seemed resolutely bent on having Josiah's promise first. Isaac knew from past experience that Josiah's character would bind him to do all that he promised, if at all possible. The grown man wept on the floor at his slave's feet.

"Promise me you'll do it, boy," Isaac begged.

In that moment, Isaac seemed absolutely dependent upon his slave. But if Josiah's heart began to soften to Isaac's pitiful condition, the cunning blacksmith had an ace up his sleeve.

With skillful precision, Isaac Riley awoke Josiah's greatest fear, explaining that the sheriff would seize everyone who belonged to Isaac, and that they would all be separated, and perhaps sold to Georgia or Louisiana.

Josiah's body shivered at the thought. He remembered his broken father, sold south to Louisiana. He thought of his mother, separated for life from five of her six children. He thought of Charlotte, and their two boys.

Josiah had faithfully served Isaac for more than thirty years, and he knew he had no choice but to accept the unknown proposition. Despite Isaac's stupidity and greed, his urgency and tears, paired with Josiah's terrifying fear of being sold south, were enough for him to promise he'd do all he could to save his master from his impending fate. And what choice did he have, anyway?

Isaac beamed, but kept his voice low so none of the other slaves would wake up.

"I want you to run away, Sie," Isaac said. "To my brother Amos in Kentucky, and take all the servants along with you."

Josiah felt Isaac might as well have just asked him to go to the moon.

"Kentucky, massa? Kentucky?" Josiah said. "I don't know the way."

"Oh, it's easy enough for a smart fellow like you to find it," Isaac replied. "I'll give you a pass and tell you just what to do."

Josiah was thirty-five years old, but he'd never traveled more than a day's journey from the plantation in his entire life. He'd never been to Virginia or Ohio or Kentucky. He'd never seen the Appalachian Mountains. All he knew were the plantation, Georgetown, and Washington. Now his master was asking him to move nearly two dozen people over 650 miles in the middle of winter, over land and water he knew nothing about.

Isaac sensed Josiah's hesitation and tried to frighten him again with the terrors of being sold south.

Some of the worst stories about the Deep South would be circulated between farms, and Josiah would have heard stories like that of William Wells Brown, who was tied up, whipped, and baked in a smokehouse.[4] There was Moses Roper, an escaped mulatto slave, who had reported that a large farmer in the Carolinas named Colonel M'Quiller had a practice of hammering nails into tobacco barrels so that the iron points protruded just inside the cask: "Into this he used to put his slaves for punishment, and roll them down a very long and steep hill," he reported. Roper believed that six or seven slaves had been killed this way, and he had heard that the terrifying idea had been adopted by several other planters.[5] And then there was the brazen account of Nash County, North Carolina, resident Micajah Ricks, who, describing one of his missing slaves in the *North Carolina Standard* on July 18 1838, said: "I burnt her on the left side of her face: I tried to make the letter M. . . ."* The *St. Louis Gazette* ran a notice on November 6, 1845, that said, "A wealthy man here had a boy named Reuben, almost white, whom he caused to be branded in the face with the words; 'A slave for life.'"

Isaac Riley pressed Josiah for hours, appealing to his pride, his sympathies, and his deepest fears. The slave owner hoped to follow Josiah in a few months and make a fresh start in Kentucky. Life would be better for all of them there. If Josiah didn't take Isaac's slaves, he said, the hungry jaws of the South would happily swallow him up.

Josiah felt he had no choice, and he reluctantly promised to undertake the long, high-stakes journey.

A FLEETING TASTE OF FREEDOM

Josiah began making the necessary preparations. There were eighteen people to transport, plus Josiah's wife, Charlotte, and their two sons, Tom

---

* Ricks also ran a similar ad in the *Raleigh Standard* on July 18, 1838, in which he specified that he "burnt her with a hot iron."

and Isaac. He readied a horse and wagon and stocked it with oats, corn-meal, and bacon, both for the slaves and the horse. He saw the impor-tance of his responsibility, and felt proud that Isaac trusted him. He would lead his master's slaves all the way to Kentucky.

Two nights after Isaac's late-night breakdown, in early February 1825, the group left the plantation under cover of darkness.

Josiah's mother, Celia, stayed behind to serve as a house maid for Matilda, likely as a way of ensuring that Josiah wouldn't try to escape.

Josiah led the slaves out of the Riley plantation at eleven o'clock at night, and they didn't stop until noon the next day. The adults marched on foot through the snow. The children rode in the wagon, and Char-lotte joined them whenever she needed a rest.

Fortunately, these people had been under Josiah's direction for decades. They were devoted and attached to him, and they knew he cared for them. Their love for Josiah, paired with their fear of being separated and sold south, was enough to keep everyone patient and alert.

Josiah and the group marched west through Alexandria, Culpepper, Fauquier, Harpers Ferry, Cumberland, and over the mountains on the newly built National Turnpike toward Wheeling. Josiah felt his sense of independence increase with every step.

❧

The air was cold and damp, and the road was muddy with melting snow as Josiah and his group made their way through Ohio. The dark branches of the bare trees seemed to claw at the overcast sky. A murder of crows squawked and fussed before taking wing over the desolate fields. Josiah's entourage approached a roadside tavern, one of many in which they had lodged each night of their winter journey.

Slaves constantly passed them in either direction. The groups were chained together, marching on foot, and driven by a white overseer on horseback. The curved wooden grip of a pistol jutted from every holster.

One overseer stopped and signaled for his group to stop alongside Josiah's. The chained slaves obediently stood by the side of the road while their master approached.

Keeping his hands visible and a smile on his face, Josiah took a few steps forward.

"Whose niggers are those?" asked the man.[6]

Josiah produced his travel pass and explained the slaves were the property of Isaac Riley of Montgomery County, Maryland.

"Where are they going?"

"To Kentucky."

"Who drives them?"

"Well," Josiah said. "I have charge of them."

"What a smart nigger! Will your master sell you?"

Josiah declined, but took pride in being looked on with such praise.

"Come in and stop with us," the drover said.

Such encounters were a regular occurrence for Josiah and the group on their way to Wheeling. After convincing skeptical whites that he was the legitimate overseer of his group, Josiah was often invited to pass the evening with the other overseers in the bar. The slaves in the other groups were kept chained in pens to keep them from running away. Josiah, meanwhile, allowed his charges to roam as they pleased.

As prearranged with Isaac Riley, Josiah sold the horse and wagon when he arrived at Wheeling. He used the money to buy a large, flat-bottomed boat, which the locals called a river skiff or yawl. Their new form of transportation was decidedly more agreeable than marching day after day. By night they stopped to camp, and by day the current floated them steadily down the Ohio River with only the need to steer and avoid obstacles, sandbars, and other vessels.

For the first time in their lives, Isaac Riley's slaves had leisure enough to rest and build up their strength. The days floating down the river, watching the towns pass by, without being beaten or compelled to break their backs in the fields, seemed like a strange and heavenly dream.

⁓≈⁓

As they floated down the river, with the slave state of Kentucky on their left and the free state of Ohio on their right, new and unexpected trouble rose up to meet Josiah. Whenever they landed for a rest on the Ohio shore, they were repeatedly told by passing travelers that they were no longer slaves but free men.

When they reached Cincinnati, free colored people gathered around them and insisted they stay with them. Their new acquaintances told them it would be foolish to surrender themselves to a new owner. They could be their own masters. In Ohio they were out of reach of being caught.

As the free men of Cincinnati presented their arguments, Josiah saw that the people under him were getting excited about the prospect of starting new lives. Josiah began to feel his own resolution weakening. He was entranced by the idea of freeing his companions and running away with his wife and children. Maybe someday he would own a house and land. He would no longer be abused or despised by white men.

Before this, although he had dreamed of gaining his freedom, Josiah had never dreamed of running away. From his earliest memory, freedom had in fact been his ultimate ambition, a constant motive to work, an ever-present stimulus to gain and to save. No other means of obtaining his freedom had ever occurred to him except to purchase himself from Isaac.

But here was an opportunity he had not anticipated. Josiah could liberate his family, his companions, and himself, with minimal risk, and with injustice to none except the one man they all hated, who had cruelly oppressed them for years, who had never shown the smallest hint of sympathy with them or their condition.

If anything, the act of escape could be seen as righteous retribution. As justice.

But it was not Josiah Henson's punishment to inflict on Isaac Riley. That was God's job. He had promised to deliver Isaac's property to his brother in Kentucky, and he would live up to the responsibility he'd been given.

Josiah ordered his people back into the boat at sunset. They'd been under his care for so long, and had grown so accustomed to obeying him, that no one resisted.

Josiah believed it was the honorable course. He'd heard ministers and religious men preach on the duties of the slave to his master as appointed over him in the Lord. Josiah was supposed to obey his master in *all* things. He felt honor-bound to fulfill his oath to Isaac, even at the expense of his freedom.

To the modern reader, this sounds absurd, of course. Josiah did the best he knew at the time, which was, frankly, almost nothing. He was brainwashed, so fully dyed in the wool of the slavery system that black and white—truth and lie—were indistinguishable.

The free blacks on land showered curses on Josiah as he pushed off from shore. His mother's fate was, no doubt, in the back of his mind. And what would happen if he escaped but was recaptured? The risk was too great. No, Josiah would improve his position on this new Kentucky plantation, and perhaps a safer opportunity for freedom would present itself in the future.

Josiah watched with longing as the free blacks of Cincinnati faded into the twilight. He had planned to stay the night in the city, but instead he camped with his party a few miles downriver. Long after his fellow slaves had gone to sleep, he sat by the water and thought about his decision. He believed he had done the honorable thing, and hadn't yet begun to doubt his choice.

Josiah had been utterly brainwashed by a toxic combination of illiteracy, indoctrination—by both state and church—and the threat of bodily harm to himself and his family. All of this, combined with his personal make-up, his fear and pride, his drive and ambition, and his desire for praise and respect, had made escape both unimaginable and seemingly unethical. Though he didn't yet realize it, Josiah had betrayed his companions to please his white master. He had the opportunity to provide freedom to his fellow slaves, but had instead re-enslaved his fellow humans.

It was a decision Josiah would regret for the rest of his life.

FOUR

DOUBLE CROSS

No pen can give an adequate description of the
all-pervading corruption produced by slavery.

—HARRIET ANN JACOBS

I T TOOK JOSIAH HENSON AND HIS GROUP TEN WEEKS TO COMPLETE
the journey to Kentucky. They arrived at Daviess County in the middle of April 1825, and Josiah dutifully delivered the entire group to
Isaac's brother Amos at his plantation.

At this time, Josiah was almost thirty-six years old. Buying his freedom seemed a far-off dream. But he had a few things to be grateful
for. Though his life had been wretched, and he had suffered greatly at
the hands of his masters, especially Isaac Riley, a few blessings had been
bestowed upon him. His body was maimed, but his mind was sharp.
Miraculously, his family hadn't been separated from each other. He was
a slave, but certainly not the lowliest.

His experience in Ohio stayed with him, and he had conflicting
emotions of complacency and outrage. On one hand, for a slave in his
relatively privileged and powerful position, it was an entirely rational
choice to "get along" and make the best of his situation until he could

legally change it. On the other hand, he knew slavery was fundamentally evil and should be abolished.

Josiah weighed the benefits of accepting his slave status and working within the system to improve his family's lot versus the risks of actively resisting. It was not an easy choice. Acquiescence would mean life, but misery. Resistance—in the form of escape—could mean freedom, but more likely death. Was it better to be a free man living in a shack than a slave in the owner's mansion?

To compound his inner conflict, Josiah's new master, Amos Riley, provided a much better living situation than he and his family had experienced previously. Amos's Kentucky plantation extended five miles north and west to the Ohio River. It comprised nearly a dozen parcels totaling at least 2,750 acres,[1] with nearly one hundred slaves to tend the handful of farms. The fields were expansive and the soil fertile, and there was a greater abundance of food.

Josiah managed the Amos Riley plantation for three years while he waited for Isaac Riley to get his affairs in order and come to Kentucky. Amos trusted Josiah to an uncommon extent. Josiah was clearly a hard worker, and he came with the recommendation of Amos's brother. Amos's trust in Josiah was evidenced by the fact that every Sunday morning before heading off to church, he sat down for a straight razor shave under Josiah's careful hand. The new slave kept the razor remarkably sharp, and yet he managed to avoid making any nicks or cuts on the older man's stubbled chin. He soon possessed a skill unequaled by most of the white barbers of the county.

Because Josiah served as the plantation's overseer, he and Charlotte were given their own cabin near the river landing on the Ohio River. The location provided them with ample diversion in the form of visitors and river traffic, and Josiah and his boys spent many evenings fishing for supper. But Amos Riley wasn't being generous to the Henson family— the spot was strategic. Josiah was the master of a little port that bustled constantly with the shipping and receiving of goods from as far north as Pittsburgh and as far south as New Orleans. Along the property's five miles from the big house to the water, several distinct farms had been cobbled together to create the massive estate. Josiah managed them all—he rode from one to the next each day—and was sometimes gone for days at a time.

Often at night, after Charlotte and the boys had gone to bed, Josiah would sit by the river and stare across at the free state of Ohio. In Maryland he'd lived within viewing distance of Isaac Riley's big house. Here he was more than five miles from Amos's watchful eye. How he longed to cross over. He knew he'd drown if he made the attempt, and there was certainly no way to do it with his family. They were just a river's breadth from freedom, yet the distance was too great.

Another reason to stay on the Kentucky side was the fact that Josiah's strapping eldest son, Tom, had been appointed to the position of house servant. As Josiah had done for Isaac Riley many years earlier, Tom tended to Amos's riding horse, polished his boots, and went on errands. Tom also kept an open ear to all that went on in the house, becoming an excellent source of information for Josiah and Charlotte whenever he was allowed to visit them.

Josiah befriended Amos Riley's children, too, just as he had befriended Frank Middleton many years before. He paid special attention to Amos Junior, knowing that someday he would inherit his father's estate, including his slaves. One could never plan too far in advance.

The advantages afforded Josiah in his post as superintendent included regular religious privileges. Since his conversion at Newport Mill, his mind had been greatly occupied by his Christian faith, and he took full advantage of this small freedom. As often as he could, Josiah attended services and camp meetings, and he paid close attention to the speaking style of the preachers. He learned how best to communicate with people, how to keep them interested, and how to point them toward redemption.

Josiah was not formally trained in theology, of course, but he was an incredibly compelling preacher. He spoke passionately of his own sinfulness and imperfection, and as he labored to improve himself, he inspired those around him to do the same. In 1828, after three years of observation, practice, and prayer, Josiah was admitted as a preacher in the Methodist Episcopal Church.

This was quite the feat, especially considering that he could neither read nor write. But Josiah was a quick study. He memorized verses as quickly as he heard them shared by others. His faith was simple, but it gave him the strength to place his heavy burdens at the feet of a higher power who offered him hope. Like many other slave preachers, he relied on his natural wit and eloquence to make up for his lack of theological training.

Life as an enslaved preacher was tricky. Most were viewed by whites with suspicion, and they had to carefully balance the demands of their conscience and the orders of their master. While some masters allowed or even encouraged their slaves to preach, others were vehemently against it. Preaching at secret meetings could result in flogging; as if that wasn't bad enough, brine would then be applied to the victim's bleeding back—it was called being "pickled." The former slave Moses Grandy wrote about the practice in his autobiography.[2]

In cases where attendance was barred, slaves did their best to avoid getting caught. They met in forests, thickets, or ravines, for example, which came to be called "hush harbors." One slave preacher, Kalvin Woods, recalled how they would hang up wet quilts around them like a "little room," "to keep the sound of their voices from penetrating the air."[3]

For many the risk was high, but, as Virginia slave Peter Randolph later described it, at these meetings "the slave forgets all his sufferings, except to remind others of the trials during the past week, exclaiming: 'Thank God, I shall not live here always!'"[4]

While Amos Riley evidently allowed his slaves to attend church services, the practice varied from plantation to plantation. As another former slave, John Brown of Oklahoma, put it: "Sunday was a great day around the plantation. The fields was forgotten, the light chores was hurried through, and everybody got ready for the church meeting. . . . But the white folks on the next plantation would lick their slaves for trying to do like we did. No praying there, and no singing."[5]

A BLINDING ENLIGHTENMENT

It had been three years since Josiah and the slaves had set out from Maryland when news arrived from Isaac Riley that he had been unable to persuade his wife to accompany him to Kentucky. He would stay in Maryland for good.

The truth was that Isaac Riley's lawsuits with Arnold Windsor were catching up with him. In a series of protracted proceedings, judgments, appeals, and countersuits, Isaac was headed for ruin, and he was willing to use every resource to stave off his inevitable collapse. He ended up arranging to sell most of his property to his sister-in-law's new husband, both to settle George Riley's estate and to pay off personal debts. But Isaac Riley had refused to vacate the house or turn over the property, and the lawsuits continued.

Isaac sent an agent to Kentucky to sell all his slaves except for Josiah and his family, who would remain on the farm with his brother. Though Josiah was exempted from a personal share in the calamity, he watched as the other slaves were prepared for the auction. He saw in them that same grief he had once seen in his own mother. As he watched each of them being auctioned off, the consequences of his earlier decision became blindingly clear, and the madness of ordering them back on the boat overwhelmed him. He had prevented these men and women from trying for their freedom in Cincinnati. His only thoughts had been about remaining faithful to his master's interests, and not of the welfare of his fellow slaves. And now they were being sold to the dreaded South, where conditions would be worse. Josiah wept. He thought of his own father, sold south to Louisiana. Was he even still alive? Had he died from old age? Hunger? Sickness? Torture?

Josiah watched helplessly as his friends were sold to the highest bidder. It was a heart-wrenching affair to watch families get torn apart forever. Former slave William Wells Brown described that horrific scene which played itself out so many times in American history: "At these auction-stands, bones, muscles, sinews, blood and nerves, of human beings, are sold with as much indifference as a farmer in the north sells a horse or sheep."[6]

Isaac Riley's slaves were treated like cattle, and they were headed south.

Josiah was irrevocably changed by the experience. It was like waking from a dream. For so long he had maintained the point of view of the slave owner, seeing himself as special, different from the slaves around him. But he was no different in the eyes of his owners and in the eyes of the law. It was in that moment that he resolved to escape, with his wife and children, to freedom. He resolved to "plot like a fox, and fight like a tiger" until he was free.[7]

TRUTH REVEALED

Josiah had been told his entire life that it was God's will that Africans should be slaves. His enslavement was surely the natural order of the universe. It was not only a religious tenet, but esteemed white scientists had offered "proof" that black Africans were not capable of handling the responsibilities of freedom. From universities to the pulpit, white proponents of slavery claimed that God and nature dictated that their place was as the slave of the white man.

In the summer of 1828, a white Methodist preacher-abolitionist visited the county and took an interest in Josiah.[8]

"You ought to be free," the preacher told Josiah, "You have too much capacity to be confined to the limited and comparatively useless sphere of a slave."[9]

The words were encouraging. Josiah knew that he was a leader with a capacity for more, but no white man had ever acknowledged it.

"It must not be known that I have spoken to you on this subject," the preacher said. "Yet if you will obtain Mr. Amos's consent to go to see your old master in Maryland, I will try and put you in a way by which I think you may succeed in buying yourself."

This was the opportunity Josiah had been waiting for.

His work slowed down in the autumn because he was no longer needed in the fields. This would be the time to do it. Still, he dreaded making the request, his hopes dangling so delicately by a thread.

ENGINEERING ACCEPTANCE

Josiah broached the subject one Sunday morning in September 1828 while shaving Amos Riley at the big house. While he lathered the man's chin with a bristle brush, he asked for a travel pass to return to Maryland.[10]

Amos Riley moved to speak, but Josiah wisely began lathering close to his mouth. The slave owner had no choice but to purse his lips.

Josiah explained that he just wanted to visit his old master. He made the point that he'd finished harvesting for the season, so it was the perfect time to go, and promised he'd be back in Kentucky well before spring.

By the time the shave was finished, Amos had heard all Josiah had to say. Much to Josiah's surprise, Amos made little objection. Josiah had been faithful to him and had earned his regard. He even told Josiah he'd earned the privilege. The thought that Josiah might run away probably never entered his mind. After all, his wife and children would stay in Kentucky.

Amos wrote out a certificate that would allow Josiah to pass and repass between Kentucky and Maryland. Armed with a travel pass and a letter of recommendation from his Methodist friend to a fellow minister in Cincinnati, Josiah left Kentucky in mid-September 1828.

⊱⋆⊰

A NEW ERA IN JOSIAH'S LIFE HAD BEGUN. FOR THE FIRST TIME, ARMED with his pass, and unencumbered by any fellow travelers, he enjoyed a freedom of movement that he had never before experienced. If he wanted to stop his horse by the side of the road to enjoy the view or a cool breeze, he could do that. If he wanted to eat at one tavern rather than another, he could do that. And if he wanted to visit a church and speak to the preacher there, he could do that. His letter of recommendation from his Methodist friend opened doors, and Josiah made a number of invaluable friends who did everything in their power to help him.

The preacher's friends arranged for Josiah to preach in three different Cincinnati churches and make his appeal for emancipation money. By all accounts he spoke eloquently about heaven and hell, and life and death. He was taking his destiny into his own hands, and those who heard him speak felt his passion.

Donations were collected throughout the great abolitionist city. Four days later, Josiah left town with more than $160 in his pocket.

Based on the preacher's advice, Josiah bought a nice suit and a horse, and for the next three months, he traveled from place to place, preaching as he went. The contrast between the abolitionist churches in Ohio and the plantations of Maryland and Kentucky were stark. Everywhere he went he was met with generosity. The crowds were warm and welcoming, and they supported his pursuit of freedom with money and words of encouragement.

By the time Josiah left Ohio for Montgomery County, Maryland, he had $275 (at least $7,000 in today's currency*), plus his horse and his clothes, and for the first time in his life, he felt like a man of dignity.

But as he would soon learn, his abuse at the hands of the Riley brothers was far from over.

SQUARE ONE

Late one evening, just a few days before Christmas, Josiah arrived at Isaac Riley's Maryland plantation. Isaac Riley greeted him with a boisterous reception, but was puzzled by his horse and suit. "What in the devil have you been doing, Sie?" he said. "You've turned into a regular black gentleman."[11]

Matilda Riley joined her husband on the steps of the big house and eyed the well-dressed slave and his horse. They asked why he'd taken months to return. He gave an account of his preaching and staying with friends, being careful to tell the truth without revealing his ultimate plan.

One thing Josiah hadn't considered was how much his new clothes would irritate Isaac, because they were better than his master's. As Josiah

---

* His $275 would be worth $7,180 today in terms of real prices. The labor value (using unskilled wages) would be $78,100, or $183,000 (using production worker compensation). The income value would be $215,000.

spoke about his trip, Isaac's face flickered with anger. He'd soon take the gentleman out of the slave.

Isaac asked to see Josiah's pass. He inspected the paper, and when he saw it authorized Josiah's return to Kentucky, he handed it to Matilda and instructed her to put it in his desk.

The cool maneuver startled Josiah. It was a stark reminder that Isaac was still his owner and master. Josiah's learning and preaching and the support from people like the Methodist minister meant nothing. All that mattered was the bill of sale that Isaac kept in his house.

Isaac instructed Josiah to board his horse and sleep in the kitchen. Josiah asked if he could visit his mother first. Isaac's voice was calm and casual as he told Josiah that his mother had died, and that he should head to the kitchen immediately. Josiah stumbled away, reeling at the news.

Josiah stood in the center of the sparse, dirt-floor kitchen. How different it was from his accommodations in the free states during the past three months. The room was crowded and filthy, the air thick with the stench of sweat and food and rot. The sleeping slaves around him were all strangers. The farm was poverty stricken and his fellow slaves looked gaunt and worn. They snored softly, their bodies thin from constant toil and malnourishment.

And his mother was gone. His sweet mother, who had saved his life, introduced him to God, and prayed for him every day.

Josiah sat down in the dirt, feeling lonelier than he had in a long time. He had to buy his freedom as quickly as possible. He knew just one friend he could ask for help—Matilda Riley's brother, Frank Middleton. The boy had come of age and started a business in nearby Washington. Josiah hoped the man would remember that he had done much to lighten Frank's sorrows when he was an abused and harshly treated boy in the big house, and that the young businessman would take an interest in Josiah's plight. It was his only shot.

At dawn, Josiah saddled his horse and rode up to the house. Despite the early hour, Isaac Riley had already gone to the tavern on his usual business of drinking and gambling.

Matilda Riley came out to inspect his horse and saddle.

"Where are you going, Siah?" she asked.

"I am going to Washington, mistress, to see Mr. Frank, and I must take my pass with me, if you please."

"Oh, everybody knows you here," she said coolly, "You won't need your pass."

Josiah knew it was the truth, but he had plans to use the paper for his ultimate return to Kentucky. Without the pass, he was bound to the Maryland plantation.

"But I can't go to Washington without it. I may be met by some surly stranger, who will stop me and plague me, if he can't do anything worse."

Josiah held his breath while Matilda thought about it for a moment, eyeing the slave with distrust. Times on the plantation had been hard, though, and her husband had told her many times that things would get better once Josiah returned. She couldn't risk her property being injured, kidnapped, or killed while he traveled to Washington.

"Well," she sighed. "I'll get it for you."

She returned a few moments later and handed him the pass.

༺⁓⁓༻

JOSIAH'S WELCOME AT FRANK MIDDLETON'S HOME WAS AS KIND and hearty as he expected. The young businessman was delighted to see him in his fine suit, and Josiah immediately told him his plan to buy his freedom.[12]

Frank thoroughly detested his brother-in-law, who he believed had defrauded him of a huge portion of his property while serving as his guardian. He immediately promised to do his best to negotiate with Isaac for Josiah's freedom.

Josiah's heart felt like it was going to escape his chest. At long last, it looked like he would be able to gain his freedom the legal way, the proper way, by buying it from his master. If this happened, he could go anywhere—to any state of the Union—as a free man, without fearing the dreaded Kentucky spies and slave patrols.

It sounded almost too good to be true.

A few days later, Frank Middleton rode over to his brother-in-law's farm and had a long conversation with Isaac about Josiah's emancipation. He told Isaac that Josiah had saved some money, and made the case that he'd faithfully served the family for almost forty years.

Isaac balked.

Josiah had paid for himself a hundred times over, and had increased yields and gotten better prices, and Frank warned that if Isaac didn't accept a fair bid when one was offered, Josiah would someday find a way to seize his freedom without Isaac's help. Isaac would lose the money as well as the slave. Plus, Frank noted, Josiah had a horse and a pass and was pretty independent already. Frank hoped his brother-in-law would grant the request and do it with good grace. But, of course, that was too much to hope.

Isaac Riley refused to budge.

Frank was tenacious, and tried to make his case again a few days later. It took nearly two months, but finally Isaac agreed to give thirty-nine-year-old Josiah Henson his manumission papers for $450.*

Josiah sold his horse and paid Isaac $350, signed a promissory note for the remaining $100, and received his freedom certificate. It was March 9, 1829. When Frank handed him the note, Josiah stared at in disbelief. He had his freedom.

The following morning, Josiah packed his bag for Kentucky. He was surprised when Isaac Riley showed up and appeared to be in a very friendly mood. Isaac asked Josiah about his plans, which were to return to Kentucky and begin saving for the remaining $100.

Isaac asked Josiah if he was going to show his freedom papers if he was questioned on the road.[13]

---

* Measured against current labor value, Josiah would have had to earn the modern equivalent of $128,000 for his freedom. Josiah thought it was a great bargain.

"Yes," Josiah said.

"You'll be a fool if you do," Isaac replied. "Some slave-trader will get hold of it, and tear it up, and you'll be thrown into prison, sold for your jail fees, and be in his possession before any of your friends can help you."

What, then, was Josiah to do?

"Don't show it at all," Isaac said. "Your pass is enough. Let me enclose your papers for you under cover to my brother. Nobody will dare to break a seal, for that is a state-prison matter; and when you arrive in Kentucky you will have it with you all safe and sound."

Josiah was grateful for the prudent advice. It was true that he could return to Kentucky with a travel pass. Slave patrols and unscrupulous sheriffs were known to arrest and imprison free blacks. It was easy to forge ownership papers and sell a victim back into bondage. Josiah figured he could shield himself from danger by pretending to be a slave.

Isaac wrapped Josiah's manumission paper inside several envelopes, triple sealed it, and addressed it to his brother Amos in Kentucky.

With his precious papers safely stowed in his carpet bag, and his travel pass in hand, Josiah Henson dared to imagine his new life as a free man.

Of course, he should have known better than to trust Isaac Riley.

FIVE

MURDER AND PROVIDENCE

*Keep him hungry and spiritless and he will
follow the chain of his master like a dog.*

—FREDERICK DOUGLASS

JOSIAH HENSON SET OFF ON FOOT FOR THE 250-MILE WALK TO West Virginia. From there he would turn toward Kentucky, snaking his way along the Ohio River. Like many solitary black men who traveled freely, he was arrested repeatedly as a possible runaway. But the time he had spent as Isaac Riley's market man among the lawyers of Washington had served him well. Josiah knew his rights. He had a travel pass from his master, and he had the right to have it inspected by a judge. Whenever he was stopped, he simply produced his travel pass and insisted on being taken before a magistrate. The hassle of involving a magistrate was enough to shake the lawmen off. And he made sure never to mention the fact that he was actually a free man with papers to prove it. It must have been hard for Josiah to keep that fact a secret, but it was far safer to continue playing the part of the obedient slave.

At Wheeling, Josiah caught a boat down the Ohio, through Cincinnati and Louisville. Now the world looked different. The sun seemed warmer, the birds friendlier, the wind cooler.

Late one evening, after weeks of travel, Josiah stepped off the boat at Amos Riley's river landing in Daviess County, Kentucky. He was supposed to carry his sealed manumission paper directly to Amos, but instead he walked directly to his family's quarters.

Charlotte and his four boys were well. Josiah had much to tell his wife, but soon discovered he had much to learn. Letters from Isaac Riley had reached the big house long before his arrival, telling Amos of Josiah's preaching and saving and bargaining for his freedom. Amos's children had eagerly shared the good news with Charlotte.

But Charlotte couldn't believe it. White men just gave him money? It took all of Josiah's powers of persuasion to convince her of the goodness of the Ohio abolitionists.

"But how are you going to raise enough to pay the remainder of the thousand dollars?" she said.[1]

"What thousand dollars?" Josiah asked.

"The thousand dollars you are to give for your freedom."

The words struck Josiah like a punch to the stomach. He immediately realized Isaac Riley's treachery. Josiah had paid $350 down, and he had promised another $100 to complete the deal he had made to purchase his freedom for $450. Evidently the Riley brothers added another zero. Now he was expected to raise an additional $650—the equivalent of him earning more than $185,000 in today's dollars—before he could receive his manumission papers.[*]

---

[*] As noted earlier, conversions to modern currency are not easy. If you compare the value of a $650 commodity in 1828 to today's values, you get a modern real price of $17,000. This is the price that Isaac and Amos would have wanted Josiah to pay in modern terms. But the numbers are different from Josiah's perspective. Compared as income or wealth in 1828, that $650 is the equivalent of unskilled labor earnings of $185,000. But $650 in 1828 gave someone the economic status of over half a million, and the economic power of $13.5 million. No matter how you calculate it, the sum was overwhelming from the viewpoint of a wage-free enslaved man like Josiah. But for the purposes of this book, I chose a $185,000 labor value, as it's the one Josiah would have felt the most. Putting ourselves in his shoes, $650, then, was like us saying today, "I need to save $185,000 in order to buy my freedom."

This was Isaac Riley's doing. If Josiah handed over his sealed manumission paper to Amos, the only evidence of his freedom would be hidden from every eye except his master's brother, who was instructed to hold it until Josiah paid the balance of what he supposedly owed. He would never be free.

Josiah was beside himself with rage and despair. The only witness to the truth, Frank Middleton, was nearly seven hundred miles away. Josiah couldn't write him a letter, and he knew no literate man he trusted to do it for him.

Josiah broke down and cried the words of Christ on the cross: "My God! my God! why hast Thou forsaken me?"

Only one thing seemed clear. Under no circumstances could his freedom papers be surrendered to Amos Riley.

But he didn't want to tell a lie, either. He told Charlotte, truthfully, that he hadn't seen his papers since he left Louisville. Maybe they were in his bag, or maybe they had been lost. If she "happened" to find them in his bag, and hid them somewhere he couldn't find them, that would probably be for the best.

Charlotte took the bag and left in darkness to hide Josiah's ticket to freedom.

❧

THE NEXT MORNING, AT THE SOUND OF THE HORN BLAST, JOSIAH went out to find Amos Riley. He found the man sitting on a fence, and as Josiah came close enough for the master to recognize him, Amos shouted out a hearty welcome.

"Why, halloa, Sie! is that you?" he said. "Got back, eh! Why, you old son of a bitch, I'm glad to see you! . . . why, you're a regular black gentleman!" Amos surveyed Josiah with an appreciative grin. "Well, boy, how's your master?"[2]

After Josiah updated Amos on the affairs in Maryland, Amos said, "Isaac says you want to be free. . . . I think your master treats you pretty hard, though. Six hundred and fifty dollars don't come so easy in old

Kentuck. How does he ever expect you to raise all that? It's too much, boy, it's too much."

Josiah realized Charlotte's information was right. The Riley brothers had added a zero to his contract price, and since Josiah didn't know how to read, his bond stood at $1,000. If only he'd had that last $100, he'd be a free man already. Instead, he owed $650 in order to possess his freedom.

Isaac Riley clearly was still unwilling to let Josiah go, and there was no way to raise the $650 if he remained under Amos's authority. Amos Riley was a relatively kind owner, but he would never let him return to the preaching circuit to earn more. Josiah was back where he had started six months earlier: he was a forty-year-old illiterate slave with no money and a rapidly dwindling future.

Amos asked if Josiah had a package of papers for him. Josiah explained, truthfully, that he'd last seen it in Louisville, but that it was no longer in his bag and he didn't have any idea where it was.

Amos sent Josiah back to the landing to retrace his steps and see if he'd dropped it along the way. The search, of course, proved in vain. This didn't bother Amos, though. "Well, boy, bad luck happens to everybody, sometimes," he said.

But Josiah's heart was burdened with grief at the trick that had been played on him. He was now back to square one. He consoled himself as well as he could and went back to work with as quiet a mind as he could muster. *Trust God. Never despair.*

SOLD SOUTH

Josiah toiled on Amos Riley's Kentucky plantation for another year. From time to time, Amos joked about the $650 and said Isaac kept writing to know why he hadn't yet paid another installment.

Both the Rileys were fairly devious, and iron sharpened iron when it came to their dealings with each other. Any money Josiah might have been able to deliver to Amos was unlikely to make it to Isaac, since his Kentucky master had no interest in having his brother grow richer while he lost the man who so expertly managed all his slaves and animals.

And then, all of a sudden in the summer of 1830, the jokes about payment stopped. Amos informed Josiah that his son, Amos Junior, was going down the river to New Orleans. The boy was nearly twenty years old, and he'd be guiding a flatboat filled with the farm's produce. Josiah was told to go with him and help him sell the goods for a good price. They would leave the next day.

Josiah's heart sunk to a new low. Trips to New Orleans were frequent, but he had never before been ordered to go along. He was sure he was being sold south.

Letters had come and gone frequently lately between the two brothers, and Josiah had been wondering why. Were they planning to sell him and divide the profits? Was Amos simply afraid Josiah would run away? Josiah would never know.[*]

He stumbled to his cabin and, like his father decades ago, collapsed in misery and despair. His fate was sealed. Nothing but horrors lay ahead.

He had little time to prepare.

Josiah asked Charlotte to find his manumission papers.

⁊ℰ∿

THE NEXT MORNING, CHARLOTTE AND THE CHILDREN ACCOMPANIED Josiah to the landing. Charlotte had sewn her husband's certificate of freedom into the cloth of his jacket near the waist. Was this goodbye forever?

Josiah stepped aboard the flat-bottomed boat bound for New Orleans. It was manned by three white men—a river captain and two hands—who had been hired for the voyage. The master's son, Amos Junior, was the only other person on board. The boat was loaded with

---

[*] In truth, Arnold T. Windsor was filing further lawsuits, and Isaac Riley was once again desperate for cash.

beef cattle, pigs, poultry, corn, whiskey, and other articles from the farm, along with produce from some of the neighboring estates. And one slave.

The items were to be sold wherever they could make the greatest profits as the group moved down the river to New Orleans.

Like his father before him, Josiah would now be separated from the love of his life and his children. By then they had four sons. Josiah stared at Charlotte as the boat pulled from shore and caught the current. He watched as her figure grew smaller on the horizon, keeping his eyes locked on her shape until she disappeared altogether.

During Josiah's voyage down the Ohio and Mississippi Rivers, each man on the boat took turns at the helm, sometimes at the direction of the captain, and sometimes on their own, when the captain needed sleep. As the only slave on the boat, Josiah was forced to take at least three turns for every other sailor's one turn.

The heat grew worse as they floated slowly south from Kentucky toward Louisiana. While Josiah sweated on deck in the harsh glare of the sun, the young Riley stayed below deck to keep cool. Josiah was often on his own, and he learned the art of steering the boat. Soon he could do it far better than anyone aboard save the captain himself. He mastered the maneuvers necessary to avoid a snag or a steamboat, shoot past an uprooted tree, or gently land against a bank. But to what end? How would he survive a life of harsh labor in this muggy heat? What slave owner would treat him well, knowing his shoulders made him useless for manual labor?

The days were long and roasting, and the boat moved so slowly that Josiah lifted his head every time a slight breeze wafted past. The captain's eyes, in the meantime, grew inflamed and swollen, which Josiah attributed to the intense sunlight and its reflection on the river. Soon the captain was unable to navigate and stayed below deck as he tried to recover from river blindness. Josiah became the acting captain of the boat carrying him south to his uncertain and likely unbearable fate.

⤜⤚⤙⤛

AFTER THE CAPTAIN STOPPED TAKING HIS TURN, THE CREW HAD to dock on shore at night, because none of the others had been down the river before, and night piloting took skill. Docking meant it was necessary to keep watch all night, to prevent being robbed of their provisions.

Josiah was wracked with fear. The slave grapevine had brought terrifying stories of life in the South up to the northern slaves. Fingers and hands were hacked off as punishment for stealing. Recaptured slaves had their knee tendons severed, so they could never run again. Some enslavers branded the letter *R* on runaways' foreheads. Flogging was common, but it didn't end there. To add further pain, and physical scarring, whip wounds were sometimes burst and rubbed with lard and ground-up bricks.

Night after night, Josiah paced back and forth on the deck during his watch. After all he had done for Isaac and Amos Riley, after all the respect they had professed for him, this was the return for his abuse and hard work. He'd been maimed for life, and now he was being sold down the river like a cow or a bushel of corn.

As time passed he felt himself growing more ferocious. The closer they got to the slave markets of New Orleans, the more Josiah was consumed with an almost uncontrollable fury. He would not go like a lamb to the slaughter. Like his father four decades earlier, he felt himself begin to change from a lively, pleasant-tempered man into a morose and dangerous slave.

❧

THE FLATBOAT STOPPED AT VICKSBURG ON THE WAY THROUGH MISsissippi. Amos Junior went to the town market to sell off some of their goods, and Josiah got permission to visit a plantation a few miles from the town. It was the new home of some of his old companions, part of the group he'd brought to Kentucky that had been sold off.

It was the saddest visit he ever made.

Their cheeks were hallowed by starvation and sickness. Josiah's friends described their daily life of toil, disease-ridden and half-naked in the marshes under the blistering southern sun. The clouds of mosquitoes and black gnats and the specter of malaria wracked their bodies with constant pain.

In his memoirs, Josiah made no mention of any anger or resentment toward him on their part, and the fact that he visited their plantation suggests he didn't expect any. How can this be?

Josiah's friends not only didn't blame him for their present condition, but some of them actually cried when they saw him, mourning the fate they knew he'd soon experience. Josiah's friends confided that they welcomed death as their only deliverance.

It is hard for the modern mind to comprehend the psychology of slavery. How could anyone's will to freedom be so pulverized? Such were the degrading conditions in which millions of enslaved people found themselves. The fear of the unknown, of punishment, torture, separation, death, and the Deep South were simply overwhelming.

In fact, there were people called "slave breakers" whose entire job was to crush the human spirit like grapes in a press. Frederick Douglass recalls being sent to a notorious slave breaker at the age of sixteen. Edward Covey used a mix of fear, violence, and extreme overwork to grind a stubborn slave's will to dust. Douglass wrote, "I was somewhat unmanageable when I first got there, but a few months of this discipline tamed me. . . . I was broken in body, soul, and spirit. . . . The dark night of slavery closed in upon me."[3] We may guess that Vicksburg had done nothing less to Isaac Riley's former slaves.

Josiah said goodbye and walked back to the boat in a sickly haze, his heart barely beating inside his aching chest. He would be forever haunted by the image of his wretched, ghostly group of friends.

⁘

AS THEY FLOATED CLOSER AND CLOSER TO NEW ORLEANS, everything Josiah witnessed seemed to feed his gloomy thoughts: wretched slave pens filled to capacity standing exposed in the blistering sun, the smell of stagnant waters, the half-putrid carcasses of horses or oxen floating in the muddy soup, covered with turkey buzzards and swarms of green flies.

Josiah's faith in Christ, which had been his firm foundation since he had first discovered it, gave way like a mudbank in a torrential downpour. *God has abandoned me and cast me off forever*, he thought. He no longer looked to God for help. He envisioned the emaciated frames of his enslaved brothers. In them he saw "the sure, swift, loving intervention of the one unfailing friend of the wretched—death."[4]

Perhaps the well-known old hymn came to mind as Josiah floated downriver toward his destiny.

> *There the wicked cease from troubling,*
> *and the weary are at rest.*
> *There the prisoners rest together;*
> *they hear not the voice of the oppressor.*

Considering his age, his maimed shoulders, and the heartbreak at the loss of his family, Josiah knew that two years of southern slavery would surely kill him. He dwelt on the thought with a bitter blend of melancholy and ironic satisfaction. *Two years.* Two years and he would be free forever. Freedom through death. Freedom had been his cherished hope, and it was soon to be realized, though not as he had thought it would come.

They brought the flatboat safely ashore, and the fellow travelers went to bed while Josiah stood watch. His mind raced as he paced back and forth on the slick deck. He was being sent to a place where his life would be made more wretched, and it would be brutally shortened. He would never live to see his children reach adulthood. He would never hold his grandchildren. He would never learn to read.

Why shouldn't he prevent this wrong by shortening *their* lives, or the lives of their agents of injustice? Doing so would be easy enough. All were asleep below deck, and they had no reason to suspect him.

The idea began to take shape. Blinded by passion, Josiah decided he would kill his four companions, take their money, sink the boat, and escape north.

Creeping down noiselessly, he took hold of a heavy ax, wiping the sweat from his hands to get a firmer grip. He entered the cabin and approached the first sleeping man. He squinted in the lantern light. His eyes fell on Amos Riley Jr.

Josiah's hand slid along the ax handle. He raised the blade to strike the fatal blow.

⁓⟡⟡⁓

THE VOICE SEEMED ALMOST AUDIBLE.

"Josiah Henson, are you a Christian? Will you commit murder?"

Josiah had not considered it murder. This was self-defense. He was preventing others from murdering him. It was justifiable, even commendable. But now, all at once, the truth rushed in. He was going to kill Amos Junior. The boy was simply following his father's commands.

Josiah had worked so hard to improve himself—not just in his day-to-day life, in practical things, but in the cultivation of his character. He'd always felt the pride of being a respected leader, but he was about to compromise his integrity in a profound way. Even if no one else ever found out, Josiah would still know that he had sinned, and it would weigh heavily on his conscience forever.

Josiah stepped back from Amos Junior's bed. He laid down the ax and crept back onto the deck as the rain continued to fall. He was still troubled, but he felt changed yet again. He was filled with shame for coming so close to murdering another person. He was afraid that the others might be able to see it on his face, or that a careless word would betray his guilty thoughts. He thanked God for giving him the strength to step away.

Instead of waking one of the men to take over on watch, Josiah remained on deck all night. He reasoned that if his life were reduced to a short span, he would at least suffer less. He knew that if he had killed them and escaped, he would have no satisfaction in his freedom. He would rather die as a slave than live as a murderer.

⁓⟡⟡⁓

THE BOAT ARRIVED IN NEW ORLEANS, WITH THE CREW NEVER LEARN-ing how close to death they'd come, and the remainder of the ship's cargo was sold. The sailors and captain were paid and sent on their way. Amos Junior booked his one-way passage on a steamboat home. Nothing was left but to sell the boat and dispose of Josiah.

Amos Junior, no longer disguising his plans, acknowledged his father's instructions to sell Josiah to the highest bidder. He promised to find Josiah a good master who would employ him as a driver or house servant, but as various owners and overseers came to inspect the slave, Josiah saw no discernible efforts being made to do so.

Josiah's speed was tested by potential buyers, who sent him on errands to see how fast he could run. Amos Junior lied about Josiah's age, and tried to avoid the subject of the man's injured shoulders. He spoke highly of his slave's mental capacity and leadership ability, in order that, as Josiah put it, "my value as a domestic animal might be enhanced."[5]

Between inspections, Josiah did everything in his power to move Amos Riley's heart. He wept as he begged him not to sell him away from his wife and children. They had often worked in the wheat fields together, laughing as they raced to cut the harvest, with the younger Amos always falling behind. Josiah talked about all the years of service to the boy's father, and the thousand little things he'd done for Amos Junior personally.

But Amos Junior was anxious to get home. The summer heat and the long journey had left him exhausted, and the humidity of New Orleans was unbearable.

Josiah even told him about the wretched conditions of the slaves in Vicksburg, but to no avail. The young man was officially entrenched in the American slave system.

❧

SOUTHERN SLAVERY COULD BE BARBAROUS ON AN UNIMAGINABLE scale. In his autobiography, William Wells Brown shared a newspaper clipping from the *Alton Telegraph* about a Missouri slave who was burned at the stake. A bystander had given this account:

After the flames had surrounded their prey, and when his clothes were in a blaze all over him, his eyes burnt out of his head, and his mouth seemingly parched to a cinder, some one in the crowd, more compassionate than the rest, proposed to put an end to his misery by shooting him. . . .

"No, no," said one of the fiends, who was standing about the sacrifice they were roasting, "he shall not be shot; I would sooner slacken the fire, if that would increase his misery. . . ."

The newspaper had dutifully reported that the speaker was "an officer of justice."[6]

The *St. Louis Republican* covered a heinous story in September 1844 involving a woman who tortured a rented child before sending her back to her owner to die:

On Friday last the coroner held an inquest at the house of Judge Dunica, a few miles south of the city, over the body of a negro girl, about 8 years of age, belonging to Mr. Cordell. The body exhibited evidence of the most cruel whipping and beating we have ever heard of. The flesh on the back and limbs was beaten to a jelly—one shoulder-bone was laid bare—there were several cuts, apparently from a club, on the head—and around the neck was the indentation of a cord, by which it is supposed she had been confined to a tree. . . . The jury returned a verdict that she came to her death by the blows inflicted by some persons unknown. . . . Mrs. Tanner has been tried and acquitted.[7]

A correspondent from the *New York Herald* followed up the report a month later, writing,

I yesterday visited the cell of Cornelia, the slave charged with being the accomplice of Mrs. Ann Tanner (recently acquitted) in the murder of a little negro girl, by whipping and starvation. She admits her participancy, but says she was compelled to take the part she did in the affair.

On one occasion she says the child was tied to a tree from Monday morning till Friday night, exposed by day to the scorching rays of the sun, and by night to the stinging of myriads of musquitoes; and that during all this time the child had nothing to eat, but was whipped daily.

The little girl had told the same story to the doctor before dying.

❧

THE STORIES OF HIS UNCLE'S FORMER SLAVES BROUGHT AMOS JUNIOR to tears, and he claimed he was sorry for Josiah. But his plans remained unchanged. For the rest of the day, he avoided Josiah as much as possible, and even refused to talk to him. As Amos marched from buyer to buyer, Josiah followed him in lockstep, pleading for a change of heart. He was begging for his very life.

Josiah fell and held the young man's knees, begging him to spare his life. Amos Junior cursed and slapped Josiah across the face. Josiah was his property—not a man, husband, friend, or father—and self-interest won the day. Amos Junior hardened his heart, just like millions of slave owners before him.

Josiah later reflected on how so young a man could already lack such mercy. "The children of slaveholders were often kind-hearted, good-tempered, and were genial companions during their childhood, before they were old enough to exercise authority," he wrote. "Then, under the influence of their circumstances, slavery would often turn the mildest disposition into a cross one, the same as thunder will turn sweet milk."[8]

A purchaser was found. Josiah would be delivered the next day, and Amos Junior would set off for Kentucky on a steamboat at 6:00 p.m. The deal was done.

A SERENDIPITOUS REVERSAL

Shortly before dawn on June 29, 1830, Amos Junior awoke with a sharp pain in his abdomen. He stood and took a few steps across the flatboat before sitting back on the bed. He called for Josiah. Josiah entered the cabin and saw the young man clutching his stomach. Josiah encouraged him to go back to bed, thinking it would pass quickly.

Amos Junior awoke an hour later and tried to stand. The pain became rapidly worse, and Josiah realized Amos had been struck with "river fever," most likely malaria. By eight o'clock in the morning, Amos Junior was unable to move from his bed.

In a moment, Josiah went from being merely property to being Amos Junior's only friend in a city of strangers. Amos was no longer the pitiless arbiter of Josiah's destiny, but a beggar, a poor, terrified young man, afraid of death and writhing in pain.

"Stick to me, Sie! Stick to me, Sie!" he cried. "Don't leave me, don't leave me. I'm sorry I was going to sell you."

In between his bouts of convulsive stomach pain, the young man insisted that he'd only been joking, and had never intended to dispose of him. He begged Josiah to sell the flatboat and get him and his possessions on board the steamer as quickly as possible.

What choice did Josiah have? If Amos Junior died, he would be trapped in New Orleans with little chance of making it all the way back north. Terrible as it was, sticking with the young man was his best chance of getting back to his family.

Josiah left the skiff's cabin. Amos Junior collapsed on the bed, his body wracked with pain as his conditioned worsened. Josiah attended to his master's requests, and by noon the young man was installed in a steamer cabin set aside for sick passengers. Josiah, too, was on board.

As the steamboat pulled into the mighty Mississippi, Josiah stood outside Amos Junior's room and watched New Orleans fade in the distance. "Away from this land of bondage and death," he thought. "Away from misery and despair. If I do not now find my way to freedom, may God never give me a chance again!"[9]

As the steamer worked its way north, Amos Junior lay on his deathbed. Josiah couldn't help but feel sympathy for the young man. Amos couldn't speak or move, but his imploring eyes followed Josiah wherever he went. Josiah nursed him carefully and constantly, but the young man's life hung by a very thin thread.

The water was seasonally low on the Ohio River, and it took twelve days to reach Kentucky. Amos Junior still couldn't speak or walk. They arrived at the landing at Daviess County on July 10, and Josiah recruited a party of slaves to construct a stretcher and relay the boy five miles to the big house.

Amos Riley looked out to see Josiah approaching with a large band of slaves carrying a strange package. When the story was told, the Rileys heaped praise on Josiah not only for saving their son, but also for taking care of the family's profits. Josiah Henson had proven more valuable than Amos Riley ever imagined.

SIX

THE GREAT ESCAPE

Those who do not move, do not notice their chains.

—ROSA LUXEMBURG

I T WAS ANOTHER FOUR WEEKS BEFORE AMOS RILEY JR. WAS WELL enough to hobble out of his bedroom chamber. Once he regained the strength to talk, some of his first words were, "If I had sold him I should have died."[1]

But Josiah Henson's service made no permanent impression on the rest of the Riley family. It never occurred to them that they held even the slightest obligation to him. He was put back to work in his old occupation as overseer.

Josiah had already paid for his freedom. If Isaac Riley had stuck to his own bargain, Josiah would have paid the money as promised. But Josiah felt that Riley's attempt to steal his money and sell him south absolved him from any obligation to pay another penny or stay another minute under a tyrant, a thief, and a liar.

After living forty-one years as a slave, Josiah's mind was made up. While Amos Riley Sr. plotted another attempt to sell him, he planned his escape from Kentucky.

Providence had beaten Isaac's scheme, but Josiah couldn't expect such luck to repeat itself. He was honor-bound by his conscience to do everything in his power to unleash himself from the conspiracies of the Riley family.

⚬⚬⚬

BUT HOW COULD HE ESCAPE WITH A FAMILY OF SIX? JOSIAH WAS CERtainly up to it, but could Charlotte make the journey? And how would they transport the young ones? There was a reason why most successful slave escape attempts were made by single adults.

There were free states in the Union, but the slave states had hidden their emissaries even in these places. Kentucky spies and slave patrols roamed the rivers and towns of Indiana and Ohio. Even if Josiah escaped across the river, he could still fall into their hands at any moment. He needed stronger protection than the northern states could provide. He knew he and his family would be safer if they were able to leave the United States.

During Josiah's happy days of preaching in Ohio, he had heard many stories of fugitive slaves and the kind men and women who helped them on their way. The British territory of Canada and its people were often featured in these stories.

On March 14, 1793, a Canadian slave named Chloe Cooley had been tied in a boat and sold across the river to Lewiston, New York. Her story was brought to the attention of the lieutenant governor of Upper Canada, John Graves Simcoe, who immediately moved to abolish slavery in the new province. Despite heavy opposition from slave-owning members of the House of Assembly, he reached a compromise on July 9, 1793, that prevented the introduction of new slaves into Upper Canada. It was the first piece of legislation in the British Empire to limit slavery, and it became the platform upon which the Underground Railroad would be built.

The British Empire's northern colony became one of the few places in North America where an American runaway could be truly safe from pursuit. Canada, that great and glorious hope for enslaved Americans, became Josiah's sole focus.

In theory, all a slave needed to do was find the Big Dipper and follow the North Star to freedom. While US census figures account for only 6,000 escapees, other data suggest that upward of 100,000 people, aided by abolitionists and their allies, may have made the harrowing journey north. In the words of Canadian author Will Ferguson, "Faced with the sheer brutality of the slave trade, a network of human decency took shape."[2]

The Underground Railroad (UGRR), started primarily by American Quakers, reached its peak in the 1850s and 1860s. By that time, safe houses were called "stations," slaves were called "passengers," and guides were called "conductors." An entire code had developed from phrases buried in hymns. "Israel" referred to the slaves. "Egypt" represented the slave states. The "pharaohs" were the slave owners, and "Canaan"—the Promised Land—was Canada. Some claim that the UGRR was itself called "a sweet chariot," and that to "swing low" meant to make your way down south to "carry me home."*

But Josiah was planning his escape in 1830. The Underground Railroad wasn't yet fully developed—it wasn't even called the Underground Railroad yet. Few "trains" ran, and few "conductors" would be able to help the Henson family on their way. In the late 1840s, and especially after the Fugitive Slave Law passed in 1850, thousands would resist the government and help their fellow man find freedom, but not yet. Josiah would have to go it alone.

Josiah knew that the North Star—like the Star of Bethlehem—announced where his salvation lay. It would guide him to the Promised Land, just as it had thousands of other hunted pilgrims.

The plan was this: From their home on the landing, they would ferry across the Ohio River to the free state of Indiana on the other side. They'd travel by night across Indiana, through Ohio, and then

---

* However, the song "Swing Low, Sweet Chariot," was not written and composed until after the Civil War, likely by a Choctaw Indian living in Oklahoma. The earliest known recording was produced in 1909, by the Fisk Jubilee Singers of Fisk University.

find a boat that would take them to Canada. In the meantime, Josiah unearthed a pair of pistols and a knife he'd discreetly purchased from a white man a while back.

He devised his plan on a Wednesday. The next three days—Thursday, Friday, and Saturday—were normal workdays. Sunday was a holiday, and Amos Riley knew that Josiah was to be away in fields far from the big house on Monday and Tuesday. If the family left on Saturday night, under cover of darkness, they could give themselves a three-day head start before anyone noticed they were gone.

When Josiah told Charlotte of his plan, she was overcome with terror. As he later wrote, "She knew nothing of the wide world beyond, and her imagination peopled it with unseen horrors."[3]

"We shall die in the wilderness," Charlotte cried. "We shall be hunted down with bloodhounds. . . . [W]e shall be brought back and whipped to death."

Josiah insisted that if they didn't run away, they'd soon be torn apart forever. He described the horrors he'd witnessed down south and explained that this was the only way they'd ever have a chance to live together as free people. Still, she refused. In frustration, Josiah told her that if she would not escape with him, he would take their oldest three sons and go without her. Charlotte cried all night at the thought.

Josiah left at sunrise, exhausted and angry, to go about his work for the day. He had not gone far when he heard her voice calling. He stopped. Charlotte ran toward him, tears streaking across her cheeks. She sniffed and wiped her nose with a corner of her dress. Despite her terror, she would go with him. Josiah wept. No matter the danger, they would go together.

❧

JOSIAH KNEW HE COULD CONTEND WITH THE PERILS OF A 640-MILE journey to freedom. But transporting his wife and children seemed nearly impossible.

Josiah and Charlotte had four boys. Tom, age twelve, could fend for himself, and could help carry the family's scanty provisions. Isaac, age ten, could march, too, with the help of his mother. The youngest children, Josiah Jr. and Peter, were three and two years old, respectively. They would have to be carried. But like their father and grandfather before them, both boys were stout and heavy for their age, and Charlotte declared that Josiah's back would break before they'd gone five miles from home.

Josiah got Charlotte to make him a large tow-cloth knapsack, big enough to fit both boys, with sturdy shoulder straps. In the nights leading up to their escape, Josiah carried them round and round the cabin, both to test his strength and to get them accustomed to this new mode of travel. To the boys it was great fun, and Josiah was pleased to see he could handle carrying them, despite his hobbled shoulders.

There was also the matter of getting Tom excused from his work in the great house as the house boy for Amos Riley Sr. Josiah would need to think up some excuse as to why Tom needed to come home.

RUN

At sundown on Saturday, September 18, 1830, Josiah Henson went up to the great house for the last time. Amos Riley Sr. sat on the porch, smoking a corncob pipe. Josiah reported on his work for the week and then headed off toward home as usual. He then stopped, appearing to have suddenly recollected a forgotten thought. He turned nonchalantly back to Amos.

"Oh, Master Amos, I most forgot," Josiah said. "Tom's mother wants to know if you won't let him come down a few days; she wants to mend his clothes and fix him up a little."[4]

"Yes, boy," Amos said. "Yes, he can go."

"Thankee, Master Amos," Josiah said.

Tom joined his father and they turned their backs on the old mansion. In spite of himself, Josiah quickly gave an emphatic farewell. "Good night, good night," he called back to his master. "The Lord bless you!"

Josiah couldn't help but chuckle inwardly at the thought of how long of a night it would be. As he and Tom walked home, he turned with an affectionate look at the well-known objects he spotted on his way. There was the old oak under which he'd enjoyed many Sunday naps. There was the pond where he'd fished many early mornings. It felt strange, this mixture of sorrow and joy, "but no man can live anywhere long without feeling some attachment to the soil on which he labors," he thought.

It was nine o'clock in the evening when the family set off. They moved quietly to the landing, where a fellow slave waited with a skiff. Josiah had convinced the man to take them across the Ohio River. It was an anxious and solemn moment. They sat still as death as the kind fellow rowed quietly through the dark, moonless night.

The rower paused in the middle of the river and turned to Josiah. "It will be the end of me if this is ever found out," the man whispered. "But you won't be brought back alive, Sie, will you?"[5]

"Not if I can help it," Josiah replied. He thought of his knife and pistols.

"And if they're too many for you, and you get seized, you'll never tell my part in this business?"

"Not if I'm shot through like a sieve," Josiah promised.

"That's all," the rower said. "And God help you."

The man continued rowing until they reached the Indiana shore. Josiah began to feel like a man in charge of his own life. He unloaded his family and turned to give the man a hearty and grateful farewell.

In a moment of astounding synchronicity, Josiah and his family landed within a few hundred yards of Lincoln Landing near Rockport, Indiana—the spot where, just two years earlier, nineteen-year-old Abraham Lincoln had embarked on a flatboat to New Orleans and there first witnessed the brutality of a slave auction.[6]

Josiah stood in the darkness with his family, listening to the oars of the skiff that propelled the boatman home. An unknown future lay before them. But there was no time for reflection. Before daylight they needed to travel as far as possible, and then hide themselves in the woods. They were to travel by night and rest by day in the woods and bushes. They were to rely solely on their own strength, with just a little foraged food and water to sustain them. They had no friends to whom they could turn for help, for southern Indiana was bitterly hostile to runaways.

Josiah led his family into the mist. He moved cautiously and stealthily, as fast as the darkness and his slow-moving family would allow. Charlotte trembled with every step. She begged him to allow them to turn back. Charlotte could attempt to swim back if she liked, but he and the boys were going on.

୶ଢ଼ଢ଼ଢ଼

THE HENSON FAMILY PRESSED ON, BY NIGHT, FOR TWO WEEKS. THE air was cold, sometimes unbearably so, and the family huddled together for warmth as they walked. The rain drenched their clothes and rattled their bones. During daylight hours, Josiah slept little. His back was starting to wear from the heavy bag and the constant chafing. Had anyone ever escaped to freedom with a wife and four children? The task seemed more impossible with each passing night.

Two days before reaching Cincinnati, after walking nearly two hundred miles, the family was at a breaking point. The children cried with hunger all night long, and Charlotte blamed Josiah for causing them such misery.

Josiah needed encouragement. His arms and legs were tired, and his back and shoulders were raw from carrying his boys in the rough knapsack. The awful fear of detection chased him constantly. He would wake suddenly in terror, his heart beating against his ribs, expecting to find dogs and slave hunters at his heels.

Had he been alone, he would have endured starvation and exhaustion rather than venture into the open to seek help from a stranger. But for the sake of the family, he had to find food. So he left their hiding place in the woods and took to the road in broad daylight. He turned south to prevent anyone from suspecting him of being a runaway. Before long he came to a house. A ferocious dog rushed at him.

Much to Josiah's relief, the surly master yelled and calmed the animal. Josiah asked if the man would sell him a little meat and bread.

"No," the man said. "I have nothing for niggers!"[7]

Josiah's luck didn't seem any better with the second house. The man of the house cursed him just like his neighbor had, but the man's wife overheard the conversation.

She scolded her husband. "How can you treat any human being so?" she asked. "If a dog was hungry, I would give him something to eat. We have children, and who knows but they may some day need the help of a friend."

The kind woman invited Josiah into the house. She loaded a plate with bread and venison. Josiah put the feast in his handkerchief and placed a quarter on the table. The woman quietly picked it up and put it in his handkerchief, along with another slab of meat.

"God bless you," she said.

Josiah felt the hot tears roll down his cheeks.

He said goodbye and continued south until he was out of sight of the house, then darted into the woods and returned to his family.

Charlotte and the children were delighted to fill their starving bellies. The preserved meat was salty, and soon the children became thirsty. They started to groan and whine for water. Josiah once again left them, this time in search of water, eventually finding a little stream.

He drank and drank and drank, replenishing his dehydrated body. He then looked for a way to carry water back to his family.

He tried filling his hat from the stream, but it leaked. He searched for large leaves, or a hollowed tree stump, but found nothing. In a moment of great ingenuity, Josiah took off his shoes, rinsed them out, and filled them with water. He carefully carried them back to his family, wincing over every sharp bramble that stabbed his feet on the return path.

The children giggled as they drank from their father's shoes. Even Charlotte smiled.

THE HENSON FAMILY ARRIVED IN CINCINNATI TWO DAYS LATER. Josiah felt comparatively at home in the bustling free town, but he couldn't take any risks, in case Kentucky spies were on the lookout. Josiah hid Charlotte and the kids in the woods and went into town in search of his friends. They welcomed their preacher friend warmly. Once night fell, Charlotte and the children were brought in with a round of cheers.

The Hensons had covered nearly two hundred miles with four children in tow. After two weeks of incessant fatigue, anxiety, rain, and chill, the comfort of rest and warm shelter were indescribably sweet. Their hosts' hospitality was not without risk. If caught, an abolitionist could face scorn from his or her neighbors, heavy fines, imprisonment, or worse. But the Cincinnati abolitionists provided for the Henson family for several days as they regained their strength.

Once the family was refreshed, they drove the Hensons thirty miles on their way in a wagon. From there, the family followed the same routine as before—traveling by night, sleeping by day—until they reached the Scioto River. Northern Ohio was far safer than southern Indiana, so they no longer needed to travel at night. They'd been told to follow Hull's Trail, the first military road in the United States. It had been built to allow a general to haul his artillery through the unbroken wilderness on his way to fight the British. Josiah found the road entrance marked by a large sycamore and an ancient elm. They entered early in the day, with fresh spirits.

Nobody had told the Hensons that the path had been cut through total wilderness. The military road was a rough passageway through an immense forest, so overgrown that even Kentucky spies wouldn't have bothered to follow them in. Although Josiah didn't know it, they were still many miles from the shores of Lake Erie. Fugitives were as likely to die of hunger or be eaten by wild animals as they were to make their way out on the other side. Josiah had neglected to bring food, thinking he could safely purchase provisions from homes along the way. Their Cincinnati friends had loaded them with provisions days ago, but all that was left was a piece of thirst-inducing salted beef.

The Hensons marched all day without seeing a soul, and lay down that night hungry and exhausted. The October nights would have been terribly cold. Rocks and brambles dug into their necks and backs, and mosquitos made restful sleep an impossibility. Wolves howled all around them. The pack was too skittish to approach the family, but the noise terrified Charlotte and the children. Josiah again slept little, keeping watch in case the wild beasts came too close.

⁓ℓℓ⁓

THE HENSONS SHARED THEIR LAST PIECE OF SALTED BEEF FOR BREAKfast, and once again they were consumed by thirst. They started on their second day's march through the rough woods. By early afternoon, the autumn sun had turned the woods into a blacksmith's furnace. The forest buzzed with flies and mosquitoes as they continued on their hot and humid tramp through the wilds.

They were starving and thirsty. The track was rough, sometimes barely visible at all. Josiah often wondered if he'd lost the way altogether. The thick brush ripped at their clothes and sapped their strength. They crawled and climbed and struggled in silence. Josiah balanced the children on his back as he navigated between branches. He looked ahead into the overgrown forest. No hope of relief could be seen.

Nevertheless, he wearily plodded ahead. The two toddlers in his knapsack squirmed and shifted, and the tow cloth rubbed away at his raw skin.

Charlotte struggled along behind her husband. She helped the other two children climb over fallen tree trunks. She encouraged them as they forced themselves through the briars, and she consoled them when the sharp thorns produced blood on their arms and legs.

Then Josiah heard Tom and Isaac yell for help. He spun around. Charlotte lay motionless on the ground.

"Mother is dying!" cried Tom.

Josiah rushed back to his wife. She showed no signs of life. Tom showed how she'd fallen while trying to climb over a log. He shook her body. No response.

Josiah listened for a heartbeat. It was slow and quiet. Her breath was shallow and uneven. He had no water, and he didn't know how to help her.

He desperately waited and prayed.

Minutes passed. She did not revive.

Then, slowly, Charlotte opened her eyes. Josiah rummaged in his bag and found a few bits of leftover meat from Cincinnati. He put them to her lips. As she chewed, her strength returned. After resting for a while, Charlotte set out once more.

Josiah Henson cheered his sad party on as best he could, but starvation in the wilderness stared him in the face. For the first time on their journey, he was almost ready to give in to despair.

∾≈∽

IN THE EARLY AFTERNOON, THE HENSONS HEARD THE SOUND OF people. They were approaching quickly, and the Hensons couldn't expect any friendly people on such a hard road. Josiah walked ahead, and a few quick steps revealed the oncoming strangers to be Native Americans with packs on their shoulders. They were so close that if the natives decided to attack, it would be useless to try to escape with four children in tow. So Josiah walked boldly.

The handful of braves were bent down and did not raise their eyes until Josiah was within a few dozen yards. When they saw the tall black man coming toward them, they howled with fear. Then they turned and ran as fast as they could.

Josiah laughed out loud. He couldn't imagine why three or four warriors would be afraid of one man, unless they supposed he was the devil in black. Josiah listened as the braves howled and ran for at least a mile.

Charlotte panicked. Surely they were running back to gather more warriors and would return to murder them in no time. She wanted to turn back immediately. Her husband reasoned that they already had a force strong enough to kill the family if they wanted to, without recruiting more help. Turning back wasn't an option—they'd already put too much road behind them. And why should both parties turn and run? It made no sense.

The Hensons pressed on, and the cries of the Indians stopped. But as the family advanced, they discovered there were more Indians staring at them from behind trees, dodging out of sight whenever they thought the family had spotted them.

Josiah, Charlotte, and the boys soon came upon their camp. A stately chief, his arms folded, waited for them amid a circle of wigwams. The chief saluted them civilly and soon decided that they were, indeed, fellow human beings and not dark spirits.

He instructed his young men to come in and overcome their fear. Curiosity prevailed. The natives wanted to touch the kids, but they were shy. Whenever one of Josiah's boys sounded a cry of alarm, the natives would jump back too, as if they thought the children would bite them. Josiah and the chief laughed at the charade.

Through hand signals and words, Josiah was able to communicate who they were, where they were going, and what they needed. The tribe offered them a bounty of food. The harvest had just come in. The Hensons finally ate, and the children were satisfied for the first time since Cincinnati. Charlotte regained her strength.

The chief led the Hensons to a wigwam and directed them inside. The domed shelter was made of thatch and covered with dried, stretched deerskins to keep out the wind and rain. It would be their home for the night. Under the kind protection of their gracious hosts, the Henson family rested for the first time in many days.

⁓∾⁓

MANY SLAVE NARRATIVES IN THE DAYS PRIOR TO AND DURING THE Underground Railroad include stories of being helped by Native Americans.[8] It made sense—rich white slave owners not only oppressed black people and the impoverished whites among them, but also Native American individuals and tribes. As American expansionism squeezed the tribes and pushed them farther and farther from their territorial lands, the ancient saying proved true: "The enemy of my enemy is my friend."

In fact, some black fugitives and indigenous people married, and their offspring were labeled "black Indians." DNA testing suggests that approximately 5 percent of African Americans have at least one Native American great-grandparent.[9]

In the late 1700s and early 1800s, some African Americans settled in Upper Sandusky with Wyandot natives, while the slaves who escaped from South Carolina's rice plantations (the Gullah people) sometimes banded with Seminole Indians in Florida and Oklahoma. Other black fugitives formed a community in eastern North Carolina with the Tuscarora tribe; later they and their descendants lived as maroons in the Great Dismal Swamp, the wetland on the Virginia border that at one time occupied about a million acres.* Many African Americans hoped that whites—who were already fearful of Native Americans—wouldn't search for them among the natives.

But not all Native American tribes were kind to runaway slaves. As the cotton trade grew in the South, the federal government urged a number of tribes—including the Cherokees, Creeks, Choctaws, Chickasaws, and Seminoles—to start farms and own slaves, in an attempt to "civilize" them.

On September 11, 1722, the lieutenant governor of Virginia gave several Native American tribes an incentive to return any escaped slaves they came across: "You sent me last year a belt of wampum as a testimony of your promise, that you would seize and carry to Virginia some Runaway Negroes," he told them. "Now I make a general proposition . . . that if any such negro or slave shall hereafter fall into your hands you shall straightway conduct them to George Mason's House on Potowmack River. . . . [Y]ou shall there receive immediately upon the delivery of every such runaway one good gun & two blankets."[10]

One famous slave narrative is that of Sophia Pooley, who was interviewed when she was in her nineties:

---

* Harriet Beecher Stowe's second novel was titled *Dred: A Tale of the Great Dismal Swamp*.

I was born in Fishkill, New York. . . . I was stolen from my parents when I was seven years old, and brought to Canada; that was
long before the American Revolution. There were hardly any white
people in Canada then—nothing here but Indians and wild beasts.
My parents were slaves in New York State. My master's son-in-law,
Daniel Outwaters and Simon Knox, came into the garden where
my sister and I were playing among the currant bushes, tied their
handkerchiefs over our mouths, carried us to a vessel, put us in the
hold, and sailed up the river. The white men sold us at Niagara to
old Indian Brant, the king.

Mohawk chief Joseph Brant owned around thirty slaves, including
seven-year-old Sophia and her sister. She described Brant's third wife as a
"barbarous creature" who beat her and left her with a knife-cut scar over
her eye. When Sophia turned twelve, Brant sold her to an Englishman
from Ancaster, Ontario, named Samuel Hatt, whose brother is credited
with establishing the nearby town of Dundas. Today the town of Brantford, Ontario, is named in the chief's honor.[11]

Ultimately, the long-standing camaraderie between Native Americans
and African Americans would not withstand the power of the United
States, which first pressed Native Americans to adopt slavery, and then,
after the Civil War, employed black soldiers to complete its conquest of
native lands.

⚬⚬⚬

THE NEXT MORNING, THE CHIEF SENT HIS YOUNG BRAVES TO GUIDE
Josiah and his family safely through the woods. The family had done
far better than Josiah could have expected. They were now only about
twenty-five miles from Lake Erie. The men pointed to where they were
to turn off the army path and head east along the lake.

The family walked toward the northern Ohio plains all morning, until they encountered a stream that had flooded the roadway. Josiah forded

the stream and ferried his family safely across, but it wasn't without great pains for the porter. Josiah removed his shirt. Hundreds of miles with the rough tow cloth on his skin had taken their toll. His back was completely raw, the skin worn away in a patch almost exactly the size of his knapsack. Charlotte gently inspected the wound, but there was nothing they could do.

The family passed another night in the woods. By late morning, they came out upon a wide, treeless plain. It was a windy day, perfect for sailing. Smoke from the village chimneys could be seen drifting away in the early light. The Hensons walked along the smooth arc of Sandusky Bay until they neared the village of Venice. About a mile from the lake, Josiah hid Charlotte and the children in the bushes.

Just inside the village, he noticed a house-like building and a small schooner. A number of men were passing back and forth between the two in a frantic hurry.

When Josiah was within shouting distance, he heard a man with a Scottish accent call to him. "Hollo there, man! You want to work?"[12]

The voice was that of a Scotsman named Captain Burnham.

"Yes, sir!" Josiah shouted.

"Come come, then!" the captain yelled. "I'll give you a shilling an hour. Must get off with this wind."

As Josiah approached the captain, the man's expression changed. He stared at Josiah's mangled shoulders.

"Oh, you can't work," Burnham said. "You're crippled."

"Can't I?" Josiah said. He grabbed a bag of corn and walked toward the men who were loading the vessel's hold.

Josiah joined the line of laborers scurrying along the plank. He positioned himself next to the only other black man. They exchanged pleasantries, and Josiah learned the man's name was Doc.

"How far is it to Canada?" Josiah asked.

The man looked puzzled for only a second.

"Want to go to Canada?!" Doc said. "Come along with us, then. Our captain's a fine fellow. We're going to Buffalo."

Josiah had never heard of it.

"Buffalo . . ." Josiah said. "How far is that from Canada?"

"Don't you know, man?" Doc laughed. "Just across the river."

Sensing he could trust the man, Josiah told him about Charlotte and his children.

"I'll speak to the captain," Doc replied.

Moments later, the Scottish captain took Josiah aside. "The Doctor says you want to go to Buffalo."

"Yes, sir," replied Josiah.

The captain was honest and frank, and the conversation cut straight to the point.

"Well, why not go with me? Doctor says you've got a family?"

"Yes, sir."

"Where did you stop?"

"About a mile back."

"How long have you been here?"

Josiah hesitated for a moment.

"Come, my good fellow, tell us all about it!" the captain encouraged. "You're running away, ain't you?"

Josiah decided to trust Captain Burnham and told him all that he and his family had been through.

"Well, go along and get them!" the Scotsman ordered.

Josiah smiled and turned to run. About fifty feet out, the captain stopped him.

"You go on getting the grain in. When we get off, I'll lay to over opposite that island, and send a boat back. There's a lot of regular nigger-catchers in the town below, and they might suspect if you brought your party out of the bush by daylight."

Josiah worked with a happiness and determination matched by no man. By afternoon the three hundred bushels of corn and grain were on board. The hatches were fastened, the anchor raised, the sails hoisted, and the ship set sail.

❧

JOSIAH HID IN THE TREES ON THE WATERLINE AND WATCHED THE vessel with intense worry. He began to fear they would leave without him. The ship sailed steadily in the strong breeze. The boat reached the spot where the captain had agreed to stop, but it continued on.

Josiah's heart sank. Captain Burnham had used him to load his ship, then taken off in the wind he'd so keenly hoped to catch. So near deliverance, only to have his hopes blasted again. They had made a game of his misery.

The sun went down. The western purples and golds faded to gray. Josiah gazed toward the Promised Land with a weary heart.

Suddenly, the boat turned into the wind. It stilled in the water. Josiah watched as a rowboat was lowered from the stern. The sailors' steady strokes aimed for the point where Josiah stood. In minutes, the rowboat slid onto the beach. Josiah's black friend Doc and two sailors jumped out, and they went to gather Charlotte and the children.

They reached the spot where Josiah had left them, but, to his horror, they were gone. He frantically searched the bushes, fearing the worst.

Had his family been discovered and carried off? The men told him there was no time to lose—he'd have to go to Buffalo alone. But Josiah couldn't leave without them if there was any chance they were still out there. He scanned back and forth in the woods. Were they gone? Had they been captured?

Almost at the point of despair, Josiah stumbled across one of his boys in the fading light. He had been gone so long that Charlotte had assumed he'd been captured. When she'd heard his voice, mixed with those of other men, she believed her husband's captors were leading him back to uncover the family. In her sheer terror she had tried to conceal herself and the boys. Now they were all together again, and they set off for the beach with the men he had met. They reached the boat, and it took no time to load the family onto it, as they had only what they were carrying. Josiah later quipped that it was "one convenience, at least, of having nothing."[13]

Doc's sailors rowed with gusto, and the little boat steadily glided toward the light that hung from the mother ship's mast. The Hensons were a pitiful sight to behold, but they were rapidly approaching freedom.

"Coom up on deck, and clop your wings and craw like a rooster," the Scottish captain yelled. "You're a free nigger as sure as you're a live mon."[14]

When Josiah was hoisted onto the deck, the crew burst into applause. Captain Burnham beamed, and every man on board seemed just as happy and willing as he was to help the Hensons make their escape.

The sails were hoisted. Wind plunged into the sheets and dragged the vessel speedily out of the harbor and on their way. Josiah and his family had endured so much these past few months: fear of slave hunters and their dogs, fear of wolves, fear of Indians, fear of drowning. They'd felt raging hunger, thirst, and pain, as well as aching feet. And on top of all that, Josiah had experienced throbbing shoulders and a ragged back.

Now he was safe on a ship with a kindhearted captain, with his whole family aboard, and heading for freedom. He broke down and wept like a child.

༄

AND WHAT OF THE RILEY BROTHERS? MANY OWNERS WHOSE SLAVES had escaped posted wanted ads, like the one that ran in *The Charleston Courier* in South Carolina on February 20, 1836, offering $300 for a twenty-five-year-old runaway named Billy. The ad suggested that "in all probability he may resist; in that event, 50 dollars will be paid for his HEAD." Others bred or hired "negro dogs" who were specially groomed to track runaways. Runaways often planned their escape with the dogs in mind, either going by river or rubbing themselves with onions or rabbit grease in an attempt to throw off their scent.*

---

* Former slave Harriet Jacobs wrote in her 1861 memoirs that the bloodhounds she had encountered "were well trained": "Their pen was spacious, and a terror to the slaves. They were let loose on a runaway, and, if they tracked him, they literally tore the flesh from his bones." Harriet Ann Jacobs, *Incidents in the Life of a Slave Girl* (Redditch, Worcestershire: Read Books, 2013). Solomon Northup confessed that he had been more afraid of the dogs than wild animals: "For thirty or forty miles it is without habitants, save wild beasts—the bear, the wild-cat, the tiger, and great slimy reptiles, that are crawling through it everywhere. I staggered on, fearing every instant I should feel the dreadful sting of the moccasin, or be crushed within the jaws of some disturbed alligator. The dread of them now almost equalled

If the Rileys sent out search parties, Josiah made no mention of it. If they posted wanted ads, or took out newspaper advertisements, none have ever been found.

Josiah had escaped on a Saturday night. Because of Josiah's rotating work schedule, Amos Riley wouldn't have discovered the family's disappearance until Wednesday. Did he simply let him go, knowing that Josiah would never stop until he found his freedom? Did Amos Junior intercede on his rescuer's behalf? Or would taking out want ads draw further attention to Isaac's ongoing lawsuits? After all, Arnold T. Windsor filed another lawsuit just two weeks after Josiah and his family escaped.

But Josiah, a crippled man traveling with a wife and four small boys, would have been easy to find. If an owner was wealthy enough, as Amos Riley was, he could hire bloodhound squads to recapture his "stolen property." Kentucky spies would fan out across the state and into Indiana and Ohio and New York. They especially watched the shorelines at places like Sandusky and Buffalo. *Especially* Buffalo.

❦

CAPTAIN BURNHAM EXPERTLY GUIDED HIS SHIP THROUGH THE NIGHT, and a smooth run brought them into Buffalo the next evening, where they moored for the night. The Henson family stayed below deck.

Early the next morning, the kindly Scotsman brought Josiah on deck and pointed across the Niagara River. "You see those trees?" he said. "They grow on free soil, and as soon as your feet touch that, you're a mon."[15]

From his vantage point on the ship, Josiah was less than half a mile from freedom. Across the treacherous, fast-flowing river was the Canadian town of Fort Erie. But the Buffalo side was crawling with slave owners and their spies.

---

the fear of the pursuing hounds." Solomon Northup, *Twelve Years a Slave* (Chapel Hill: University of North Carolina Press, 2011), 101.

Captain Burnham guided Josiah and his family down to the Black Rock* ferry, just fifteen miles from Niagara Falls, and twenty miles south of where Harriet Tubman crossed near Whirlpool Rapids.[16] Burnham and the Hensons walked down Niagara Street, turned onto Ferry Street, and descended a steep hill. They crossed over the Erie Canal—which had been completed just five years earlier—and Black Rock Harbor on bridges to the ferry dock, which was built atop Bird Island Pier, a narrow line of huge stones stretching south toward downtown Buffalo.

It was a good spot from which to cross over to Canada. Thousands of boats came and went, and workers of all nationalities were employed on the docks. It wasn't unusual to see African Americans around the ferry, and Buffalo had a sizable population of free blacks, too. As the mass exodus of fugitives grew, the Black Rock ferry became the most important part of the Underground Railroad.[17]

"I want to see you go and be a freeman," the captain said. "I'm poor myself, and have nothing to give you." He didn't actually own the boat, he explained, but had sailed it for wages. "But I'll see you across," he promised.[18]

The captain turned to the ferryman, a man named Mr. Green. "What will you take this man and his family over for? He's got no money."

Green agreed to take them across on the horse-powered boat for three shillings, the modern equivalent of about twelve dollars. It was not unusual for men like Green to assist men like Josiah. According to one source, "Black Rock's ferry boat captains were often willing to convey fugitives across without question and sometimes at no charge."[19]

Captain Burnham paid the man. He then took a dollar (worth about $25 today) from his pocket and gave it to Josiah. He reverently put his hand on Josiah's head.

"Be a good fellow, won't you?"

Josiah was overcome with emotion.

---

* Josiah's memoir says he sailed into Buffalo, but the ship actually moored at Black Rock, a town named after a triangular outcropping of black limestone extending three hundred feet into the Niagara that had been blasted from the river in the early 1820s to make room for the canal. The City of Buffalo annexed the town in 1853.

"Yes," he nodded. "I'll give my soul to God."

The captain smiled and stepped back. As the ferry pushed off from shore, the Scotsman took of his hat and waved to the Henson family.

Josiah stood at the edge of the boat and called back to the captain.

"I'll use my freedom well!"

FREE SOIL

On the morning of Thursday, October 28, 1830, Josiah Henson's feet touched the Canadian shore for the first time.* He threw himself on the ground and rolled in the sand. He grabbed fistfuls of free soil and kissed them. He danced circles around Charlotte and the children until a crowd of onlookers stopped to watch the madman. A well-dressed gentleman pushed through the crowd. Colonel John Warren was the customs collector, and he stopped short at the sight of this large black man, covered in sand, whooping at the top of his lungs. Warren scanned the scene and explained to the crowd, "He's some crazy fellow."[20]

Josiah scrambled to his feet and rushed to the colonel.

"Oh no, master!" Josiah explained. "Don't you know? I'm free!"

Colonel Warren burst into laughter. "Well, I never knew freedom make a man roll in the sand in such a fashion!"

Josiah couldn't control himself. He hugged and kissed Charlotte and the boys and continued to dance in the sand before the growing crowd.

After 15,109 days—over forty-one years—in slavery, Josiah Henson was a free man.

---

* Josiah most likely landed next to the Old Ferry Wharf, which Warren operated from 1802 to 1832. The colonel's job was to inspect all vessels coming over and charge them tax if necessary. Thus, the ferry would have landed near his customs house, which was located on the Niagara River between Lavinia and Catherine Streets.[21]

SEVEN

THE STRUGGLE
FOR LIGHT

He who does not help us at the
right time does not help us at all.

—ATTRIBUTED TO GOETHE

T HE NEXT MORNING, JOSIAH SET OFF IN SEARCH OF A JOB. HE
described himself as "a stranger in a strange land," referencing a
phrase from the Book of Exodus spoken by Moses after he had left Egypt,
when he was dwelling in the land of Midian.[1] Canada was not yet a
nation—it was called Upper Canada at the time and had a population of
just 213,156. Though it had been surveyed, it was virtually a backwoods.
The land was filled with forests and wild animals, and a population consisting of First Nations and a smattering of pioneer settlers.

Josiah didn't understand Canadians or their culture, but as soon as he
arrived, he kept his eyes and ears open, just as in his days as a Washington
market man. He asked anyone he met if they knew of anyone who was
hiring. By noon the same day, he learned that a man named Mr. Hibbard
might be interested. Hibbard, who lived seven miles from Black Rock,

was considered rich for a Canadian. He had a large farm with some small tenements that he rented to his laborers. If hard and honest work would satisfy Hibbard, Josiah was certain they'd get along.

Josiah found Hibbard in the afternoon and struck an agreement for his employment. He asked if there was a house he and his family could live in. Hibbard showed him an old two-story shanty. Pigs had broken through the lower level, and by the looks of things, they'd been there a while.

Josiah evicted the pigs and prepared the house for its new tenants. If he was going to bring Charlotte and the boys here, he needed to make it nice. After all, this was home.

So he borrowed a hoe and a shovel from Hibbard and cleaned out the manure. He boiled water and mopped the floor as best he could. By midnight, the place was in a tolerable condition, and only then did he sleep with weary contentment. The next morning he returned with Charlotte and the boys, later joking that his family members were "the only furniture I had."[2]

The family had nothing but bare walls and floors, but even Charlotte admitted it was better than their log cabin with a dirt floor and a cloud of oppression overhead. Josiah found logs and built boxes in the corners of the room and stuffed them three feet thick with straw. The Henson family, for the first time in their lives, had beds.

To his great delight, Hibbard discovered that Josiah's work was more valuable than what he received from most of his hires. His new employee worked harder and smarter than the average farmer. Josiah gained favor with Hibbard, and Hibbard's wife took a liking to Charlotte. All their needs were met. Food and firewood were abundant, and the Hensons were, at last, full and warm and safe.

Josiah worked for Hibbard for three years. Sometimes he worked for wages, and other times for a share of the produce. With his profits, the family bought some pigs, a cow, and a horse. The family's conditions gradually improved, and Josiah began to feel that their sacrifices had been worth the trouble.

An old friend from Maryland escaped to Canada and came to visit. This friend, remembering Josiah's wonderful sermons, started spreading the word that he was good in the pulpit. Soon Josiah developed a reputation. As the requests came in, he couldn't help but say yes. The invitations came from churches with members from all walks of life, and soon Josiah labored in two fields—in Hibbard's farms, and in the pulpits of churches across the region. He was invited to speak to rich and poor, black and white, literate and illiterate, and to all alike he spoke about their duties to God and to each other.

But an old problem bothered Josiah. Despite the fact that he was often called upon to minister to highly educated folk, he still didn't know how to read. He knew that religion wasn't so much about knowledge as it was about wisdom, and yet he still craved knowledge.

Hibbard, in a kind display of generosity, enrolled Josiah's eldest son, Tom, in two quarters of school. The schoolmaster, in his own kindness, added two more. Tom was able to read the Bible to Josiah every evening. On Sunday mornings, he would read a passage and Josiah would memorize it before heading off to preach.

One summer Sunday morning, Josiah asked Tom to read to him.

"Where shall I read, father?"[3]

Josiah didn't know where to direct him. "Anywhere, my son."

Tom opened to Psalm 103. "Bless the Lord, O my soul: and all that is within me, bless His holy name."

As Josiah listened for the first time to what he later described as "this beautiful outpouring of gratitude," he began to weep. All his memories rushed back in a flash. All the pain, the hardship, the abuse. All the evil that the Rileys had done. Of his father, sold south. Of his mother, long passed. Of his harrowing journey to freedom.

Bless the Lord, O my soul. It was all he needed to express the gratitude he now felt.

Tom finished the passage. "Father, who was David?" He looked up at Josiah and saw the tears running down his cheeks. "He writes pretty, don't he?"

Josiah smiled and nodded.

"Who was David, Father?"

Josiah was unable to answer the question. He had never heard of David, but he couldn't bear to acknowledge his ignorance to his own son.

"He was a man of God, my son."

"I suppose so," Tom said. "But I want to know something more about him. Where did he live? What did he do?"

Josiah saw that evasive maneuvers couldn't outwit his sharp little boy. He confessed that he didn't know.

"Why father?" Tom asked. "Can't you read?"

The question was worse than the rest. All pride drained from Josiah's heart.

Josiah shook his head and admitted he couldn't.

"Why not?"

"Because I never had an opportunity to learn, nor anybody to teach me."

"Well, you can learn now."

"No, my son, I am too old, and have not time enough. I must work all day, or you would not have enough to eat."

"Then you might do it at night."

"But still there is nobody to teach me. I can't afford to pay anybody for it, and, of course, no one can do it for nothing."

"Why, father, I'll teach you!" Tom said. "I can do it, I know. And then you'll know so much more that you will be able to talk better, and preach better."

Josiah's ambition to be a great leader, and his deep desire to learn, were strong. He agreed to try.

Starting that night, and every evening to follow, by the light of some hickory bark or a pine knot, Josiah began to learn to read. His progress was slow, and Tom was discouraged. He would complain about his father's slowness, or bark at him like a schoolmaster with a troublesome student. Sometimes Josiah fell asleep in the middle of their lesson. His days were long and tiresome, and they had just a few minutes each night to work on the project.

But father and son persevered, and by winter Josiah had learned to read. By spring, his newfound ability was a great comfort. Until he learned to read, Josiah had never comprehended the cruel nature of the owners who kept their slaves in the dark. This gross injustice made him hate slavery even more, and he decided it was time to do something to elevate others who were suffering the same oppression.

SELF-IMPROVEMENT

After three years with Hibbard, Josiah found new and better employment. He was hired by a gentleman named Benjamin Riseley in the autumn of 1833. The new boss was progressive in his thinking, and the two men talked about the challenges facing new refugees in Canada.

Josiah knew he and his family were not the only ones to escape from America and settle wherever they first arrived in Canada. Hundreds of black people lived in his neighborhood. But even after gaining their freedom, their way of life hadn't improved much.

Newly free slaves, delighted in their emancipation, often accepted the first job offers they received and settled for wages far lower than what they could have earned. For generations, the word "no" had never been an option, and they'd been trained to believe they were incapable of accomplishing the same things as white people. They entered into unprofitable agreements, such as renting wild land on short-term contracts and committing themselves to clearing a certain amount of acreage. Their leases would expire by the time they cleared the land, and the landlord would happily raise himself a bountiful harvest. Then the tenants would move on and start all over again. Others, tempted by the high prices paid for tobacco, raised nothing else, eventually flooding the market. The price of tobacco crashed, while the prices of wheat and corn rose.

Josiah knew many men who were no further ahead in ten years than when they'd first arrived. They were happy to get paid for their work, but that was the height of their ambition. They didn't dream of becoming independent landowners themselves. Josiah made it his mission to arouse ambition in the hearts of his fellow escapees. They needed to organize, diversify, and learn how to negotiate.

Riseley agreed with Josiah's views and allowed the preacher to hold meetings at his house. Josiah invited a dozen of the smartest black workers he knew, and they discussed the subject. He pointed to how white men, for two hundred years, had taken a course of bold action, and in doing so, had, in his own words, "acquired an indestructible character for energy, enterprise, and self-reliance."[4]

Over the next year, Josiah hosted a number of meetings in Riseley's home and convinced about a dozen free men to join with him and invest their earnings in land. The plan was that, like the white men before them, they would find a piece of land and colonize it. They would settle some wild parcel, something they could call their own. On this land, every tree felled and every bushel of corn raised would bring profit to their own families. For the first time in their lives, they would truly be their own masters.

The group deputized Josiah to explore the country and find a suitable place. They all agreed they'd go wherever Josiah himself was willing to settle.

It was time to find a home.

SEARCHING FOR DAWN

After the harvest of 1834, Josiah set out on foot to travel the region between Lake Ontario, Lake Erie, and Lake Huron. He hitched rides whenever possible. A minister named Benjamin Cronyn recorded in his diary that he gave Josiah a lift in his covered wagon in Brantford, on his way to Hamilton.[5] When Josiah came to the territory east of Lake St. Clair and the Detroit River, he felt the soil's fertility was far better than anything else he'd seen. The township's name was Dawn. Could this be home?

Josiah returned and reported his findings to the group. Wisely cautious, they encouraged him to revisit Dawn in the summer of 1835, to see if the land was still good in the opposite season. While he waited for time to pass, he discovered a large tract of government land near Colchester, Ontario, about thirty miles southeast of Detroit on the Canadian side of Lake Erie, and about 250 miles from where he had first crossed into Canada.[6]

The land had been granted, "with conditions," to a man named Mr. McCormick, who had rented it out to settlers for as much as he could squeeze from desperate people. They had all since moved on—or rather, it's likely that McCormick had run them off once they'd done the hard work of clearing his land.[7]

Josiah's tiny community couldn't afford to miss a season by clearing and preparing land; here was land ready for planting. A dozen or so families decided to join him and temporarily rent McCormick's land while they saved up to purchase the piece of Dawn that Josiah had discovered.

The families moved in the spring of 1836 and were soon rich in wheat and tobacco. It turned out to be incredibly profitable—so much so that they stayed for seven years. But it was not their own land. The government, which had taken back the land from McCormick—presumably he had not fulfilled the conditions stipulated in the land grant—could put it up for sale at any time and they'd likely be driven off by wealthier buyers. All their improvements—irrigation, fencing, buildings—would be lost. It was hard to both settle land and save for the future at the same time, but Josiah's heart was now set on Dawn.

Meanwhile, the population of escaped slaves in Upper Canada increased rapidly. They spread throughout the towns and into the interior. Immigration from America was constant, and some of it was, in fact, Josiah's own doing.

⁓♾⁓

JOSIAH HAD PROMISED THE SCOTTISH BOAT CAPTAIN, BURNHAM, that he would use his freedom well, and he had made good on that promise. But he felt he could do more. There were still so many who lived in captivity. Josiah had paved a path to freedom and wanted to help others escape. When he preached, he preached on the "importance of the obligations they were under; first, to God, for their deliverance; and then, secondly, to their fellow-men, to do all that was in their power to bring others out of bondage."[8]

One Sunday, after Josiah had preached such a sermon, a young man named James Lightfoot approached him and begged him to rescue his brothers in Kentucky. Josiah wrestled with the proposition for days. It would mean a difficult journey—four hundred miles on foot through the free states of New York, Pennsylvania, and Ohio, and on into Kentucky. But this was what it meant to use his freedom well. Ultimately, his mission would prove successful—not only did he rescue the Lightfoot brothers, but he helped another group escape to Canada as well.[9]

Josiah, of course, wasn't the only emancipated black person who saved others. William Still, a wealthy coal merchant born to freed Maryland slaves, served as a clerk for the Philadelphia Vigilance Committee, a citizen band of freedom fighters.[10] In his fourteen years as an Underground Railroad conductor, Still helped almost eight hundred slaves escape. He documented many of the stories of these rescues in his 1872 book *The Underground Railroad Records.*[*]

After her escape from Maryland to St. Catharines, Ontario, Harriet Tubman made more than a dozen trips back to America to help at least seventy people escape to Canada, earning her the nickname "Black Moses" for leading so many people out of slavery. A legend persists that southern slavers offered a $40,000 bounty for her capture, "dead or alive." This figure is highly unlikely, considering that a typical slave sold for a few hundred dollars, and a prime male might fetch $1,000. An $800 reward was posted for Peter Pennington, who escaped with Tubman's help on November 16, 1856. If a $40,000 reward had been offered, it would

---

* William Still was the youngest of fourteen children born to Charity and Levin Still. Although William was born in the free state of New Jersey, his mother was a Maryland runaway; thus, her son was still legally considered a slave under federal law. Charity and Levin's oldest sons, Levin Jr. and Peter, were sold from Maryland to Kentucky and on to Alabama. Peter and his family escaped when he was about fifty, but Levin Jr. was whipped to death for visiting his own wife without permission. Thanks to William Still's meticulous records, he had the pleasure of reuniting his brother Peter with their mother after a separation of forty-two years.

have made national news, as it would be the equivalent of more than $1 million today. The US government offered $50,000 for John Wilkes Booth, Abraham Lincoln's assassin, in 1865.[11] The $40,000 figure was likely concocted by Sallie Holley, a New York antislavery activist, for an 1867 newspaper article.[12] The only published notice that's been found concerning a reward for Tubman's capture is an October 3, 1849, advertisement in the *Cambridge Democrat* offering a $300 reward for the return of "Minty [Tubman's birth name was Araminta Ross] and her two brothers, Ben and Harry."[13]

The Underground Railroad ran north to Canada and south to Mexico and the Caribbean. Some escapees were transported in wagons, boats, and trains, but many walked on foot. Approximately 100,000 people made the journey in all, many of them led by conductors. It was a dangerous choice to return to the South and rescue slaves, but people such as Tubman and Josiah did so repeatedly. Although we don't know how many trips he took during his first decades in Canada, Josiah returned to America again and again, by his count rescuing 118 people* from the strangling grip of merciless slaveholders.

⁓ℰ⁓

As more and more slaves escaped to Canada, the supply of cheap labor became a windfall for some already-established Canadian pioneers. Josiah saw it all around him. Clearing and settling the woods of Upper Canada was labor intensive, and there was a serious demand for workers. He and other self-emancipated blacks weren't afraid of hard work, but they were still selling themselves short.

Though he had no formal training, Josiah started lecturing on crops and wages and profit and loss. He insisted that each man should raise his own crops, save his wages, and secure the full profits of his labors.

---

* The number 118 is peculiar. Josiah had denied 18 slaves their freedom when he brought them from Maryland to Kentucky. Did he feel he needed to make up for what had been lost? Was this number achieved purely by chance, or did Josiah set out to reach this particular number?

He didn't try to hide what he was doing, and the traders whose exorbitant profits he was trying to diminish often attended his speeches. Josiah reasoned that their overall profits wouldn't shrink if free black men followed his advice. Rather, they would have more people with whom to trade.

Realizing that for many, finance was a tricky topic to navigate, Josiah handled questions carefully. His sensible and kind nature never offended his opponents, and the white landowners soon realized that he wanted to benefit everybody involved in the nation-building effort. In Josiah's view, the future of Canada would be inclusive of black people, white people, and native people alike. They would own their own farms, educate their children, and cultivate true independence.

But war with American settlers was brewing, and Josiah would first need to defend what they had built so far.

REBELLION

Nearly a thousand Canadian rebels with American sympathies were growing tired of Great Britain's colonial rule. They joined together with American adventurers into a secret organization called Hunters' Lodges.[14] Membership swelled to as many as 80,000, and small groups began to make raids into Canadian lands along the Detroit River. It was a threat to Upper Canada's sovereignty, and hundreds of black Canadians volunteered for service during the rebellion. They helped create fighting units called the "Coloured Corps" in Toronto, Hamilton, Windsor, and Chatham, the area where Josiah lived.

A far later version of Josiah's autobiography reports that during the Canadian rebellion he was appointed captain of the 2nd Essex Company of Coloured Volunteers. No external record has been found to confirm this statement, but it is not outside the realm of possibility. Rev. Jermain W. Loguen, another black preacher, also claimed he was invited to command a black company, and a free black man named William Allen boasted that he was the first black captain in British North America. He was later awarded a special sword for his outstanding leadership during the rebellion.[15]

Although Josiah perhaps served in the war, his captaincy might be an autobiographical embellishment made by his editor, as white officers typically commanded black companies at the time. That said, it seems reasonable that natural leaders like Josiah would be placed in charge of their fellow soldiers, and the motivation for black men in Canada to fight against the Hunters' Lodges would have been extremely high. These free men were willing to help defend the nation that had given them a home and refuge from slavery.

Josiah's autobiography states that, though he couldn't shoulder a musket, he carried a sword, and that his company held the highly strategic Fort Malden, in Amherstburg, Ontario, from Christmas 1837 until May 1838. It also mentions that his company captured a schooner, called *Ann* or *Anne*, along with its three hundred arms, two cannons, musketry, and provisions for the rebel troops.

The *Ann* incident might be the only time in history that a company of foot soldiers captured a sea vessel.[16] On January 9, 1838, American patriots attempted to raid the town of Amherstburg by crossing the Detroit River on the schooner. Thanks to a quick drop in the Canadian temperatures during the skirmish, the schooner froze solid in ice floes and was easily boarded by all three of the town's regiments, including bands of militia and First Nations warriors. The Canadians successfully defended their town, capturing twenty American prisoners, including their commander, Brigadier General Edward Alexander Theller.* After the rebellion, both sides returned to the status quo.

---

* Another version of the story states that Brigadier General Edward Alexander Theller fired cannon at Amherstburg. The local militia, completely ignoring the fact that they were out-gunned, peppered the schooner with musket fire. Their bullets tore the rigging to pieces and killed the helmsman, which caused the schooner to run aground. According to one source, "the Canadian militia waded to their armpits in the freezing January water, boarded the schooner, and captured Theller and his crew."[17]

A PARTNERSHIP FOR PROSPERITY

Prior to the rebellion, while Josiah lived and farmed in Colchester, he had met a white Congregational missionary from Massachusetts named Hiram Wilson. As a boy, Hiram had attended a manual labor school called the Oneida Institute, and then he enrolled at the recently founded Lane Theological Seminary in Cincinnati. When the school refused to discuss slavery as part of its theological conversations, he moved to Ohio and earned his degree at Oberlin Theological Seminary. Hiram then moved to Upper Canada as an agent for the American Antislavery Society. He was an abolitionist and a dreamer, and over the next six years he raised and borrowed enough money to start at least ten schools for free black people in Upper Canada. He recruited fourteen teachers, mostly fellow Oberlin graduates, and soon gained the attention of a Quaker philanthropist named James Canning Fuller, an Englishman living in Skaneateles, New York.

Hiram Wilson took an interest in Josiah's community and promised to do whatever he could to help them acquire land in order to start a permanent settlement. He wrote to Fuller and asked for the philanthropist's help. On a visit to England in the summer of 1840, Fuller convinced many of his friends to support Hiram's cause. He returned with $1,650 to benefit freed slaves in their new land.

Josiah's small community—and blacks throughout the region—were overwhelmed by the sum. Many members of Josiah's group couldn't even comprehend the figure. But Josiah and Hiram knew exactly how they wanted to spend the money, if they could convince the community to go along with their plan. The two men decided the fastest way to reach consensus was to call a meeting. They sent word to all the black settlements in the area and invited them to send delegates, and together they hosted a convention in London, Upper Canada, in June 1838.

At the meeting, Josiah and Hiram urged the group to spend the funds on establishing a manual labor school, so their children could gain a theoretical *and* practical education. The school would have all the benefits of a grammar school plus a robust hands-on component. Girls would learn domestic skills such as cooking and sewing. Boys would be taught mechanical arts, such as blacksmithing, mill working, and carpentry.

Despite being known as a land free of slavery, Canada was still rife with prejudice. In many districts, it was impossible to overcome the racism of white settlers, and black children were often barred from attending local schools. Starting their own school would not only train up their own people to then train others, but it would gradually enable black people to become independent of white men for their intellectual progress and physical prosperity.

There were some at the convention who opposed the Wilson-Henson plan, likely wishing to simply divvy up the proceeds among the various settlements. But over three days of debate they came to a consensus that they would build something of permanent usefulness. Hiram and Josiah's proposal was unanimously adopted. The Canada Mission Board appointed a committee of three to choose and purchase land for the school, with Hiram and Josiah as the leading men. Fuller likely served as the silent partner, though some speculate that a man named Henry Shelby was the third man who joined in the search for the perfect property.

Hiram and Josiah traveled for several months, but no site seemed as good as the one Josiah had seen years earlier: Dawn.

The area, today the city of Dresden, Ontario, was nothing but wild forest prior to 1790. There were no roads or highways, just trails to various First Nations camps. The land teemed with deer, bears, wolves, foxes, and wild turkeys, as well as fish in the lakes and streams, and would make an attractive spot for settlers.

In May 1790, Alexander McKee, a deputy agent of the British Indian Department, negotiated with the Wyandot, Ottawa, Chippewa, and Potawatomi First Nations to acquire title to what is now much of southwestern Ontario. The British government paid in goods worth £1,179 13s. 9d. in Quebec or Halifax currency for all their lands, including the Dresden area, in the form of 39 gallons of rum, 400 pounds of tobacco, plus guns, ammunition, blankets, clothing, and other useful items.[18]

The first settler in Dresden was Gerard Lindsley, who purchased the lot that would become Dawn in 1825.[19] The pioneer had sailed up the

Sydenham River and landed at his forest lot.* He quickly located a fresh-water spring and built himself a log cabin nearby. Lindsley was completely isolated, and he remained sole monarch of all he surveyed for several years, with only an occasional native visitor.

The first black settlers to put down roots at Dawn arrived by at least 1823, when freedom seekers Weldon Harris and Levi Willoughby purchased Lot No. 3 on the 3rd Concession, a fifty-acre parcel that extended north to the river flats.

Several more black families soon followed. As early as 1839, when Dresden was still a dense forest, settlers of all races and creeds from a forty-mile radius would meet on the flats of the southern banks of the river for religious camp meetings. The meetings could often run a week or more, with families bringing tents along with "stands for the preachers, seats for the sinners, and pens for the saved." The camp site continued to be used for river baptisms until at least 1949. The Christian connection may have been what drew Josiah to the Dawn area in the first place, and there's a chance that he may have participated in the gatherings on his scouting trip.[20]

Dawn was a loose society, at best, but by the time Josiah arrived, around fifty black families lived in the area, and he would have found the community inviting. The land itself was heavily forested, and there were wetlands and grasslands that would provide game to feed the community, along with rich land and dense hardwoods. It would be a good place to call home.

THE BRITISH AMERICAN INSTITUTE

In November 1841, Hiram and Josiah used a portion of Fuller's funds to purchase two hundred acres on the Sydenham River. It was fine, rich soil, densely covered with black walnut and white birch trees. The price was $4 per acre.

---

* Prior to being named the Sydenham, the river was known as Bear Creek, and before that, by its native name, Jonquakamik, meaning "Milky River." Visitors to modern-day Dresden will immediately agree that the first name best describes the sleepy, white chocolate river.

Josiah also purchased the adjoining lot of two hundred acres, with his own money, and prepared to move his family to their very own piece of land.

Thirteen months after their initial purchase, just a few weeks before Christmas in 1841, the British American Institute (BAI), a manual labor school, opened its doors. The BAI started with twelve students and Hiram Wilson as their teacher. His wife, Hannah Maria Hubbard Wilson, also became a teacher at the school. The school's board of trustees, consisting of six men—three white and three black—signed a Declaration of Trust leaving Hiram Wilson, as BAI president, and an executive committee to realize the BAI vision. Josiah's exact role in the first two years is not known, but it's likely that he spent much of that time building a home and clearing the trees from his own land in order to provide farmland to feed his family. It's also likely that in the first year, there would still be a final crop from their Colchester lands.

The school's mission was to integrate basic education and profitable labor to ex-slaves of all ages, and to introduce them to the economic system so they could become self-sufficient freed people. The institution also provided temporary living space for refugees who had just arrived in Canada. Hiram and Josiah's plan was to make the BAI a self-sustaining institution. Students would help to work the BAI land as a means of paying their own way.

The BAI was funded by Christians, Quakers, abolitionists, and several organizations. Significant funding came from the American Baptist Free Mission Society (ABFMS) and the Canada Mission Board, and Hiram Wilson made sure to lay out his dream in a letter to his supporters south of the border:

> At this Institution a suitable selection is made of the most promising characters among the negroes, to be trained up in habits of industry, and to receive a secular and religious education suited to their capacities and future prospects, so as to qualify them to become teachers and benefactors to their deeply injured and suffering brethren. The value of these labours will appear still more important, when it is

recollected that it is only by improving the intellectual and moral condition of the colored race, that prejudice against color can be overcome, on account of which they are now suffering in their newly adopted country.[21]

⁓⁓⁓

JOSIAH MOVED HIS FAMILY TO LOT NO. 3 ON THE 4TH CONCESSION of Dawn in 1842, and many of his friends soon joined him. Like some of the other early investors in the Dawn area, in time he would grow to own several lots and houses (likely for his adult children). He also built up a successful farm operation that employed others. Perhaps because grooming Isaac Riley's horse had been one of his first jobs, Josiah seems to have always liked horses, and at some point he began to invest in and breed fine stallions as well. This flourishing home base allowed him to travel far and wide in his efforts to elevate the plight of black refugees in Canada and raise funds on behalf of the British American Institute.

Until now, Josiah felt that black families had only been able to share the miseries of society, but now they would share in its blessings. Economy and education were the two great means by which their oppressed race could be elevated to equality in civilization. The new school at Dawn could train up generations of newly freed blacks to become independent and self-sustaining. The institute could prove that blacks were, indeed, equal to whites, both in education and industry. The BAI could become a beacon of hope for those who were still enslaved.

Once work began in earnest, the members of the new community made progress quickly. By March 12, 1843, Hiram and the community had cleared and mostly fenced twelve acres, built three houses, and constructed a 1.5-story schoolhouse that sat up to sixty students and slept twelve in the loft above.

The plan was for students to work three to four hours per day on the farm in order to raise food for their own support. Unfortunately, many students treated the BAI as a charity built for their benefit and didn't seem to realize that it was a working farm. They came for the winter school term, when their labor was basically useless, and left in the spring to work on steamboats or other paid summer jobs, making use of their newly acquired education. Many who did remain had to work at clearing the densely wooded land, which meant that expenses needed to be covered by outside donors.

The institute was growing at a rapid pace, but James Canning Fuller's startup funds were quickly depleted. The BAI was chronically short of funding.* Hiram Wilson traveled to England in May 1843 to solicit more money, leaving his wife and others to care for the BAI in his absence. He was gone for nearly five months, managing to raise £258 after costs. This was enough to float the operation and purchase one hundred acres from Josiah. By 1844 the British American Institute was three hundred acres in size, and there were high hopes that it would be enough land to sustain its work.[22]

On September 30, 1843, Hiram wrote that the school had "sixteen adults and about twenty youths," and that "their improvement has been highly satisfactory." He added, "A steward is engaged to superintend the manual labour, and two teachers are employed in giving a sound English education."[23]

The BAI continued to grow rapidly. By 1844, American abolitionists were publicizing Dawn. Levi Coffin, the Quaker abolitionist from Cincinnati known as the "president" of the Underground Railroad—which was now nearing its peak—made his first visit to the school that year. By the following year, Hannah Wilson was teaching seventy students.

Although there hadn't been many black settlers in the area before Josiah's arrival, the abolitionist press quickly made Dawn and the BAI a magnet for fugitives and a major destination on the Underground Railroad. The advantage of community and the opportunity of a practical education attracted refugees at a rapid rate. It would be a mistake to say that Josiah started Dawn, or that he alone was to be celebrated for its success. Josiah was the spiritual and celebrity leader of Dawn, but the

---

* An 1856 report says they ran a deficit of $120 in 1841 and of $331 in 1842. The entire property at that time was worth $1,000.

settlement was far bigger than any one person. Dawn wasn't a community with a master plan—it grew naturally. Farms were cultivated, businesses blossomed, churches were erected, and mission outposts served the poor, all independent of the school.

At the time, the Sydenham River was deep enough that boats of up to three hundred tons could navigate directly into town from Detroit and the Great Lakes. Naturally, homes and businesses sprouted along its banks, and it's not unlikely that the community developed a marine route for the Underground Railroad that led straight to Dawn's doorstep.

But what was Dawn, exactly? There was as much confusion about it then as there is today. Dawn was not the BAI, nor was the BAI Dawn. Josiah raised funds for the BAI, but he also personally helped the settlers at Dawn. The BAI had a board, while Dawn was a free-form, grassroots community. The nearby town of Dawn Mills was not Dawn. The surrounding township of Dawn was not Dawn. Dawn was something more spiritual, more of an idea and an area of refuge than a place with well-defined borders. It was a vision.

Still, the BAI unquestionably played an integral role in attracting people to the area. In 1845, a developer named Daniel R. VanAllen, of nearby Chatham, bought the original Dawn settler Gerard Lindsley's seventy-acre farm, just northeast of the BAI lands. In November of the same year, VanAllen, who is now considered the founder of Dresden, turned twenty acres of his land into more than sixty one-eighth-acre lots. The main street of Dresden ran (roughly) in a straight line, dodging stumps and quagmires along the way. Around the same time, an Irish-born developer, William Wright, started building another village, Fairport, just southeast of Dresden.[24] Between the BAI, Dresden, Fairport, and all the surrounding farms that made up the settlement, Dawn was, indeed, starting to rise.

⁓◦∞◦⁓

DAWN WASN'T THE ONLY FREE BLACK SETTLEMENT TO SPRING UP IN southwestern Ontario, of course. While most refugees initially landed at places like Fort Erie or Windsor, in time, like Josiah, they, too, moved farther inland to build their own lives. Black colonies emerged. While some black people settled in cities such as Chatham, London, Hamilton, Toronto, and Colchester, there were those who felt it necessary to give fugitives a chance to acclimate to freedom before thrusting them into the wider Canadian society.

In a way, all the black settlements were like refugee camps, in that they lacked a definite sense of permanency and were supported predominantly by white outsiders. The newcomers faced prejudice— many Canadians were hostile to the black settlers—and the life of land-clearing and city-building was incredibly arduous. These small pockets of freedom continued to develop nonetheless. Other well-known colonies included the Elgin Settlement near Buxton, Henry Bibb's Refugee's Home Society near Windsor, the Wilberforce Colony, and settlements at Port Royal, Shrewsbury, and rural locations in be-tween.* Each of these colonies was supported by white abolitionists, Christian denominations, and wealthy patrons. The Elgin Settlement was likely the largest—at 9,000 acres—and certainly the most orga-nized. But Dawn was easily the most influential and best known of the settlements, thanks in part to the British American Institute.[25] In time, however, the settlements had to compete for an ever-shrinking pot of donor money both at home and abroad. It is hard to imagine the cost of resettling tens of thousands of abused, illiterate, uneducated, hungry former slaves on wild land not yet a nation. Each of the black colo-nies required a huge amount of sustainable funding, and there never seemed to be enough to go around.[26]

WITHERING GROWTH

The Dawn community continued to grow through the summer of 1845. Former slaves from Virginia introduced tobacco and hemp, and the BAI

---

* The Elgin Settlement, which was supported by the Presbyterians, rang a donated Liberty Bell every time a new freedom-seeker arrived in town.

started a brickyard that was said to have produced almost 100,000 bricks in its lifetime.[27]

The trustees and the executive committee, with Josiah and Hiram as their fundraising agents, did their best to make the school self-supporting, hiring the students to work the land and build businesses to increase income. But it was never enough. The Dawn Settlement ballooned to more than five hundred inhabitants, and the BAI itself grew far too quickly. The need was great, and the institute's expenses far exceeded the donations that Hiram and Josiah could solicit.

As the debts mounted, the BAI came under heavy attack. At least some of the controversy arose from disagreements over how much former fugitives should be set apart from society. Some felt that by providing shelter for the students, where they could live and learn away from the rest of society, the BAI was advocating colonization. They held that fugitives should instead be fully integrated into society, and above all, that they should not beg for money. It was a war that no one would win.

The BAI could likely have become a self-sufficient enterprise had it been given time and support to grow slowly. But the influx of refugees from America was constant, and the school's leaders simply weren't up to the task of keeping pace with the growth. Hiram Wilson was a visionary dreamer, not a manager, and Josiah Henson, though a man of remarkable intelligence and talent, was an uneducated former slave who could barely read and couldn't write, let alone run a college. There were the costs of employing teachers, building mills and houses, feeding the poor, and the additional overhead of simply running the BAI. The institute and its leaders took on debt at an alarming rate. They were working with an unsustainable business model, and something drastic was needed to fix it.

The American Baptist Free Mission Society saw this financial predicament brewing and moved to hire a capable leader to help right the ship. William P. Newman was an escaped slave from Richmond, Virginia, who had studied at Oberlin College before becoming a minister at Union Baptist Church in Cincinnati. The ABFMS offered Newman the job of secretary of the settlement's executive committee, and he arrived at Dawn in June 1845.[28]

Unlike the people-pleasing Josiah, Newman was aggressive and decidedly partisan. The two men were bound to clash far sooner than later. For now, Newman's job was to reorganize the BAI's executive management, and by the late fall, he believed he had turned things around.

On October 4, Newman reported to Dawn's patrons that sixty acres of timber had been cleared and cultivated in the previous three years. Josiah's community had built a large schoolhouse, several houses, and a barn. They were starting on a potashery, likely for making soap, glass, and fertilizer. They had also erected two large buildings that would be ready by December 1, presumably as expanded boarding and teaching space.[29]

Newman informed the patrons that Josiah had raised $220 to help pay the BAI's deficits, and that he had spent the summer preaching among the black settlements at his own expense. The school had eighty students, and Newman predicted they would reach one hundred by winter. They could triple that number if only they had space to house them all, he noted.

Newman ended by saying that "in the fullness of confidence and fraternal solicitude, we commend to the kind consideration and sympathy of the benevolent public our beloved brethren, Hiram Wilson and Josiah Henson[,] as the accredited agents for our Christian enterprise."

Less than three weeks after his appeal, Newman wrote, "The institute is in a better condition than ever before. We have now some 90 students and they are coming in almost daily." However, he went on to mention that when two ladies had arrived the previous day, there was nowhere to house them; they had to turn away another man due to housing and food shortages. Rather casually, he noted that "Brother Wilson and Henson have left on an agency and should they fail to obtain help, we must stop operations in a few weeks for the want of food." How could the BAI be both doing better than ever and on the verge of collapse? The letter is baffling.

Things went downhill quickly. Before the end of 1845, and despite his kind words just a few months earlier, William Newman charged the executive committee, Josiah and Hiram included, with maladministration. He had examined the financial records and believed something was amiss. Newman asked Josiah to return from one of his New England preaching trips to discuss the missing money. Josiah and Hiram defended themselves at a public meeting, and they were unable to produce an exact account of all the funds they had collected. Nevertheless, the executive committee declined to prosecute.

Newman resigned from the BAI and returned to his Cincinnati congregation later in 1846, though that didn't stop him from continuing to attack Dawn's leadership. He claimed that the black residents of Dawn disliked Hiram Wilson. He tried to use Frederick Douglass's antislavery newspaper, *The North Star*, to denounce both Hiram and Josiah. For Newman, the battle had inexplicably become personal.

Hiram certainly didn't help resolve the controversy surrounding the BAI, and with it, the Dawn Settlement in general. He was an able organizer on his own, but he was a terrible team player. He was careless with finances and easily flattered. Moreover, he was an inveterate people-pleaser.

Both Hiram and Josiah believed the BAI should remain factionless, and tried to make all sides happy. There was a group within Dawn that obviously didn't want them running things. The leader of this group was, of course, William P. Newman.

It was only a matter of time before the "moderate" British abolitionists who supported Josiah and the "extremist" American abolitionists who supported Newman would wage battle for total control of the British American Institute.

PREACHER MEETS POET

After several years without a discernible position within the BAI, Josiah was authorized as an official fundraising representative for the institute. Fundraisers typically earned a 20 to 25 percent commission for their efforts. The commission covered their expenses, served as a salary, and compensated them for having to be away from their own farms back home for long periods while traveling.

Josiah was bold in his fundraising efforts and managed to elicit the support of some very influential men. Henry Wadsworth Longfellow recalled meeting Josiah on June 26, 1846, when the preacher visited Craigie House in Cambridge, Massachusetts, to convince the famous poet to sponsor the BAI: "In the evening Mr. Henson, a Negro, once a slave, now a preacher, called to get subscription for the school at Dawn, in Upper Canada, for education of blacks. I had a long talk with him, and he gave me an account of his escape from slavery with his family."[30]

Though he was new to fundraising, Josiah was well-spoken and had a great presence. Longfellow wrote: "There was never anything more childlike than his manner. . . . The good-natured ebony face, the swarthy-bearded lip, the white teeth, the whole aspect of the man so striking and withal so wild,—It seemed as if some Egyptian statue had come to life; and sat speaking in the twilight sonorous English not yet well learned." Josiah evidently made quite an impression, as Longfellow's account books record that he donated to "Father Henson" many times over the next thirty years, including $10 on June 5, 1856, and $20 in March 1875. Altogether, he donated the combined equivalent of around $10,000 by today's income standards.[31]

MILLS WITH A MISSION

Despite the controversy with Newman, Josiah's good reputation remained intact. Now a Methodist Episcopal elder with a three-hundred-mile district under his care, Josiah preached constantly. He lectured on justice and equality for black people and raised awareness and funds for the work of the BAI at Dawn. He was quickly becoming a leading figure in the abolitionist movement, and was revered by abolitionists throughout the nation. Soon people gave him a new name: Father Henson.

During this financially challenging time for Dawn and the BAI, Josiah looked for new ways to produce income for the settlement and institute. The lands on which the Dawn community had settled were covered with a beautiful forest of hardwoods, but the settlers didn't need trees. They needed arable ground to raise crops to feed their families. When the former slaves cut down the trees to clear the land, they were burning the piles of wood simply to get rid of them.

Burning down forests could in fact be an easy way to make money, though perhaps it was not the best way to profit from trees. Starting in 1845, farmers in the area realized they could raze their forests, collect the ashes, and sell them to the newly constructed ashery in Dresden. The facility leached the ashes, boiled the lye into a gritty powder, and shipped it in barrels to Chatham, and then on to England and Ireland, for bleaching linens.

Josiah often roamed through the forest, and the waste appalled him. He wasn't the only one. When a new settler named Parker Smith arrived, he noted that the locals grazed cattle in the forests all winter to forage for elm branches when they ran out of hay. He found it even more difficult to see Canadians use premium "curled maple and splendid walnut stuff" as mere cooking fuel.

Josiah needed to find a way to convert this abundant natural wealth into money. He left home for America in the autumn of 1847. Mills in New York sawed logs just like those in Dawn's forests into lumber and then sold it for huge profits. In New England, he found a market hungry for black walnut, and birch in particular, both of which were plentiful and being wasted back home.

Josiah reached Boston and reported his findings to some of the philanthropic men he'd met on previous preaching trips. A minister named Ephraim Peabody introduced him to Samuel Atkins Eliot, a prominent Boston politician, who was kind enough to hear Josiah's ideas and draw up a business plan for him. Josiah then presented this plan to Amos Adams Lawrence Jr., the son of the wealthy merchant-philanthropist Amos Lawrence Sr.

This Amos Junior was far kinder than the men named Amos that Josiah had known in Kentucky. A Unitarian from Boston, he was a well-known figure in the US abolitionist movement. Josiah's plan was presented to several men of similar means, all leading Bostonians, and they contributed about $1,400 to help Josiah with his new enterprise, around $500,000 by today's standards.

Josiah returned with the money to Canada and immediately started constructing a building for a sawmill in Dawn. The improvement to the community's morale was astonishing. Rather than selling ashes, they'd be selling hardwoods. More money would soon be on the way. People began to work with renewed vigor, and the clearing and cultivation of the land became a happy affair.

Unfortunately, Josiah's financial planning skills again fell far short. By the time he finished framing the mill, his funds were exhausted. The sawmill would sit idle for more than a year while he figured out how to raise the funds to complete it.

Despite the setbacks with the sawmill, the Boston philanthropists connected deeply with Josiah and supported his efforts, and they funded several of his other initiatives. Josiah, for example, realized the community needed a grist mill to grind corn. He wrote that a man had to walk three or four miles (likely to the gristmill at nearby Dawn Mills) "with two or three bushels on his shoulders, through paths in which the mud was knee-deep, leave his corn at the mill, and then go repeatedly after it in vain; he would be put off with a variety of excuses till he was quite discouraged, and would conclude that it was almost useless for him to raise any grain; and yet there was no other way for him to have a bit of bread or corn-cake."[32] Josiah decided he would personally build a grist mill in 1846. He returned to his Boston friends, raised $5,000, and oversaw construction of a steam-powered mill on the BAI lands. He was soon proud to report that "in a short time we ground the corn for the entire neighbourhood, and this venture was a decided success."[33]

⁓⁓

THINGS WERE NOT GOING SO WELL FOR HIRAM WILSON. HE BECAME seriously ill in early 1847, going so far as to write that he was "nigh unto death." Hiram went to England for the spring on a health respite. By the time he returned to Canada, his wife, Hannah, had died, leaving four motherless children behind.

It was a severe blow to the passionate missionary. The BAI's debts continued to spiral upward as more and more people in need arrived at Dawn. Josiah and others took on personal debt to help carry the institution, but by the summer of 1848, no one but Hiram had any credit left. There had never been enough money to adequately sustain the BAI, let alone bring it out of the red.

Hiram and Josiah's plan had been to create income sources from within the Dawn community, but they'd come to rely heavily on loans they simply couldn't repay. The idea of a manual labor school was sound, but neither of the founders had understood the importance of long-term financial planning. Perhaps if they had turned more people away, they could have remained solvent. But the pair seemed unable to grasp the school's finite financial capacity. Both men wanted to help all who were in immediate need, but their choices imperiled the long-term sustainability of the BAI.

Another death struck a blow to the institute. James Canning Fuller, Hiram and Josiah's silent partner in the founding of the BAI, passed away. The Quaker philanthropist had been a lifelong friend of Hiram's and a longtime trustee for the school.

Hiram decided to resign from the BAI, citing his extremely poor health, but he also complained to the board about his "lack of discretionary and controlling power." Like Newman before him, he claimed bad leadership and mismanagement as part of his reason for leaving, which was true, but he was unable to recognize that as one of the leaders, he had been a large part of the problem.*

---

* Hiram Wilson remarried and went on to establish another fugitive haven in St. Catharines, Ontario, in 1849. He opened an American Missionary Association school, housing approximately 125 refugees in his own home between 1850 and 1856. Though Hiram was described as "a distinguished, self-denying philanthropist," his career was always mired in problems. He continuously sought funds to support his ambitious plans, and continued his long-standing feuds with Newman and another Presbyterian minister, named Isaac J. Rice, not realizing it would ruin the reputations of all three men. Benjamin Drew, *A North-side View of Slavery: The Refugee; or, The Narratives of Fugitive Slaves in Canada, Related by Themselves, with an Account of the History and Condition of the Colored Population of Upper Canada* (Boston: John P. Jewett, 1856), 18.

The BAI's leadership now faced great challenges. Fuller and Hiram Wilson were gone. Money had stopped flowing in from England, in part because funds were being diverted to the Irish Potato Famine. Meanwhile, Americans and Canadians were reluctant to give to a settlement so obviously mired in conflict.

With no clear leader, something desperately needed to be done to save the institution. As Hiram Wilson wrote, "The Manuel [*sic*] Training Institute here ran well for a season, and accomplished much good; but since my resignation . . . it has run down, and can hardly be resuscitated again without a miracle."[34]

It was clear that William P. Newman wished to gain total control of the BAI on behalf of the American Baptists—likely for good reasons. He would also do whatever was necessary to accomplish his purpose, including ruining Josiah's reputation.

Josiah would have to find a miracle.

CLEARING LAND, CLEARING DEBT

The BAI's board of trustees convened again on July 10, 1848. The financial situation was so grave that the board of trustees, which usually left the operations to the executive committee, intervened. The institution carried huge amounts of debt, and two of the trustees gave public notice that they would not be held responsible. With all their strongest means of support dead or gone, the BAI's best hope was to find a new sponsor.

Deciding to take drastic action, the trustees decided to break the BAI into two separate entities. One of them would own the school, most of the buildings, and all the arable farmland. The other would own all of the BAI's debts, plus the sawmill and some forested land, to be used to pay off the institute's debts over a period of four years.

Despite the fact that Josiah did everything in his power to help carry the BAI's burdens on his own shoulders, he was not capable of running such a vast and growing enterprise, even with the executive committee's help. Splitting the institution into two was a drastic but necessary decision, if only to shield the school from the mill's debts.

It would be relatively easy to find someone to take over the school, but who would be willing to take over a debt-laden, nonoperating sawmill?

By early 1849, the BAI's lumber industry was estimated to be worth up to $11,000, but the overall institution owed somewhere between $4,000 and $7,500, and no one wanted to take it on as their personal responsibility. Amos Lawrence of Boston finally reached out to Josiah and offered to extend a loan to pay the debt. In a letter, he outlined his three conditions. First, Josiah needed to find forty people willing to commit $100 each to pay off the debt. Second, Josiah would have to agree to be in charge of the lumber mill to ensure steady cash flow for the BAI. Third, Josiah would have to travel to England to solicit funds to help keep the school afloat, since their American donations had dwindled significantly.

Josiah agreed to travel to England, but he wasn't able to find forty volunteers at Dawn willing to go in with him on the debt. In a last-ditch effort to secure Lawrence's loan to save the BAI, he agreed to personally carry the BAI's debt, in equal partnership with an original BAI trustee, Peter B. Smith, on the condition that Smith would oversee the mill's day-to-day operations while Josiah traveled overseas.

Josiah also needed funds to complete the sawmill itself. Though certainly discouraged, he returned to Boston to raise funds. Three men in particular—Amos Lawrence, H. Ingersoll Bowditch, and Samuel Atkins Eliot—again agreed to help with the sawmill. The Unitarian abolitionists encouraged Josiah in his business enterprise, and the approval of these eminent men was like a salve for his soul.

Josiah ended up borrowing $2,800 for which he was personally responsible. He returned to Dawn, where he and his sons completed the sawmill. They installed steam-powered machinery. Although Josiah personally carried the loan, the mill belonged to the BAI and was rented back to him for $500 per year.

Josiah decided to put his sons in charge of the mill's operation, while he turned his attention to how to discharge his towering debt, the equivalent of perhaps ten years of income.

Josiah chartered a boat, loaded it with 80,000 board feet of prime Dawn-milled black walnut from his own land, and hired a captain to deliver it to Oswego, New York, and then on to Boston. Josiah was able to sell the entire load to a man named Jonas Chickering for $3,600. He tried to pay off his loan to his Boston friends, but they encouraged him to reinvest it in the lumber business. Josiah returned to Dawn, and later that summer he brought a second large load of lumber by the same route. Sadly, the market had turned, and it appears he struggled to make a profit.

At some point during his trips to Boston in late 1849 and early 1850, Josiah was invited to become a Freemason. Upon his return to Canada, he joined the Mount Moriah Lodge No. 4—he would be listed as its secretary in 1866. The African Lodge had been founded by Prince Hall on July 3, 1776. Hall had previously met with General George Washington about the enlistment of 5,000 black soldiers, and he was one of the few black men who had fought at the Battle of Bunker Hill. Today, Prince Hall is considered the father of black Masonry.[35]

For men like Josiah, fraternal organizations such as the Masons would have been a safe place to share struggles, discuss ideas, and help each other. The principal tenets of Freemasonry—brotherly love, relief, and truth—were desperately needed in those dark times, and former slaves as well as Christian leaders flocked to the organization.

Take, for example, Richard Allen and Absalom Jones, the founders of the African Methodist Episcopal (AME) Church. By the end of the nineteenth century, most AME bishops and many ministers were Prince Hall Masons. One minister, Jordan W. Early, used his Freemason association as a means of escaping a branding. The pastor was riding his Shawneetown, Illinois, preaching circuit when he was cornered by well-armed white men. Early showed them the sign of Masonic fraternity and they let him go on with his work.[36]

Black church leaders obviously understood the need for racial equality, solidarity, and self-improvement, and they saw Freemasonry as a tool to bring these values into black society. Many of the internationally known abolitionists, such as Dr. Martin Delany, Rev. Thomas Stringer,

Abraham D. Shadd, Rev. Thomas Kinnard, and Rev. Benjamin Stewart, were Masons and assisted fugitives on their journey to freedom. Several lodges became Underground Railroad way stations, and Masons that were ministers, including "Father Henson," became heavily involved.

During one of his trips to Boston, Josiah became friends with Samuel Atkins Eliot. An abolitionist, Eliot had been the seventh mayor of Boston and had served in the Massachusetts House of Representatives and the Massachusetts Senate; he would later serve in the US House of Representatives.

Eliot, impressed with Josiah, had helped him pay for the sawmill, and now he offered to pen the story of Josiah's life. Josiah told his story to Eliot, who wrote it up and then read it back to him for his approval. Josiah's autobiography, entitled *The Life of Josiah Henson, Formerly a Slave, Now an Inhabitant of Canada, as Narrated by Himself*, was published in Boston in early 1849 by Arthur D. Phelps.

Henry Bibb and J. W. C. Pennington also penned slave narratives that year, but there were those in the abolitionist community who wished they hadn't. Frederick Douglass, for one, was critical of narratives that divulged too much information. After all, if free slaves openly shared their methods and escape routes, it could be a huge disservice to those who were attempting to follow a similar path. Josiah's memoir, to his credit, is light on specific details that could compromise others, including his own brother who remained in slavery in Maryland. Josiah tells the harrowing story of his time in slavery, but when it comes to his escape, speaks in general terms. He even left out the names of his former masters.

Josiah had no way of knowing then that his story would help spark the Civil War.

⁓⁂⁓

JOSIAH'S LITTLE BOOK GARNERED SOME ATTENTION AT THE ABOLItionist reading room in Boston as well as in abolitionist households throughout the north. One of those readers was likely a young woman who was about to begin researching and writing a book of her own. On one of his trips home from Boston, Josiah made a fourteen-mile detour to visit this woman who would shortly change the course of history. As a later edition of Josiah's memoir recalls:

> I was in the vicinity of Andover, Mass., in the year 1849, where Mrs. Harriet Beecher Stowe resided. She sent for me and my travelling companion, Mr. George Clark, a white gentleman, who had a fine voice for singing, and usually sang at my meetings to add to their interest. We went to Mrs. Stowe's house, and she was deeply interested in the story of my life and misfortunes, and had me narrate its details to her. She said she was glad it had been published, and hoped it would be of great service, and would open the eyes of the people to the enormity of the crime of holding men in bondage. She manifested so much interest in me, that I told her about the peculiarities of many slaveholders, and the slaves in the region where I had lived for forty-two years. My experiences had been more varied than those of the majority of slaves, for I was not only my master's overseer, but a market-man for twenty-five years.[37]

EVERY BLACK A FUGITIVE

By the time of the 1850 census, there were almost 23.2 million Americans, of which more than 3.2 million were enslaved. But how does one count a slave, exactly? Was a black slave equal to a white man? Certainly not in the eyes of the government. While many Americans believed that those of African descent were still human, the pervasive belief was that they were somehow lesser so. How much less? According to the law, 40 percent less.

In what was surely one of the most racist pieces of legislation in history, the Three-Fifths Compromise set into American law the principle that a person of color was only worth 60 percent of his white counterpart when being counted in the US census. The census helped determine each state's number of seats in the US House of Representatives and played a role in taxation. Enshrined in the US Constitution at the 1787 Constitutional Convention, the "compromise" allowed the Founding Fathers to satisfy the southerners, who wanted the extra representation in Congress, as well as the northerners, who didn't want southern states to have this advantage based solely on a large slave population. But the deal was anything but democratic—it still gave southerners more power in the legislature while reducing their overall tax burden compared to counting slaves as full people.[38] The outcome did not, of course, ingratiate the North to the cause of southern slaveholding.

Throughout the mid-1800s, slaves continued to pour north. Some made it to Canada, while others settled in the free northern states. The American South grew more and more agitated with each passing month, and soon the northern states were feeling pressure to stop helping escapees.

In June 1850, the *Ohio Statesman*'s editor considered using military force against the Underground Railroad. A large number of fugitives had crossed into the free state, and the newspaper speculated that a time might soon come when, "in order to preserve the peace of the State among them, it may be necessary to call on the light troops in the vicinity, and even upon the militia."[39]

On September 18, the US Congress passed the Compromise of 1850. Congress's goal was to preserve the unity of the American nation by addressing the concerns of both slave and free states, but historians disagree as to whether the agreement diffused any of that tension or further entrenched both sides. Regardless, the safety of all African American refugees was suddenly put at risk.

The new law included a ban on slave-trading—but not slavery—in the nation's capital. But it also amended the Fugitive Slave Act to allow anyone to declare ownership of an escaped slave by affidavit alone. No longer was proof or evidence needed, just a statement that the individual in question was an escapee. The act now emboldened kidnappers to chase free black people on behalf of supposedly aggrieved slaveholders, and some went so far as to attempt to kidnap at least two AME bishops.

Any black man, woman, or child could simply be grabbed from the street and hauled before a federally appointed commissioner. The already lax approach to due process was obliterated. Under the new law, new judges were paid five dollars for every person they released, and *ten* dollars for every person they sent south.

The act was incredibly invasive even toward white people. Aiding runaways had been illegal since 1793, but now everyone—law enforcement and ordinary citizen alike—was *required* to help catch fugitive slaves. It was illegal for any American to "withhold knowledge he might possess of any chance meeting with the fugitive." Not only could someone be arrested for helping a slave escape, but even those who refused to assist slave-catchers could spend six months in prison and be fined up to $1,000, the modern income equivalent of nearly $250,000—for an average laborer, an impossible figure to pay.[40]

For northerners in free states, the new law brought the issue far closer to home. No longer could they try to ignore southern slavery. The Fugitive Slave Act galvanized the antislavery movement. Antislavery groups and free black people rightly argued that the system openly bribed commissioners to send kidnapped people into slavery while forcing citizens to participate in the brutal system. Frederick Douglass averred that the Fugitive Slave Act created a crisis of faith as the country became "the enslaver's hunting ground." When the law passed, Rev. Daniel Payne, an AME bishop, visited Canada, and Father Henson himself gave him a tour of Dawn and the area to help him determine whether "Canada would be a safe asylum for our people."[41]

Harriet Beecher Stowe, the woman who had been so interested in hearing Josiah's story, was absolutely furious about the Compromise of 1850 and the Fugitive Slave Act. She believed her country was forcing its citizens to support an immoral and unjust system. She had come by her activism honestly: She had been raised in a Christian family that debated social justice issues every single night over supper. Her preacher father, Lyman Beecher, favored the "back to Africa" colonization movement and the creation of Liberia as a new nation for freed slaves.* Stowe's grandmother kept African American servants who had probably originally been slaves. Prior to the Compromise of 1850, as a young wife and mother, Stowe had met other formerly enslaved people while living in Cincinnati. Whenever she crossed the Ohio River to the slave state of Kentucky, she witnessed the cruelty firsthand. When she discovered that her recently hired servant was a runaway, she hid the woman until her husband and brother could help the woman escape to Canada.

In 1850, Stowe's husband, Calvin Ellis Stowe, accepted a position at Bowdoin College, and the family moved to a rented house in Brunswick, Maine. As before, Harriet Beecher Stowe continued to hide runaways. But now she was a criminal, and she railed about the injustice to her family.

Harriet's sister-in-law, Isabella Porter Beecher, wrote several letters in which she urged Stowe to write a piece on the evils of slavery, saying, "If I could use a pen as you can, Hatty, I would write something that would make this whole nation feel what an accursed thing slavery is."[42]

Stowe knew that slavery was a topic that could split communities in two. She saw what was happening to the nation. She understood the stark divide between the free state of Ohio and the slave state of Kentucky. Even her father's Christian college, Lane Seminary, had witnessed riots and rebellion over the contentious issue. But Stowe could stay silent no longer.

Her sister-in-law's encouragement won her over, and in December 1850 Stowe made her decision: "I shall write that thing if I live," she wrote in a letter to her husband.[43]

---

* Liberia was the brainchild of the American Colonization Society (ACS). Established by Robert Finley in 1816, the society supported the migration of free black people back to Africa, where ACS founded a colony on January 7, 1822. Though those favoring colonization were mainly Quakers and evangelicals, even some proslavery groups were in favor of "repatriation." Within forty-five years, the ACS had helped 13,000 Americans move back to Africa. At one point the colony was even called the *Republic of Maryland*. The settlement remained a colony of the ACS until it declared its independence in 1847; the United States recognized it as a sovereign nation fifteen years later, in 1862.

FLAUNTING FREEDOM

Josiah brought a third shipment of lumber to New England in the late autumn of 1850, but this time he wisely eliminated the costly middlemen. Despite the fact that the Fugitive Slave Law had just passed in Congress, and it was a serious offense to harbor or help fugitive slaves, he shipped his lumber directly to Boston via the Saint Lawrence River, where, without an agent or other third party, he paid his own border duties and got the lumber through the Custom House.

When the customs officer gave him the bill for the import duties on his lumber, Josiah remarked that the officer might find himself liable for having dealings with a fugitive slave. He joked that it might be better if the officer let him through without having to pay any tax.

"Are you a fugitive slave, sir?" the officer asked.[44]

"Yes, sir," Josiah replied. "And perhaps you had better not have any dealings with me!"

"I have nothing to do with that," the official said. "You have acted like a man, and I deal with you as a man." Josiah enjoyed making a scene, and the bystanders enjoyed it, too. If he felt any fear, he doesn't mention it in his memoirs. Josiah was always a very bold man, but perhaps he didn't fear the new law because if he had been arrested, his wealthy Boston friends would have seen to his immediate release. Josiah paid the officer and went on his way.

❧

DESPITE JOSIAH'S BEST EFFORTS, THE LUMBER INCOME SIMPLY WASN'T enough to cover both his own debt and the BAI's ongoing expenses. A new sponsor had to be brought in, and one was ready.

Pursuant to the trustees' decision of 1848 to split the BAI into two entities, the school was passed to the American Baptist Free Mission Society, which hired Rev. Samuel H. Davis, the black pastor of Detroit's Second Baptist Church, as headmaster. By June 4, 1851, there were about sixty scholars. By most accounts, Davis was a good man and a solid teacher, but he was never more than the nominal Baptist leader at Dawn, especially after William P. Newman decided to return to Canada. Passage of the amended Fugitive Slave Law had rattled the American preacher, and in 1850, he wrote an angry letter to Frederick Douglass's newspaper venting his frustrations with the federal government and the terrible decision Congress had made, asking, "Would not the Devil do well to *rent out hell* and move to the United States . . . ?"

Sadly, Newman also used his letter to Douglass's newspaper to officially abandon his belief in pacifism, stating, "I am frank to declare that it is my fixed and changeless purpose to kill any so-called man who attempts to enslave me or mine."[45]

Josiah's pacifism and Newman's militarism stood at odds, but somehow the men still managed to work together, albeit with great tension.

While Davis and Newman and the Baptists now ran the institute, Josiah, a Methodist, was still seen as Dawn's visionary leader and spokesperson. And true to his promise to Amos Lawrence, he began to prepare for his trip to England. Lawrence and his charitable Boston Unitarians would pay for the voyage. They hoped he'd bring in significant donations on behalf of the BAI.

In the following year the ABFMS would take over the farming tenancy of the BAI land. Despite all his other duties, William P. Newman assumed Josiah's lease and the operations of the sawmill. The BAI now seemed securely locked into the hands of the American Baptists.

Above: Isaac Riley's big house.

Below: Dr. McPherson's inventory, which includes Josiah, his mother, and brother. Celia, age 50, listed as infirm and worth $50. Josiah, listed as "Sye," age 9 and infirm, valued at $30. John, age 12, is likely Josiah's brother.

Bryce Litton. (Page 33.)

Depiction of Bryce Litton, who broke Josiah's arms. Drawn 1879.

At the request of Josiah Henson the above manumission was recorded the 9th day of March, 1829.

The Crystal Palace at The Great Exhibition of the Works of Industry of All Nations in London, 1851, which Josiah attended to exhibit his high quality lumber while fundraising for the work at Dawn.

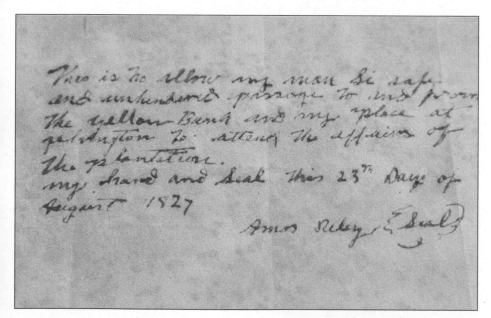

A travel pass from Amos Riley, allowing Josiah to travel to town and back to the farm, August 23, 1827. It reads: This is to allow my man Si safe and unhindered passage to and from the Yellow Bank and my place at Yelvington to attend to affairs of the plantation. My hand and seal this 23rd day of August 1827. Amos Riley.

Harriet Beecher Stowe, author of *Uncle Tom's Cabin*.

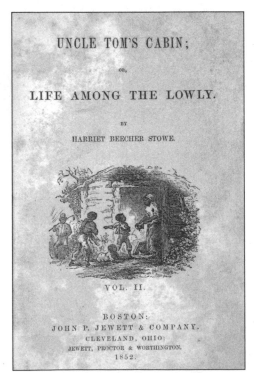

First edition of the *Uncle Tom's Cabin* novel, 1852.

Runaway slave ads from *The New Orleans Picayune*, March 20, 1852.

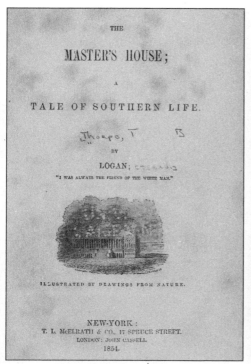

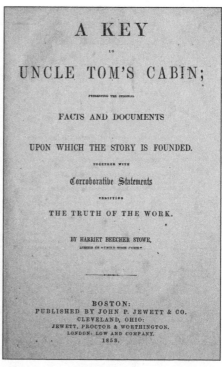

At left: One of the many anti-Tom novels of the era.

At right: *A Key to Uncle Tom's Cabin*, the book in which Stowe identifies Josiah as the Tom character, 1853.

British abolitionist John Scoble, the man who precipitated Dawn's ruin.

Josiah and his second wife, Nancy, whom he married sometime after the autumn of 1856.

Josiah and his editor, John Lobb, likely 1876.

At left: Josiah Henson with original signature, 1858. His actual birthdate is unknown, but it is thought he was around 69 years old here.

Above: Josiah as the first African-American on a Canadian stamp, 1983.

Josiah Henson, age 87, photographed in Boston on June 17, 1876.

Josiah's cabin at Dawn.

Josiah's gravestone in Dresden, Ontario.

EIGHT

THE GREAT EXHIBITION

I've heard "Uncle Tom's Cabin" read, and I tell
you Mrs. Stowe's pen hasn't begun to paint what
slavery is as I have seen it at the far South.

—HARRIET TUBMAN

ON JUNE 30, 1849, QUEEN VICTORIA'S HUSBAND, PRINCE ALBERT, who was president of the Royal Society of Arts, hosted a planning meeting at Buckingham Palace. There, he conceived of an international exhibition where nations from around the world would come together to display the technological inventions of the age. Though typically listed as the first World's Fair, it was not a new idea. There were at least twenty-two other major industrial exhibitions before 1851, dating at least as far back as Prague's 1791 celebration of Leopold II's coronation. Paris alone had hosted eleven previous expositions, and even the United Kingdom had held an exhibition just two years beforehand.

Regardless, the 1851 fair would be so grand it would set the standard for all similar events to follow. Prince Albert put his people on an unbelievably tight timeline to stage the event, which was titled the Great Exhibition of the Works of Industry of All Nations. In January 1850, a committee was formed to choose a building design. Within three weeks, 245 entries were received and rejected. The committee members made an ethically questionable attempt to cobble together many of the ideas from the submissions into their own master plan, which was ultimately overambitious. The design they came up with would have required the use of 15 million bricks, and it would be a challenge to get it built in time—their building plan was overcomplicated, and the fair was to begin in just fifteen months.

After learning of the 245 failed entries, a man named Sir Joseph Paxton took a walk through Hyde Park, made a quick sketch, and within two weeks submitted his detailed plans. With a price tag of only £150,000, the committee heartily approved.

Paxton was a magazine publisher, railway speculator, and member of Parliament with no formal engineering qualifications, but his many hobbies included architecture and gardening. He had already created the world's largest gravity-operated fountain and cultivated the Western world's most popular banana, the Cavendish.

Made from cast iron and glass, the exhibition pavilion was erected in less than nine months. It was officially called the Palace of Industry for All Nations, but the London writer Douglas Jerrold dubbed it the "Crystal Palace," a name that stuck. It was an architectural marvel and an engineering triumph well befitting the event. When it was finished, the building was about twice as large as St. Paul's Cathedral, and four times the square footage of St. Peter's Basilica in Rome. While it's typically said to have been 1,851 feet long—to represent the year of the event—the building came out closer to 1,848 feet in length. It boasted the first major installation of public toilets, cheerily called "Retiring Rooms."

The palace grounds were equally impressive, covering 26 acres of Hyde Park just south of the Serpentine River, with flowers, shrubbery, and fountains. The latter were especially impressive, with two massive water towers to propel the 250-foot twin jets.[1]

It was going to be a glorious six months.

A FUGITIVE ABROAD

Josiah was now sixty-one years old, with a floundering educational institute and a settlement of free black people looking to him for leadership and hope. But there was potential salvation in his trip to London. Amos Lawrence had seen the potential of the high-quality products made by his walnut lumber operation and sent Josiah to the Great Exhibition in London as a way of finding new customers and bringing in more revenue.

Josiah set out from Dawn in the late winter of 1850 accompanied by his son Josiah Jr., now a young man.[2] He was furnished with letters of introduction from nine of his North American friends to their British associates. These nine men included John Rolfe, a minister from Toronto; Sir Allan MacNab, the builder of Dundurn Castle in Hamilton, Ontario, and the last premier of Upper Canada before Confederation; and Detroit's Rev. Dr. George Duffield, a member of the Board of Regents of the University of Michigan. Thanks to their glowing letters, their British acquaintances warmly welcomed Josiah. They quickly introduced him to what he deemed to be "the very best society in the kingdom."[3]

On the Sundays leading up to the fair, Josiah preached from several notable pulpits, quickly becoming a well-known figure in London. He knew this opportunity would open doors to raise funds for Dawn and the BAI, so he asked his new friends to appoint a special committee of twelve men to carefully examine his enterprise. This committee comprised many of London's leading men, including Samuel Morley; George Hitchcock; George Sturge; Lord Ashley, Earl of Shaftesbury; and John Scoble, the secretary of the British and Foreign Anti-Slavery Society.

The committee appointed a subcommittee of three men and a treasurer to receive every farthing the public donated to Josiah. They would then appropriate the funds to the BAI as they saw fit. This arrangement was a wise and shrewd move on the part of Josiah and his domestic backers. Perhaps subconsciously, he had an aversion to both Americans and Baptists. America was the land that had enslaved him. Isaac Riley had been a Baptist. It was a Methodist minister who had helped him earn his freedom, and the British colony of Canada that had made it a reality. Many of his new supporters were wealthy British Methodists and Congregationalists. By aligning with them against William P. Newman's American Baptists, Josiah likely thought he would have the power to swing the BAI back to the national, denominational, and racial equality he so desired for the school. He was also stubborn and competitive.

The British leaders were very kind to Josiah and introduced him to many people of high rank within the empire. Banker-philanthropist Samuel Gurney even arranged for him to have a meeting with the archbishop of Canterbury, John Bird Sumner. Gurney told Josiah that the second-highest-ranking man in the empire might grant him fifteen minutes during their visit at Lambeth Palace, but when they met, the two men hit it off immediately. Half an hour into the conversation, after Josiah had described the struggles faced by black people in Canada and his plans for Dawn and the BAI, the archbishop asked him, "At what university, sir, did you graduate?"[4]

Josiah's answer was equal parts humorous and brilliant: "I graduated, your grace, at the university of adversity." Josiah told Sumner that he'd never gone to school and hadn't learned to read until adulthood. He also explained how he'd come to his faith through the baker's sermon and the prayers of his mother.

Sumner asked Josiah to repeat the baker's sermon text, which he'd learned by heart: "He, by the grace of God, tasted death for every man."

The archbishop didn't try to hide his tears. After an hour and a half of conversation, the archbishop walked Josiah to the door, shook his hand, and handed him five golden sovereigns, the modern equivalent of over $6,700. Josiah was off to a good start.

THE CANADIAN CAPTIVE

The Great Exhibition opened on May 1, 1851, with a private ceremony for the 25,000 season ticket holders. Prince Albert gave a speech. The archbishop of Canterbury said a prayer. Choirs performed Handel's "Hallelujah Chorus," accompanied by two organs. Queen Victoria wrote in her journal that evening: "This day is one of the greatest and most glorious of our lives. . . . It is a day which makes my heart swell with thankfulness. . . . The Park presented a wonderful spectacle, crowds streaming through it,—carriages and troops passing. . . . The Green Park and Hyde Park were one mass of densely crowded human beings, in the highest good humour."[5]

There were 14,387 exhibitors displaying over 100,000 objects atop more than 8 miles of display tables. Charles Goodyear's "India-rubber" goods made their debut, along with what was likely the world's first voting machine. There was a steam hammer that could both forge steamship bearings and gently crack eggs. There was a "stiletto umbrella" for self-defense. The French sent porcelain, the Russians sent furs, and Chile sent a 110-pound lump of gold. The American exhibits included chewing tobacco, false teeth, and Colt's repeating pistols.

Although the exhibition most certainly did not represent "all nations," nearly half the exhibitors were non-British, with exhibitors from twenty-eight countries in attendance, including the United States. And therein lay an amusing problem.

Josiah had selected four of his best walnut boards from the cargo he had shipped to Boston. His friend Jonas Chickering had then carefully packed them into boxes and shipped them to England on an American vessel full of American products for exhibition. Each board measured seven feet long and four feet wide. Josiah had had them planed and French-polished by none other than William P. Newman, who had taken over the Dawn sawmill. Newman was apparently quite good at his job, because Josiah noted that they reflected light like a mirror.

The commissioner for the American Department of the exhibition was Edward Riddle, a carriage maker and auctioneer who held a weekly auction every Saturday at 11:00 a.m. at 65-73 Union Street in Boston, beside America's oldest tavern, the Bell in Hand. Riddle insisted that Josiah's lumber be exhibited in the American section of the exhibition because it had been carried over in an American ship.[6]

Josiah objected. He lived in Canada, his boards were from Canada, and there was a section of the palace specifically set aside for Canadian products. He requested his boards be relocated. Superintendent Riddle refused. "You cannot do it," he said. "These things are under my control. You can exhibit what belongs to you if you please, but not a single thing here must be moved an inch without my consent."[7]

Josiah couldn't understand why they wouldn't just make the change. What he didn't know was that the Americans had insisted on a vast amount of exhibition floor space—40,000 square feet, more than any other nation except France and Britain itself—despite having far fewer goods to display. The young nation wanted a global stage from which to prove its superiority over the Old World, but it had overreached. Though it contained some of the most practical pieces in the entire building, the American exhibit was embarrassingly sparse. London's satirical magazine *Punch* was brutal in its assessment: "By packing up the American articles a little closer, by displaying COLT'S revolvers over the soap, and piling up the Cincinnati pickles on top of the Virginia honey, we shall concentrate all the treasures of American art and manufacture into a few square feet, and beds may be made to accommodate several hundred."[8]

The magazine also directed its witty wrath at American artist Hiram Powers's *Greek Slave*, a scandalous nude in marble that was to become one of the most famous sculptures of the nineteenth century: "Why not have sent us some choice specimens of slaves? We have the Greek captive in dead stone—why not the Virginia slave in living ebony?"

Such writing was indicative of the growing separation between American and British values. America was still highly entrenched in slavery, which had been illegal in Great Britain since 1833.

Edward Riddle's edict threatened to put a damper on Josiah's mood, but his wit won out. If the Americans insisted on holding his goods hostage, at least he could tell the world who owned them. Early one morning, Josiah hired a painter to write in large white letters across the tops of the boards:

THIS IS THE PRODUCE OF THE INDUSTRY OF
A FUGITIVE SLAVE FROM THE UNITED STATES,
WHOSE RESIDENCE IS DAWN, CANADA.

The American superintendent made his rounds later in the day and found Josiah at his post. Riddle read the inscription with dazed astonishment. Josiah resisted the urge to laugh.

The man was furious. "What, under heaven, have you got up there?"[9]

Josiah shrugged innocently. "Oh, that is only a little information to let the people know who I am."

"But don't you know better than that? Do you suppose I am going to have that insult up there?"

English folk began to gather around the dueling pair, chuckling with semi-suppressed delight at the American's wrath.

"Well, sir," Riddle said, "do you suppose I brought that stuff across the Atlantic for nothing?"

"I never asked you to bring it for nothing," Josiah replied. "I am ready to pay you, and have been from the beginning."

"Well, sir, you may take it away, and carry it where you please."

The crowd continued to grow.

Josiah said, "I think, as you wanted it much, I will not disturb it. You can have it now."

"No, sir; take it away!"

"I beg your pardon, sir, when I wanted to remove it, you would not allow it, and now, for all me, it shall remain."

The next day, the boards were moved to the Canadian part of the exhibition at no expense to Josiah. The Canadian commissioner, Henry Houghton, was happy to install Josiah in his rightful place. In the Official Catalogue of the Great Exhibit, Josiah's entry appeared as follows: *Henson, J. Dawn.—Black walnut plank. Indian corn in the ear.*

Of all the wood products on display, Josiah's received the most attention. When Queen Victoria and her entourage stopped in front of his display, Josiah removed his hat and saluted her respectfully, and she nodded in return. As she continued on, Josiah overheard her ask a member of her retinue, "Is he indeed a fugitive slave?"

"He is indeed . . ." came the reply.[10]

A WARM RECEPTION

In the evenings, Josiah continued to mix and mingle among London's leading abolitionists. A soiree was held at the Freemasons' Hall, on Lincoln's Inn Fields, at 6:00 p.m. on May 19, with Josiah speaking on slavery.[11]

In late May he attended a Ragged School meeting chaired by Lord Anthony Ashley Cooper, the Earl of Shaftesbury.* A few days later, on June 2, he attended a Sunday school meeting at Exeter Hall. *The Anti-Slavery Reporter* wrote that Josiah was "received by the audience with tumultuous greetings." He told his story and spoke at length on the importance of education for children, something he had not received. He thanked his new friends for their kindness and ended with an invocation of sorts:

> *Honor to the brave,*
> *Freedom to the slave,*
> *Success to British liberty,*
> *And God bless Queen Victoria.*

The paper reported that "Mr. Henson then resumed his seat amid the applause of the assembly."[12]

A SEED IS PLANTED

On the other side of the Atlantic, true to her word and despite the constant distractions and duties of motherhood, Harriet Beecher Stowe had started writing furiously. In March 1851, she wrote to Gamaliel Bailey, editor and publisher of a Washington antislavery paper called *The Na-*

---

* Ragged Schools provided education and other services for poor children.

tional Era, and offered him the story she had been working on, which she thought would run for three or four installments.

The plot is familiar. A Kentucky farmer runs up large debts and is forced to sell two of his slaves. But the master's conversation is overheard. One of the slaves attempts to flee north, while the other, Uncle Tom, is transported down the Mississippi River, where he is eventually sold to a vicious Louisiana plantation owner. Tom's faith nearly falters, but a pair of visions places him back on firm ground. His original master's son heads south to buy Tom's freedom, but he is too late: after encouraging two women to escape north, Tom is beaten to death when he refuses to reveal where they've gone. The owner's son returns to Kentucky, and when his father dies, he sets them all free, encouraging them to remember Tom's sacrifice whenever they see his cabin.

Uncle Tom's Cabin debuted on June 5, 1851, and it ran for forty-one weekly installments over the next ten months. *The National Era*'s subscriber base grew by 26 percent, and at least 50,000 people read Stowe's story in serial form. Even if the story had never been printed as a book, it was already one of the most widely read novels of the nineteenth century.

WILD ACCUSATIONS

Back at the London exhibition, the summer crowds were massive, but in true British form they kept in perfectly ordered queues. Josiah discussed his walnut boards over and over again, and he was probably on his feet for twelve or more hours each day. The event was to last a full six months, so Josiah settled into the task at hand—until one afternoon he discovered a pamphlet that was being circulated around the city. It claimed that "one styling himself Rev. Josiah Henson was an impostor, obtaining money under false pretences; that he could exhibit no good credentials; that whatever money he might obtain would not be appropriated according to the wish of the donors, and that the said Josiah Henson was an artful, skilful, and eloquent man, and would probably deceive the public."[13] The notice went on to list a handful of resolutions, supposedly from the black community at Dawn, denouncing their leader and his actions.

Josiah was shocked. Who would say such a thing?

He believed that the BAI should remain completely free from sectarianism, whether by skin color or religious denomination, and this had earned him the wrath of some of the American Baptists. Josiah suspected that the pamphlet was the work of people who wanted to take over the BAI for political reasons, or at least wreck his influence and connection with it.

As it turned out, William P. Newman had taken advantage of Josiah's absence in Canada to call a meeting in Chatham, where those assembled had passed a number of resolutions against Josiah's fundraising mission. The notes from the meeting had been published in *The Liberator*, the newspaper founded by abolitionist William Lloyd Garrison, who had some followers among the Baptists.

Newman, along with a Baptist minister named Edward Mathews, had charged that Josiah did not speak for the BAI trustees and that his financial management skills were faulty. Mathews then went to London and called a meeting of the special committee that had been formed to work with Josiah. In that meeting, Mathews claimed that Josiah was essentially a thief and a crook, that he didn't represent the BAI or Dawn, and that a convention back in Canada—in reality the Chatham meeting—agreed. Josiah, he said, was not their agent and had no authority to raise funds for black Canadians. Mathews went so far as to claim that Josiah hadn't even built a black settlement in Canada.

Josiah stood up and restated the facts of the previous investigations. He reminded the committee members that any man who devotes himself to doing good will be misunderstood by his enemies. Finally, he explained the true motives of Mathews, Newman, and the American Baptists as he understood them—they wished to control the British American Institute.

Mathews's story quickly fell apart. He was forced to admit that residents of Dawn hadn't even attended the Chatham meeting. Worse still, he admitted that he had forged the most damning resolution and inserted it into the damning pamphlet himself.

The London committee rejected the Chatham allegations that Josiah was an imposter. The members assured Josiah of their complete confidence. But they had needed to clear up these aspersions on his character, especially since the allegations had been so public. They proposed that John Scoble, the secretary of the British and Foreign Anti-Slavery Society (BFASS), visit Canada and determine the facts about Josiah's personal character, and that Josiah go with him to answer any questions that might arise.

John Scoble was a legendary abolitionist who had been a forceful Congregational minister before being appointed as a full-time lecturer for the Agency Committee of the Anti-Slavery Society in 1831, and later as secretary of the more radical Society for the Universal Abolition of Slavery and the Slave Trade.[14]

As a skilled researcher and orator, he was the right man to determine if Josiah was innocent or guilty of all the breaches of trust the American Baptists claimed. The two men left for Canada immediately. Josiah later wrote that he didn't mind having to leave his boards on exhibition and return home for a while. He had already raised close to $1,700, which remained in the hands of the British committee's treasurer. Josiah's son, Josiah Jr., remained in England, presumably to man his father's booth in his absence.

Proven Innocent

Back at Dawn, a public meeting was called at the BAI premises in the autumn of 1851. One of the BAI's founding trustees, Toronto Congregationalist minister John Roaf, presided over the assembly. The London committee had sent Scoble to investigate the conniving ways of Newman and Mathews before making any decisions about how the British could best help the Dawn community, and it turned out to be a battle of nation versus colony.

Mathews, who had rushed back to Dawn after his disastrous meeting with the British and Foreign Anti-Slavery Society, accused Scoble of trying to take the BAI away from the American Baptists in order to serve the British society's interests. A colleague of Garrison's, Samuel J. May Jr., wrote to the editor of the *National Anti-Slavery Standard* saying that Scoble was "a crafty villain who would not be worth 120 pounds on a Richmond auction block." He promised to supply documents to support Mathews's accusations. (Later, he would say that Garrison had lost them.) Others at the meeting also claimed that Josiah and the anti-Garrisonian Lewis Tappan were trying to put the British back in charge.

The convention made a thorough examination of the institute's records and could find no fault with Josiah's mission of raising more funds to help it. As Josiah matter-of-factly reported in his memoir, "The originator of the slander against me, denied having made it; it was proved upon him, and the whole convention unanimously repudiated the false charges."[15]

Hiram Wilson later supported Josiah in a letter to a friend. He wrote: "That money was spent there unwisely and not with good economy there is no doubt. [But] [t]hat funds have been perverted or dishonestly applied has never yet been proved, and I believe never can be."

John Scoble told Josiah that a bank draft was waiting in the hands of Amos Lawrence, and whenever Josiah wished to return to England, the cost of his journey would be completely covered.

A CHANGE OF DIRECTION

John Scoble was a forceful and self-assured man. He liked being in charge and was well-acquainted with success. The school was doing better under William P. Newman and the American Baptist Free Mission Society, but it was still debt-ridden, and it had a backwoods feel to it.* The great abolitionist saw an opportunity to build an entirely new school.

On September 12, 1851, Scoble invited Josiah to join him in Toronto, where he gathered the six BAI trustees for a meeting to discuss the

---

* Frederick Douglass said that the track into Dresden was "no velvet road," and newcomer Parker Smith remarked that his neighbors used dried peas as a substitute for coffee.

institute's future. The meeting was held in the basement of a church run by Rev. John Roaf, the chairman of the board of trustees.

According to Josiah, Scoble envisioned Dawn as "a glorious moral lighthouse, a beacon whose illumination should be perpetual." Scoble told the trustees that the BAI "could be made the brightest spot in the garden of the Lord, if there were only an efficient manager at its head to control it."[16] Scoble suggested that he was the man for the job.

Josiah liked Scoble; in fact, he was in awe of him. Not only had Scoble cleared Josiah's name, but he was a strong defender of the emancipation cause. Scoble painted a promising picture, and Josiah was dazzled.

Scoble promised the trustees that he'd clear Dawn's debts and insinuated that the British and Foreign Anti-Slavery Society would be the official backer in helping him to place the school on a permanent foundation. One of the BAI's trustees, James C. Brown, later recalled that Scoble told them he would make the BAI a "blessing to the fugitives"—*if* the trustees signed over the institution to his care.

Josiah evidently thought it was a great idea, and used his considerable powers of persuasion to convince the trustees that it was a good move. John Scoble had proven himself a winner, in many countries and many contexts, and Josiah felt he could do incredible things with their struggling settlement.

James C. Brown was completely opposed to the idea of the British Congregationalists taking control, as he was firmly in Newman's American Baptist camp.* Another board member, George Johnson, was also leaning toward keeping the current arrangement. Roaf, the BAI chairman, had previously acknowledged the Baptists had done their duty to the students, teachers, and ministers, but he was converted to Scoble's

---

* Brown was the president of the Cincinnati Colonization Society and had been one of the first settlers at the Wilberforce Colony, a black settlement established in 1829 just north of London, Ontario, after the 1829 race riots in Cincinnati. According to his report in Benjamin Drew's *North-Side View of Slavery*, published in 1856, he had stayed only briefly at the colony before moving to Toronto; then he had returned to Cincinnati for a little over a year. After Cincinnati, he returned again to Toronto, where he claimed to be a gunner during the 1837–1838 troubles. He moved to Dawn to help start the work, then moved to Chatham in 1849, where he remained for the rest of his life.

camp in that basement meeting. Roaf promised Brown and Johnson that all the Baptists' expenses for running the BAI would be covered if they moved on.

That evening, with Josiah's help, Scoble won the support of five of the BAI's six trustees—including the chairman—on the condition that the British and Foreign Anti-Slavery Society take on the BAI's debts and carry out the original educational purposes outlined in the BAI's declaration of trust. At that time the debt amounted to $7,000. Scoble agreed, and the five trustees signed over their voting rights to the famed Englishman. Only James C. Brown refused to budge. Josiah was delighted with the outcome. Hope had returned to Dawn.

On October 1, as John Scoble prepared to return to England, a large reception of refugee slaves and their friends gathered to congratulate him on his visit and wish him a speedy return. In his speech, he encouraged them to grow in self-respect and to get educated, emphasizing the importance of education in breaking down prejudice and gaining the respect of others. He talked briefly about the abolition of slavery in the West Indies. One attendee said he was "highly instructive and truly eloquent. It was received with showers of applause by the entire audience, and will make a good and lasting impression on the minds of our people."[17]

William P. Newman immediately began to plot his revenge.

A MEDAL FOR THE MAN

Josiah returned to England as quickly as possible. The exhibition was still in progress, with the crowds as big as ever.

Despite the constant flow of people, the mass of humanity was almost exclusively white. Although there were exhibitors from all over Europe, Asia, and the Americas, according to a *London Times* column, among the crowd there "was a single negro exhibitor. All he had to display were four black walnut boards, but they were of the finest grain and texture."[18] With the exception of a few men who were actually *in* an African exhibit, Josiah was the only black man presenting at the World's Fair.

By the end of the exhibition, on October 11, 1851, Josiah considered his mission a success. He had managed to raise £1,000 for the BAI school, which he gave to the London committee's treasurer. It was enough to cover a good portion of the school's debts.

The Great Exhibition had admitted a total of 6,039,722 guests, at a time when Britain had little more than 15 million citizens. Season ticket holders visited an average of thirty times each. Many luminaries attended, including Charles Dickens, Charlotte Brontë, Charles Darwin, Lewis Carroll, and George Eliot.

Much later, after his return to Canada, Josiah received a large book containing a full description of all the objects presented at the exhibition. In it he found his own name, along with a bronze medal for his lumber and a portrait of Queen Victoria and the royal family. It became one of his most prized possessions.

EARTHQUAKE

Harriet Beecher Stowe's slavery story had been well-received as a serial publication, so John P. Jewett and Company decided to publish it as a novel in two volumes of 312 pages each.

Uncle Tom's Cabin; or, Life Among the Lowly was published on March 20, 1852, and it sold 3,000 copies on its first day in print. Frederick Douglass reported that 5,000 copies—the entire first print run—were purchased within four days. The book was a runaway bestseller. By the end of the week it had topped 10,000 copies sold. Within two months it had sold 50,000 copies. By May 3, the *Boston Morning Post* declared that "everybody has read it, is reading, or is about to read it."[19] By week eleven, 80,000 copies had flown off the shelves, and *The Liberator* pontificated to its readers, "Its gifted author was moved to take up the subject of slavery . . . by the passage of the Fugitive Slave Law. So does a just God overrule evil for good."[20]

Stowe's book was so successful that it took seventeen printing presses running continually to keep up with demand. By the end of its first year in print, the book had sold over 300,000 copies in America alone. The sales figures were particularly astonishing when you consider that the entire US population was just 24 million at the time, and much of it was illiterate. Additionally, most of the South couldn't be counted as purchasers—both because of the huge population of illiterate slaves, and the fact that many southern communities simply banned the book outright.

The first British edition was printed by Samuel Orchart Beeton in April 1852; the American and British editions combined sold more than 1 million copies in the book's first year in print. *Uncle Tom's Cabin* would go on to become the best-selling novel of the nineteenth century.

The book generated an astounding amount of press. On May 13, the *New York Independent* reported that "the demand continues without abatement. . . . [I]t has taken 3000 reams of medium paper, weighing 30 lbs. to the ream—90,000 lbs. of paper; and . . . three or four of Adams's power presses have been kept running at the most rapid rate, day and night, stopping only on the Sabbath; and . . . from 125 to 200 bookbinders have been constantly at work in binding."[21]

The following day, the *New York Times* reported that Stowe had "received $4,000, as her share of the sales already made of that work. She receives 10 cents on each copy sold, and a Bangor paper says she has been offered $10,000 for the copyright of the book."[22]

It was wise of Stowe to decline the offer, because on July 15 the *National Anti-Slavery Standard* informed its readers that "Mrs. Stowe received from her publishers . . . the sum of Ten Thousand Three Hundred Dollars . . . the largest sum ever received by any author."[23] By declining the buyout offer, Stowe earned the modern equivalent of many extra millions.

Many years later, the *Washington Post* reflected on Stowe's meteoric rise in unsurprisingly chauvinistic terms: "When Mrs. Harriet Beecher Stowe was given a royalty check for $10,000 by Mr. Jewett, three months after 'Uncle Tom's Cabin' was issued, she didn't know what to do with it, and the publisher was obliged to go with her to a bank, into the mysteries of which she was initiated."[24] Although accurate royalties may never be known, the *New York Times* speculated that Stowe earned somewhere between $25,000 and $30,000 from the sale of her book, the equivalent of upwards of $9 million today.

Others made even more money off of Stowe's main character. Minstrel shows, called "Tom shows," were racially driven plays or musicals based on an inverted version of the novel's plot. Tom was played by white men in blackface, who exaggerated and stereotyped black people to the point of buffoonery and caricature. They made him appear as an old hunchback with poor English who would happily sell out his own race to curry favor with his master. Even though the novel was the best-selling book of the century, considerably more people saw one of these racist reenactments than read the book. There were thousands of performances.

Having grown up in a religious home, Stowe's family believed that stage plays were immoral. She refused requests to authorize a dramatization of her book. However, after so many unauthorized stage versions became so wildly popular, she relented and wrote a script for "dramatic readings." These were performed by Mrs. Mary E. Webb, a free woman of mixed origin. The play, entitled *The Christian Slave*, was not a huge success.

The unauthorized plays could have been another source of income for the abolitionist author if today's copyright laws had existed. So many of them were put on that she could have earned $30,000 (at least $9 million in today's currency) from charging royalties.

People profited from Stowe's work in other ways, too. The *New York Times* reported that a certain Rev. Alfred Thomas Wood was arrested for obtaining money by false pretenses. He apparently told people that George and Eliza Harris, two characters in *Uncle Tom's Cabin*, were members of his church in Liberia, and had taken up an offering to support the ministry.

The book may not have been considered a literary masterpiece, but its contents were explosive. Its characters fully represented the range of people living in the South, and the North was riveted by it.

The early reviews in abolitionist or abolitionist-supporting publications were glowing:

"THE STORY OF THE AGE!" —*The National Era*

"Spread it around the world!" —*The Independent*

" . . . a deep and thrilling interest, increasing in intensity
to the finishing stroke."—*The Liberator*

"The deepest spirit of piety, and the largest spirit of humanity
prevail on every page . . ." —*The Christian Inquirer*

"ILIUM FUIT—the deed is done, and the South done for."
—*The Literary World*

The British reviews, too, were unapologetically positive. The *New York Independent* declared that "the English press is literally alive with enthusiastic encomiums of this celebrated book."

The *Davenport Independent* summed up the general British abolitionist feeling: "It is a truly wonderful production, and will, we believe, do more towards ridding America of the foul stain of slavery, than has yet been done by any other effort."[25]

And that, of course, was the entire reason Harriet Beecher Stowe had written *Uncle Tom's Cabin* in the first place. The political impact of her book was both immediate and massive. Simply put, Stowe's novel became the epicenter of an enormous cultural shockwave that rattled the relationship between black and white people in America.[*]

Despite its many challenges, 1852 was a year of great steps forward in the racial equality cause. On Thursday, April 29, a Canadian named Robert Sutherland, who had been born in Jamaica around 1830, became the first known person of African descent to graduate from a Canadian university. Sutherland won fourteen academic prizes and went on to become British North America's first known black lawyer. He'd often said that at Queen's University he felt he had always been treated like a gentleman. Twenty-six years later, in 1878, Sutherland would save his

---

[*] It was also the first time that a slave had been so "sympathetically" described in literary fiction. Unknowingly, Stowe had created a new archetype that, despite its flaws, set the standard for many African American characters to follow.

beloved Queen's from bankruptcy with a $12,000 bequest, an amount that would be equivalent to at least $2 million today.[26]

An Enticing Offer

Josiah stayed in England all winter and spring, and while there, he took an interest in the Ragged School movement. As in Dawn, Christians in England provided free education to destitute children, and Josiah was invited to attend many of their events.

Josiah spoke frequently at schools and churches about the conditions of slavery. At the anniversary of one Sunday School union, he heard an eminent Pennsylvania preacher boast that there was no racial discrimination in American Sunday schools. Josiah felt compelled to contradict him, and publicly hammered the man with questions in front of a packed audience. When the preacher faltered, Josiah informed the crowd that "the great body of the coloured people were almost entirely neglected, and in many places they were excluded altogether" in the southern states.[27] Josiah's words brought great attention to his work at Dawn, and the name "Josiah Henson" became well-known around London.

In May 1852, Josiah fell in with Lord Henry Grey, son of the former prime minister Charles Grey.* Like his father before him, Henry Grey was opposed to slavery; he even resigned a junior ministerial post in 1834 when he learned that the government planned to emancipate slaves gradually instead of immediately. As current secretary of state for war and the colonies, the statesman hoped to move the United Kingdom away from consuming American slave cotton, although his motives were not entirely altruistic. He offered Josiah a well-paid position as superintendent in his efforts to introduce an American-style cotton culture to India. He was trying to do the same thing in Egypt as well. Effectively, Grey wanted to shift the British Empire from slave cotton to colony cotton—which perhaps produced cotton with slightly less injustice, but

---

* Famous for introducing the world to Earl Grey tea.

certainly in a way that was more profitable for the motherland. One can only imagine how tempting the offer would have sounded, especially after the public hammering that Josiah's reputation had received. A prominent, well-paid, overseas job was alluring. But Josiah was committed to ensuring the BAI's success, and he declined Grey's offer. He had too much to do at Dawn.

A SUNDAY SCHOOL SURPRISE

In June 1852, Josiah was invited to join a large company of Sunday school teachers for a day at Lord John Russell's property in Richmond Park. Russell, the prime minister, was the wealthy scion of a powerful family, and his park was stocked with deer and hare, along with colorful birds and fish.

Pembroke Lodge, a Georgian mansion on the property, began as a one-room mole catcher's cottage in 1754. It had undergone upgrades over the years. Queen Victoria granted the property to Russell shortly after the start of his second term in 1847. The prime minister used the grounds for government business, but he also entertained visiting royalty there, as well as writers such as Dickens and Tennyson, and, on that sunny afternoon, Josiah Henson and his happy band of Christian brothers. It was an afternoon picnic of sorts, but instead of each person bringing his or her own food, locals were allowed on the property to sell cakes, pies, and fruit to the three hundred Sunday school teachers and others in attendance. Josiah spent the afternoon strolling the grounds, enjoying the wildlife and panoramic views across the Thames Valley, and chatting with his fellow guests. It's likely that he visited the highest point in the park, King Henry's Mount, with its legally protected view of St. Paul's Cathedral.

At five o'clock the group was unexpectedly invited to come inside the mansion, and the guests filed into the massive dining hall for a surprise party. The tables were laden with every delicacy in the land. Josiah was invited to take the head of the table, and the group opened supper with a song:

Be present at our table, Lord,
Be here and everywhere adored:
These creatures bless,
And grant that we may feast
In Paradise with Thee![28]

Josiah rose and gave an impromptu toast.

"First to England. Honour to the brave, freedom to the slave, success to British emancipation. God bless the Queen!"

Cheers and laughter were followed by the customary English exclamations, *"Up, up, up again!"*

Always the showman, Josiah rose a second time and toasted the Queen.

"May she have a long life, and a happy death. May she reign in righteousness, and rule in love!"

More cheers, assuredly.

And then, to her illustrious consort, Prince Albert: "May he have peace at home, pleasure abroad, love his Queen, and serve the Lord!"

Josiah considered it one of the best days of his life.

CLEARED

On July 12, 1852, the London committee that had been looking into the allegations about Josiah ruled that Edward Mathews's claims were nothing but "an attempt to ruin the character of Mr. Henson."

John Scoble then revealed his plans to return to Dawn as an agent of the British and Foreign Anti-Slavery Society and take over the British American Institute and its debt. It was a risky proposition, but it's likely that Scoble believed he could quickly turn the school around and make it profitable both for himself and for the community. He told the committee members that he had assumed they would endorse his work, but one shrewd businessman, Samuel Morley, shook his head, saying, "We did not authorize you to represent that we would shoulder the responsibility of the school, and we cannot do it."[29]

This was a shock to Scoble, no doubt, but after some negotiation, the men decided they would be supportive of the BAI, though they would not carry any financial responsibility for it. With great expectation on Josiah's part, John Scoble set off to revitalize the BAI.

It would be a short honeymoon.

A STORY RETOLD

Josiah's time in England had been a great success, and the future looked bright. Many of the English philanthropists he had met over the past year had encouraged him to rerelease his memoir, with none showing greater enthusiasm than Samuel Morley and George Hitchcock.

Samuel Morley was nicknamed "the Philanthropic Merchant." He was the world's largest woolens manufacturer, but he was also a radical dissenter and abolitionist. His strong-jawed caricature was published in *Vanity Fair* in 1872, one of many caricatures of famous people published by the British magazine during the era. Morley chaired the inauguration of Homerton College, endowed Morley College, published London's *Daily News*, and served as a Liberal member of Parliament for Nottingham for eighteen years.[30]

George Hitchcock had revitalized an old firm of drapers in St. Paul's Churchyard in what was then the Cheapside shopping district. A young man named George Williams joined Hitchcock in 1841, soon after they'd both converted to nonconformist Christianity. Together they grew the business into a successful operation that treated workers well—a rarity in London at the time. Hitchcock became involved in the Ragged School movement for poor children. He was strongly antislavery. Along with folks such as Sir Arthur Conan Doyle, the author of the Sherlock Holmes stories, he lobbied for shorter work hours for retail workers. Williams married Hitchcock's daughter, became a partner in the firm, and convened the first meeting of the YMCA in their offices near Temple Bar in 1844.* Josiah had lunch with one of the two men every day at 1:30

---

* By the time Williams died, he was the president of thirty-nine charitable societies.

p.m., alternating back and forth between them all summer. His friends published a new, British edition of his slave narrative in London and Edinburgh under the title *The Life of Josiah Henson, Formerly a Slave: As Narrated by Himself*. It was a slightly altered version of the original edition, with a new preface by Thomas Binney, the minister of the King's Weigh House Congregational Chapel on Fish Street Hill in London; Binney was known as the "Archbishop of Nonconformity" for his opposition to the traditional Anglican Church. Binney's dissident congregants had taken a particularly strong interest in Josiah's cause and had given generously. The British edition came with an appendix on fugitives in Canada and an appeal for £2,000, following a style common to abolitionist works.[31]

Josiah finished editing and updating his memoir in early September, and two thousand copies were printed. At four o'clock on the afternoon of September 3, 1852, he received a letter from his family in Canada. Charlotte, his wife of forty years, was on her deathbed. Her life had been strenuous, and the journey to freedom had been a difficult one for her.

Josiah's heart flooded with emotion. She was his life companion, the woman with whom he had shared his joys and his sorrows. In the letter, she begged him to return immediately. Josiah was panicked. He was four thousand miles from home. What if he didn't make it back before she passed away? He left London for Liverpool the next morning and the following day caught a steamer bound for Boston.

⁘

JOSIAH ARRIVED IN CANADA TWO WEEKS AFTER HIS DEPARTURE FROM London, on September 20, 1852. He rushed to Dawn, but approached his home fearfully. He had heard nothing since the letter and didn't know if Charlotte was still alive.

As he walked toward home, he thought about their journey from slavery to freedom, how sad and lonely and sore she'd been. Charlotte had been a kind, affectionate, and supportive wife for four decades, and she had tirelessly and lovingly raised their eight children.

Josiah reached the yard of his house. His four daughters rushed into his arms, absolutely delighted by his unexpected return. Charlotte was still alive.

He rushed to her bedside. Charlotte embraced her husband with calmness and strength, and he found it impossible not to break down and cry. Despite her weakness, she teased him for his display of tears.

Josiah was profoundly thankful to have made it home while Charlotte was still alive. Charlotte was perfectly calm, and had surrendered herself to the will of God. As Josiah later wrote, she waited "with Christian firmness for the hour for her summons."[32]

The loving couple reminisced about their life together, recalling the moments of sorrow and trouble, as well as the many bright and happy days they had shared. They talked until Charlotte was exhausted, and she sank into a quiet sleep.

Josiah's return seemed to lift Charlotte's spirits, and he hoped that she would soon be restored to health. But it was not to be. Josiah wrote that "God in His mercy granted her a reprieve, and her life was prolonged a few weeks. I thus had the melancholy satisfaction of watching day and night by her bed of languishing and pain. . . . She blessed me, and blessed her children, commending us to the ever-watchful care of that Saviour who had sustained her in so many hours of trial; and finally, after kissing me and each one of the children, she passed from earth to heaven without a pang or a groan, as gently as the falling to sleep of an infant on its mother's breast."[33]

Josiah closed her eyes. Charlotte had been a sincere and devoted Christian and a faithful and kind wife. Even on the day of her death, she had arranged with her daughters to care for all the family's domestic matters so that Josiah would be comfortable and happy without her. But who can bear such sadness alone?

A HERO RETURNS

John Scoble resigned as secretary of the British and Foreign Anti-Slavery Society in September 1852, but returned to Dawn on the society's behalf. Now in charge, he immediately ousted the American Baptists and ordered Newman and Davis off the property. Reports later circulated that it was a forceful eviction, with Scoble either breaking or adding a few locks, depending on the story. Whichever way it went, it was not a brilliant introduction.

There were now five hundred people living in the Dawn community, and there were sixty students attending the school, including some white and First Nations children. The American Baptist Free Mission Society retained the farming tenancy into 1853, but the school was now in British hands. Thus ended the brief reign of William P. Newman and the American Baptist Free Mission Society.

Scoble's plans for the British American Institute were vast and grand. He told Josiah, "I am going to renovate this place '*de novo*.'"[34] Those words sounded so grand to Josiah's ears. Scoble explained that he was going to start fresh and build an institution of which they could all be proud. The land was in great shape, and Scoble could turn it into a model farm for the world to see.

One of Scoble's first orders was to tear down the schoolhouse. He explained that it was too small and rough, and that he'd soon replace it with a far bigger, far better building. It was a terrible omen, but Josiah was blind to it at the time. Several people in the Dawn community objected to Scoble's rash move, but Josiah defended his friend's actions. He assumed the man would be good to his word. As he later wrote, "I upheld him in all these suggestions, for I had a kind of respect for the man that almost amounted to veneration."[35]

Scoble made it his policy to discourage American and British donations to the BAI. He believed that local financial support must come first—ideally, he said, the BAI would become a financially sustainable organization that could pay its own way. To that end, he attempted to incorporate the institution. Perhaps he believed it would open them up to government funding, so that they would not have to rely on fickle patrons and unreliable donors. Scoble also argued that incorporation would get rid of individual liability in the event the BAI went bankrupt.

This strategy did not go over well with James C. Brown, the only trustee who had refused to surrender his trust to the London committee. Josiah, Samuel Davis, and local businessman William Whipper all supported the idea of incorporation, but Brown blocked Scoble at every turn. It's easy to understand how Brown could be worried—Scoble could have ulterior motives, and with the incorporation, Scoble might be able to seize control of the BAI for personal profit.

With the BAI "safely" in Scoble's hands, Josiah began traveling once again to help change public sentiment in the North about slavery. He was soon traveling constantly, not only throughout Canada, but also into Maine, New Hampshire, Vermont, Massachusetts, Connecticut, and Rhode Island.

Meanwhile, although slavery was still considered a permanent institution of the South, the earthquake from *Uncle Tom's Cabin* was starting to break up its foundations. Slave owners had grown up with the system, and it was profitable. Why let it go because some Yankee said so? Anti-slavery ideas certainly weren't popular in the South; nor had they fully taken root in the North.

NINE

THE REAL UNCLE TOM

A man's character is his fate.

—HERACLITUS

JOSIAH IMMEDIATELY UNDERSTOOD THE IMPORTANCE OF *UNCLE Tom's Cabin* and later wrote of its launch: "When this novel of Mrs. Stowe came out, it shook the foundations of this world. It shook the Americans out of their shoes and of their shirts. It left some of them on the sandbar barefooted and scratching their heads, so they came to the conclusion that the whole thing was a fabrication."[1]

The backlash against Harriet Beecher Stowe's novel came rapidly and rabidly. Critics argued that Stowe's writing was far too emotional to reflect events in the real world. After all, it was a novel. It wasn't based on facts. And in any case, she'd overlooked many of the "benefits" of slavery. In early 1853, even some northerners and abolitionists opposed the novel. The most liberal antislavery advocates didn't think the book was strong enough in its call for immediate emancipation. Others were dismayed that it casually endorsed colonization instead of abolition. Still others thought the main character, Tom, simply wasn't a strong enough black man.

Stowe wasn't concerned about the politics. For her, slavery was a religious and emotional challenge. Her stated goal was "to awaken sympathy and feeling for the African race."[2] On this point she certainly hit her mark, with many moderate antislavery advocates praising the book for putting a human face on slavery. The American masses, for the first time, were feeling sympathy, and maybe even empathy, for their brothers and sisters in chains. The Fugitive Slave Act had been a tipping point, and *Uncle Tom's Cabin* was a hard shove toward enlightenment.

Naturally, proslavery advocates saw the novel as sectarian propaganda. They insisted that slavery was sanctioned in the Bible, and that Stowe had fabricated an unrealistic, one-dimensional picture of slavery in the South.

The Daily Dispatch in Richmond opposed Stowe's entire premise in an August 1852 editorial, saying, "In the name of justice and propriety, to what are we coming, if such a course is to be pursued? What can Southern men expect as the fruits of such a literature?" The editor lamented the book might lead to "the ultimate overthrow of the framework of Southern society."[3]

Proslavery newspapers were mocking and sarcastic in their reviews, which had titles such as "More Anti-Slavery Fiction," "A Few Facts for Mrs. Stowe," and "Uncle Tom Mania." Editors lamented that "Uncle Tom's Cabin seems fated to be an ever-springing fountain of discord," and "We tremble for the traditional chivalry of the South."

One New Orleans publication shared the story of a doctor who left twenty-one of his slaves with the option to return to Liberia one year after his death if they so wished, and the newspaper quickly and confidently concluded that "not only do these circumstances contradict Mrs. Stowe's book, but in what contrast do they stand to her mercenary conduct!"

The Daily Picayune complained that Stowe had amassed tens of thousands of dollars from the sale of her novel, but hadn't spent any of it in "purchasing the freedom of a meritorious slave."

A "Georgian gentleman" wrote anonymously to *De Bow's Southern and Western Review* that *Uncle Tom's Cabin* was "one of the most incendiary papers ever issuing from the American press. It is insulting to the South, because Mrs. Stowe wants the world to believe that all she has written is true!" He went on to estimate that the current value of all the southern slaves "amount[ed] in round numbers" to $1 billion, and that they produced $120 million per year in cotton, rice, and tobacco alone: "If Mrs. Stowe and her associates in America and Great Britain, think that the Southern people are so inconsiderate as to give up their property for nothing, and then keep the negroes in a state of idleness as they are kept in Jamaica, they are certainly mistaken." The Georgian racist ended by reminding his readers of the Pharisees who put heavy laws on their people but never lifted a finger to help. He signed his letter to the editor with *Veritas*—Truth.[4]

In addition to newspaper editors, fiction writers in both North and South said Stowe's story was an exaggerated and flawed depiction of slavery. They responded by writing proslavery, anti-Tom novels as a rebuttal.

In 1852, Mary Henderson Eastman published a book called *Aunt Phillis's Cabin; or, Southern Life As It Is.*[5] Henderson had been born to one of the so-called First Families of Virginia, and had grown up in elite planter society. Her best-seller, published in Philadelphia, sold upward of thirty thousand copies, making it a strong commercial success.

A more direct counter to Stowe's work was W. L. G. Smith's *Life at the South; or, "Uncle Tom's Cabin" As It Is: Being Narratives, Scenes, and Incidents in the Real "Life of the Lowly."* In this iteration, Uncle Tom is convinced to run away by a northern abolitionist schoolteacher. Tom soon realizes the abolitionists want to enslave him, and he tries to escape after being mistreated in Illinois. He eventually ends up in Canada, where his master is waiting to "rescue" him and take him back to "good old Virginia."

In New York, Charles Scribner published Rev. Bayard Rush Hall's *Frank Freeman's Barber Shop*. The tale centers around a slave named Frank who is convinced by abolitionists to run away from his idyllic life on a southern plantation, with promises of freedom and a prestigious career. Frank realizes he's been deceived when he ends up running a barber shop frequented by his new abolitionist "masters." Frank is then rescued by members of the American Colonization Society, who pay for his passage back to Liberia, where he can live happily ever after.

These supposed "sequels" generally had three things in common. First, they presented slave owners as benign, if not helpful and kind, toward their slaves. Second, the slaves were presented as satisfied, and often happy and grateful, with their treatment. Slaves who were loyal and obedient to their masters were well-fed, well-dressed, and well-housed. Third, the abolitionists, sometimes called "philanthropists," were depicted as villainous agitators who stirred up trouble with tall tales and promises of riches and freedom in the north.

❦

ONE OF THE ARGUMENTS AGAINST STOWE'S NOVEL WAS THE IDEA that slave owners might possibly whip a slave to death. Many newspapers denounced this outcome as unlikely, if not impossible. Stowe, however, asked her readers to consider the case of *Souther v. the Commonwealth of Virginia*.[6]

On September 1, 1849, a Virginia slave owner named Simeon Souther, in the presence of two other whites, murdered a slave named Sam. He had learned that Sam had gotten drunk, and as punishment Souther had tied his victim "with ropes about his wrists, neck, body, legs, and ankles, to a tree" that morning. Once he was bound, Souther whipped the prisoner with apple and peach tree switches. He then beat the slave with a flat wooden board. When he grew tired, he forced two of his slaves—one male, one female—to hit their fellow slave with the shingle as well.

While still tied to the tree, Sam endured a beating in which Souther "did strike, knock, kick, stamp, and beat him upon various parts of his head, face, and body."

Souther then "applied fire to his body, back, sides, belly, groins, and privy parts" before washing Sam with warm water that had been steeped with red pepper pods. He then forced his two slaves to wash Sam with the fiery liquid.

"After the tying, whipping, cobbing, striking, beating, knocking, kicking, stamping, wounding, bruising, lacerating, burning, washing, and torturing," Souther untied Sam and threw him to the ground, where he "did knock, kick, stamp, and beat [Sam] upon his head, temples, and various parts of his body."

In the afternoon, Souther had Sam carried indoors. He forced one of his slaves to lock Sam's feet in a pair of wooden stocks and tie a rope around his neck, which he fastened to a bedpost, "thereby strangling, choking, and suffocating" the slave. Souther continued to "kick, knock, stamp, and beat him upon his head, face, breast, belly, sides, back, and body," and he forced his two slaves to "apply fire to the body" until Sam died.

Souther *and* the prosecuting attorney demurred the indictment, but the court overruled them. Souther then filed an abatement, stating he hadn't been properly examined, and "prayed judgment that the indictment be quashed."

Souther was convicted of second-degree murder and sentenced to prison by a jury, but he immediately moved for a new trial on grounds that "the offense, if any, amounted only to manslaughter." When this request was denied, he moved twice that the court clerk not charge him for the per diem cost of the jury that had ruled against him.

The very fact that Souther performed much of his abuse in the presence of two white witnesses suggests he may have had no idea that his behavior was either wrong or illegal. Moreover, the court record indicates that Souther "frequently declared while the said slave was undergoing the punishment, that he believed the said slave was feigning and pretending to be suffering and injured, when he was not."

Souther pled not guilty, and his lawyer argued that an owner couldn't be indicted for malicious, cruel, and excessive whipping of his own slave, as there was a precedent case for this. If that excessive punishment killed the slave, it wasn't the owner's fault. It wasn't premeditated, and therefore, it wasn't a crime.

In the end, the court ruled that "it is believed that the records of criminal jurisprudence do not contain a case of more atrocious and wicked cruelty than was presented upon the trial."

Souther served just five years for torture and murder.

Stowe's book was not an exaggerated account of the evils of slavery, of course. In fact, the true depths of slavery's violence and cruelty have never fully been told.

Such appalling crimes never saw the light of an honest courtroom, because even if a slave survived such heinous torture, they weren't allowed to testify against a white man in a court of law. Justice, as the powerless know well, is blind in one eye.

⚬⚬⚬

THE ATTACKS AGAINST HARRIET BEECHER STOWE WERE VILE AND wide-ranging, and often they became appallingly personal. She was labeled a socialist, anti-Christian, and plain ugly.

The Daily Dispatch said Stowe's "very name has grown to us distasteful in the extreme." It went on to complain about abolitionism in general: "What a hell of a world these poor maniacs would make if they were just allowed to fashion it after their own notions."[7]

The *Southern Literary Messenger* printed an epigram about Stowe:

> *When Latin I studied, my Ainsworth in hand,*
> *I answered my teacher that Sto meant to stand,*
> *But if asked, I should now give another reply,*
> *For Stowe means, beyond any cavil, to lie.*

Other attacks were simply chauvinistic. One newspaper nicknamed her "Mrs. Breeches Stowe." A *Memphis Daily Appeal* reader anonymously wrote that "Harriet Beecher Stowe terms the abolition crusade against the South a 'holy war.' It should be remembered she is a strong-minded woman."

Worst of all, perhaps, was an entry in the *Daily Picayune*. The New Orleans publication reported on June 15, 1853, that Mrs. Stowe had taken a trip during which she was taunted by a Mr. Justice Haliburton, who showed her his leather razor strop, which was supposedly "made of nigger skin."[8]

THE FEMALE FRONT

Harriet Beecher Stowe went to London to secure the copyright for her books, both *Uncle Tom's Cabin* and her upcoming novel, *Dred: A Tale of the Great Dismal Swamp*. She was virtually mobbed wherever she went in the city, and was wined and dined by royalty. On May 7, 1853, Stowe spoke at the Stafford House, the London home of the Duchess of Sutherland, where the Countess of Shaftesbury presented her with a gigantic petition titled "An Affectionate and Christian Address of Many Thousands of Women of Great Britain and Ireland to Their Sisters the Women of the United States of America."

The petition, oddly, had been conceived and drafted by a man, albeit a rather illustrious one. The Earl of Shaftesbury, on behalf of British women, implored the daughters of America to raise their voices against slavery. The British plea concluded with a powerfully sympathetic appeal: "We acknowledge with grief and shame our heavy share in this great sin. We acknowledge that our forefathers introduced, nay, compelled the adoption of slavery in those mighty colonies. We humbly confess it before Almighty God; and it is because we so deeply feel and so unfeignedly avow our own complicity that we now venture to implore your aid to wipe away our common crime and our common dishonor."

The document circulated throughout the British Isles. Volunteers had collected the signatures of British women from all walks of life, and many of them had likely read *Uncle Tom's Cabin*. In total, more than 563,000 women signed the document, which was leather-bound in twenty-six massive folio volumes.

Neither Great Britain nor the United States permitted women to vote, but the women of Britain had made their voices heard. Stowe, calling it "a singular monument of an international expression of a moral idea," promised to establish a committee of women in America who would attempt to get a petition going back home.

CRITICS CHECKED

Stowe, for her part, seems to have remained strongly antislavery and devotedly Christian throughout the highs and lows of her novel's warm reception and scalding resistance. She truly believed in the justice of her stance, and that the task of writing *Uncle Tom's Cabin* had been assigned to her by a higher power. As she wrote in the preface to an 1879 edition of the novel: "I did not write it. God wrote it. I merely did his dictation."

But Stowe went further in early 1853. Rather than letting the anti-Tom novels gain attention and discredit the truths behind her novel, she decided to fight fire with fact. Her response to critics was a book called *The Key to Uncle Tom's Cabin: Presenting the Original Facts and Documents upon Which the Story Is Founded, Together with Corroborative Statements Verifying the Truth of the Work*.[9] The book was a giant annotated bibliography of her sources, pointing to hundreds of documented cases of real-life incidents that were similar or identical to those portrayed in her story.

Although the book is more like an encyclopedia than anything else—it was called "ponderous (and rather unsaleable)" by one critic[10]—it sold more than 90,000 copies within a month of being published.

The Key to Uncle Tom's Cabin contained facts and figures, along with newspaper clippings, quotes, book excerpts, letters, slave inventories, interviews, and wanted ads. One of her primary sources of information was T. D. Weld's book *American Slavery As It Is: Testimony of a Thousand Witnesses*. Published in 1839 by the American Anti-Slavery Society, it was a compilation of horrific stories. It had been a best-seller more than a decade earlier.

Once again, the rebuttals to *The Key* came fast and furious. One newspaper titled its review simply "Mrs. Stowe Again." Another review was titled "Southern Slavery and Its Assailants." *The Southern Literary Messenger* wrote, in June 1853, that "Mrs. Stowe obtrudes herself again upon our notice, and, though we have no predilections for the disgusting office of castigating such offences as hers, and rebuking the incendiary publications of a *woman*. . . ."[11]

A New Orleans newspaper started its review with "Mrs. Stowe and her books together have sunk so low. . . ." It went on to rationalize that dead-or-alive wanted posters weren't actually to be taken seriously, but were simply "mere pieces of bravado on the part of masters." This, of course, was a serious misdirection, as wanted posters themselves often told of previous abuse suffered by runaways. Consider a July 23, 1836, wanted ad posted in the *Mississippi Gazette*:

> A negro man who says his name is Josiah, that he belongs to Mr. John Martin, living in Louisiana, twenty miles below Nathchez. Josiah is five feet eight inches high, heavy built, copper colour; his back very much scarred with the whip; and branded on the thigh and hips in three or four places thus: "J.M." The rim of his right ear has been bitten or cut off.

In addition to the evident physical abuse the wanted ads inadvertently confessed, the very fact that they existed proved that slaves were considered property. A New Jersey slave owner advertised in his local paper for "the return of his nine-year-old Negro girl who was stolen by her mother."[12]

Although there exists the argument that southerners weren't really racist, but had simply grown up with the belief that black people were inferior or inhuman, misses the point entirely, for that belief was the very essence of racism. In reality, antebellum America was profoundly racist. In the year Stowe's novel was published, a Philadelphia outfit published *Bone Squash's Black Joke Al-Ma-Nig*, a deeply racist almanac containing "new an' original nigga' stories, black jokes, puns, parodies, serenades, songs, coon's cons, cun-un-ori-fums, cuts ob great coons, portraits of great possums, an' dog-berry-o-types ob fun."[13] It wasn't the only one. The American—and global—psyche was, as it still is, in many parts, cruelly opposed to the rights and freedoms of minorities.

Although *Uncle Tom's Cabin* helped awaken Americans to the fact that slave owners were both wrong and racist, something fundamentally new had occurred with the publication of Stowe's *Key*. Rather than simply sweeping aside the "fiction" of a novel, editors were forced to justify and defend every story and fact presented, like a criminal attorney suddenly put on the defensive. Stowe cited real stories of real people, of events and situations that could be corroborated and proved.

Harriet Beecher Stowe had named names. She had described the various people who had inspired the characters of Mr. Haley, George Harris, Eliza, Legree, and the rest. One of those characters, of course, was of particular interest. Who was Uncle Tom?

Stowe wrote in *The Key*: "The character of Uncle Tom has been objected to as improbable; and yet the writer has received more confirmations of that character, and from a great variety of sources, than of any other in the book." Stowe spends several pages describing the inspiration for various scenes in Uncle Tom's story, and then she declares: "A last instance parallel with that of Uncle Tom is to be found in the published memoirs of the venerable Josiah Henson . . . now pastor of the missionary settlement at Dawn, in Canada."[14]

Josiah Henson would soon be world famous.

⤜⤏⤜⤏

HARRIET BEECHER STOWE MENTIONED JOSIAH'S NAME ON EIGHT occasions in *The Key to Uncle Tom's Cabin*.[15] She even quoted the passage in his memoir where he raised the ax to kill Amos Riley Jr. on their journey by boat to New Orleans.

Josiah isn't the only historical person whose life contained scenes similar to Tom's, of course. There were striking parallels between Stowe's novel and the life of Solomon Northup, and although Stowe also compares Josiah to another character in her novel, George Harris, her use of Josiah's life story is largely focused on Tom's character.

Josiah and Tom were also dissimilar in many ways. Tom was private, Josiah very public. Tom was not ambitious or successful in the sense of worldly achievements, while Josiah was very much both. Tom turned down Legree's offer to become overseer, while Josiah accepted Isaac Riley's offer. Tom witnessed the flogging of his wife, while Josiah recounted his father's torture. Tom murdered his overseer, but Josiah couldn't bring himself to fell the ax on his master's son. Tom escaped slavery by dying. Josiah simply escaped.

But there were significant overlaps between the lives of Josiah Henson and Tom, and readers who were familiar with Josiah immediately saw them. Their real-life and fictional slave masters both separated a mother from her child while she begged him not to tear the family apart. Both Josiah and Tom lived on plantations in Kentucky. Legree constantly beat Tom. Tom was sold to pay his owner's debts; Josiah nearly met that fate. Tom was sent to Louisiana, a fate Josiah just barely escaped. Both escapees crossed the Ohio River. Above all, it was Josiah's faith in God in the face of hardship that fused him to Stowe's hero, for both Tom and Josiah were strongly religious men.

Indeed, it was faith that drove Stowe to write *Uncle Tom's Cabin* in the first place. As she explained in an 1853 letter, "I wrote what I did because as a woman, as a mother, I was oppressed and broken-hearted with the sorrows and injustice I saw, because as a Christian I felt the dishonor to Christianity—because as a lover of my country, I trembled at the coming day of wrath."[16]

Without question, faith and religion played a crucial role not only in Stowe's work but in the battle between North and South in general. America has, until recently, always considered itself a Christian nation, but Frederick Douglass begged to differ, writing, "Between the Christianity of this land, and the Christianity of Christ, I recognize the widest possible difference—so wide, that to receive the one as good, pure, and holy is of necessity to reject the other as bad, corrupt, and wicked. . . . I love the pure, peaceable, and impartial Christianity of Christ; I therefore hate the corrupt, slaveholding, women-whipping, cradle-plundering, partial and hypocritical Christianity of this land."[17]*

The character of Uncle Tom was inspired in part by the Christ-like character and faith of Josiah Henson. The fact that Josiah never resorted to violence to win his freedom spoke volumes to Stowe. Josiah represented all that was good and truly faithful in American religious life. He had, in some sense, become a living hero.

On April 15, 1853, Martin Robison Delany, who was one of the first three black people admitted to Harvard Medical School, and would go on to become the only black officer who received the rank of major during the Civil War, wrote a letter to Frederick Douglass in which he confirmed Stowe's estimation of Josiah. He wrote, "It is now certain, that the Rev. JOSIAH HENSON, of Dawn, Canada West, is the real Uncle Tom, the Christian hero, in Mrs. Stowe's far-famed book of 'Uncle Tom's Cabin.'"[18]

Delany, who was also the first African American male to publish a novel, suggested to Douglass that perhaps Stowe owed Josiah something more substantial than a citation in her book: "Since Mrs. Stowe and Messrs. Jewett & Co., Publishers, have realized so great an amount of money from the sale of a work founded upon this good old man, whose *living testimony* has to be brought to sustain this great book . . . would it be expecting too much to suggest, that they—the publishers—present Father Henson . . . but a portion of the profits? I do not know what you may think about it; but it strikes me that this would be but just and right."[19]

Josiah was not, of course, Uncle Tom in the flesh, but the moniker stuck from the moment it was mentioned. Unfortunately, no monetary

---

* The American doctrinal chasm was deep and wide, and often proslavery Christian beliefs were immensely twisted, while others simply didn't make much sense. The self-purchased former slave Olaudah Equiano wrote in his autobiography, "One man told me that he had sold 41,000 negroes, and that he once cut off a negro man's leg for running away. I told him that the Christian doctrine taught us to do unto others as we would that others should do unto us. He then said that his scheme had the desired effect—it cured that man and some others of running away." Olaudah Equiano, *The Interesting Narrative of the Life of Olaudah Equiano, or Gustavus Vassa, the African, Written by Himself* (London, 1789).

gift was ever sent to him, and money problems would continue to plague the BAI and Josiah personally. His debts now included the cost of Charlotte's funeral and burial.

Still, Josiah was honored to have played a small role in Stowe's colossal work. He later reflected:

> After Mrs. Stowe's remarkable book, "Uncle Tom's Cabin," was published and circulated in all parts of America, read openly at the North and stealthily at the South . . . many thought that her statements were exaggerations. She then published the Key to the book, to prove that it was impossible to exaggerate the enormities of slavery, and she therein gave many parallel cases, and referred to my published life-story, as an exemplification of the truth of the character of her Uncle Tom. From that time to the present, I have been called "Uncle Tom," and I feel proud of the title. If my humble words in any way inspired that gifted lady to write such a plaintive story that the whole community has been touched with pity for the sufferings of the poor slave, I have not lived in vain; for I believe that her book was the beginning of the glorious end. It was a wedge that finally rent asunder that gigantic fabric with a fearful crash.[20]

A FALLEN FRIEND

Josiah's foray into the sawmill business had turned out to be an utter disaster. He had begged and borrowed to raise the money for the mill, and he and his sons had worked hard to build a high-quality operation that could benefit the community. The mill had been very profitable when Josiah and Newman had held the lease, as the Sydenham River connected them with a world market hungry for lumber.

The mill could have remained a highly profitable entity for years to come, but after Newman and the Baptists left, John Scoble rented the sawmill to an unnamed third tenant in 1853. The lessee employed more than forty men, but when, after a few years, there was a recession, the subtenant claimed bankruptcy, fleeing to America without paying his workers. The starving employees took out their anger on the mill itself and tore it to pieces for firewood. Josiah, reflecting sadly on the mill's demise, wrote, "Thus they ruthlessly destroyed this valuable building, the establishment of which had cost me so many anxious hours, and had proved to be such a valuable piece of property in my hands. When it was gone, I felt as if I had parted with an old idolised friend."[21]

A HOPEFUL SPRING

Armed with a request from the British and Foreign Anti-Slavery Society and the money Josiah had raised in England the previous year, John Scoble and Rev. John Roaf cleared all the BAI's debts. Josiah reported that Scoble paid back some of the liabilities at full price and bought up other debts for as little as sixty-two cents on the dollar.

Josiah had personally borrowed $2,800 from Amos Lawrence, Samuel Atkins Eliot, and J. Ingersoll Bowditch to finance the sawmill, and the lenders knew he had "exerted himself faithfully" to make it a success.[22] He had tried to pay them back earlier, but they had insisted he reinvest it. The mill was now gone, but Josiah's debt remained. Scoble appears to have liquidated the debt in late June 1853 for $1,500, but in the process he turned the lenders against Dawn. Eliot spoke for the trio in saying that he believed Scoble should have raised funds to pay off the BAI's debts, rather than making them take a loss. In a letter, he wrote that they were "immensely disgusted with the behaviour of the London gentlemen."[23]

Although the debts were paid, the BAI remained in a poor position. The institute's school was gone, and its sawmill lay in shambles. But the Dawn community, Josiah included, placed their hopes in John Scoble, saying, "Surely he will commence building next year."[24]

ॐ

WILLIAM P. NEWMAN'S AMERICAN BAPTIST FREE MISSION SOCIETY resented John Scoble's control of the BAI's school. Its members decided to give up the society's farm tenancy to the BAI's lands. In 1853, New-man and his fellow Baptists departed the BAI, taking anything that was portable with them.

Facing extensive repairs and unable to find a farm tenant that met his requirements, Scoble decided to farm the property himself. But he had never farmed before, and he wasted a huge amount of money building up his new enterprise. Scoble bought expensive farming equipment to work the farm "scientifically." He often bought the most expensive cattle in the market, without accounting for the fact that he didn't have enough to feed them once they were brought to his stables.

Scoble often asked Josiah to accompany him to the market. Josiah occasionally suggested that the new purchases of cattle would require a large amount of feed to make it through the long Canadian winter, but although Scoble often asked for his opinion, he invariably ignored it. Josiah wrongly concluded that the abolitionist knew what he was doing and must have had past farming experience.

Looking back from the vantage point of more than two decades, Josiah wrote of Scoble's early days: "It is my candid opinion that, in the beginning, he intended to benefit the coloured race, and to have a splen-did school which should be the pride of the neighbourhood. If he had been a practical instead of a theoretical farmer, he doubtless would have accomplished those blessed results."[25]

Although the BAI was making little visible progress in the hands of John Scoble, a number of prominent abolitionists and their families invested in the Dawn area. When William Whipper, then the wealthiest black man in North America, visited Dawn, he was so impressed that he invested heavily in nearby Dresden. Starting in 1853—with his sister and brother-in-law, James and Mary Ann Hollensworth, managing his investments—Whipper built a flour mill and a dock for ships, purchased an inn, and helped to establish key industries with his banking and de-velopment talents. He lent money to both black and white people, and he contributed thousands annually to the Underground Railroad. He personally helped hundreds of slaves escape in train cars and a steamboat that he owned.[26]

James and Cornelius Charity started a crockery shop and a corn mill. They also owned a ship and some rental housing, along with four hundred acres of farmland. Surveys from the time list three ministers, two grocers, two dry-goods store owners, a barber, two innkeepers, a lye factory, and the area's first medical doctor. Every single one of these local leaders was of African descent.

But Dawn wasn't simply a refugee community for escaped slaves. White entrepreneurs also came to the region. Alexander Trerice and his Irish father-in-law, William Wright, the founder of Newport, for example, built a lime kiln and a sawmill on a bend in the river. Dawn was open to people of all colors. The area included poor white people, First Nations people, Scottish, Irish, and German families, and, according to the 1871 census, one man from South America named Don Juan E. Barbero.

Dawn would soon encompass several thousand acres, cobbled together from hundreds of land purchases by former slaves, including those in Josiah's little group. Hundreds of farmers raised livestock, grew corn and wheat, and cultivated apple orchards. The next decade added more shops to Dresden, including its first ice cream parlor, called Sweet Briar Cottage.

By the end of 1853, John Roaf and John Scoble had cleared away all the BAI's liabilities. Even though a few jealous detractors spread rumors to the contrary, Scoble seems to have received no monetary kickbacks from the settlement of accounts. The British abolitionist was lauded for his swift and decisive actions.

Many at Dawn praised Scoble, and the community's growing success seemed assured. Despite the BAI's new debt-free position, however, the institute's long-term survival was anything but assured, and there were a few who remained unconverted.

A NEW ENEMY EMERGES

Mary Ann Camberton Shadd Cary was born on October 9, 1823, in Wilmington, Delaware. Shadd was the oldest of thirteen children born to free black parents. When it became illegal to educate African American children in the state, the Shadds moved to Pennsylvania, where Mary Ann attended a Quaker school.[27]

After graduating, Mary Ann started a school for black children in West Chester, Pennsylvania, and later taught in Norristown, Pennsylvania, and New York City. After passage of the Fugitive Slave Law of 1850, Shadd attended the first North American Convention of Coloured Freemen, held on September 10, 1851, at St. Lawrence Hall in Toronto.[28] Hundreds of black community leaders attended. The event was hosted by prominent abolitionist figures, including Josiah Henson and Henry Bibb. Bibb was a fugitive slave who, along with his freeborn wife, Mary, ran a newspaper called *The Voice of the Fugitive*.[29] The Bibbs met Mary Ann at the convention and convinced her to accept a teaching position near their home in Windsor.

Mary Ann Shadd and her brother Isaac moved across the American border to Canada. Shortly thereafter, backed by the American Missionary Association (AMA), Shadd started a racially integrated school. Henry and Mary Bibb favored segregation for black children, and the dispute informed many editorials written by both sides in *The Voice of the Fugitive*. The public dispute caused Shadd to lose her AMA school funding, but the fight had taught her a valuable lesson about the immense power of the press.

Starting on March 24, 1853, Shadd began printing an antislavery newspaper called *Provincial Freeman*, and in doing so, became the first female editor in North America. The paper's motto was "Self-Reliance Is the True Road to Independence."

Shadd's weekly publication was intended to encourage black emigration while reporting on the lives of blacks in Canada. Shadd was one of the first people to advocate for African Americans to flee the United States and immigrate to Canada; like many others, she idealized Canada as a haven for black people, calling it the "New Canaan." She promoted Canada as a nation with strong antislavery views and no legal racial discrimination, though neither were entirely true—she herself faced persecution.

Shadd moved the paper to Toronto the following year, bringing her small staff with her. Their first edition in their new location arrived on March 25, 1854. Her brother Isaac ran the day-to-day operations, while Shadd and her coeditor, Samuel Ringgold Ward, wrote much of the content. Shadd signed her work as either M. A. Shadd or M. A. S. C. and wrote in an aggressive, gruff, masculine voice as a way to hide the fact that she was a woman.

Nearly from the beginning, Mary Ann Shadd loathed Josiah Henson. Their paths couldn't have been more different. She was an educated free woman; he was a nearly illiterate fugitive slave. Shadd was an American; Josiah was now staunchly Canadian. Shadd advocated for full racial integration. As a teacher and freewoman, she believed in education and self-reliance—to her, segregated settlements like Dawn were obvious fodder for criticism. Shadd hated "begging" above almost anything else, because she believed that fundraising cast poor blacks in an unfavorable light. Because he was so well known as a speaker and fundraiser, Josiah was a particularly easy target for a newspaper in need of attention. While Henry Bibb would suffer some of Shadd's wrath via her *Provincial Freeman*, most of her vituperation would be saved for Josiah Henson and John Scoble.

Part of the controversy stemmed from the fact that Dawn and the BAI were often confused with each other. Hundreds of letters and newspaper columns from the time intermix the terms "Dawn Institute," "BAI settlement," "Dawn School," and so forth. Many believed the institute was owned by the citizens of Dawn, which it was not. James C. Brown, one of the original board members, insisted that the BAI should be owned by "the coloured people of Canada" in general, instead of the people of Dawn specifically.[30] Shadd, like most others, simply didn't understand that Dawn and the BAI weren't one and the same. In reality, the BAI was an independent school set within the general area known as Dawn, and it was owned by *no one*—it was controlled only by whatever trustees happened to possess the powers of stewardship at any given moment.

It didn't help that, by the summer of 1854, William P. Newman began actively informing Shadd about the troubles at the fledgling institute he'd so recently lost to the British. Where was the new school they'd been promised? Josiah himself later admitted that he had "silenced the questionings and murmurings," as he still believed in Scoble's integrity and purpose.[31] But unfounded rumors circulated that Josiah had been raising funds for the BAI, taking a big commission, and then giving the rest to Scoble to pay for his increasingly comfortable lifestyle. Henson and Scoble were in cahoots. The institution had become their personal slush fund.

Mary Ann Shadd paid a visit to Dawn in the summer of 1854 and printed a report in her newspaper on July 22: "I find myself in the flourishing settlement called Dawn. . . . In the village of Dresden, carpenters are busy completing the fine buildings owned by [William] Whipper, smiths, waggon-makers all are at work." As for the BAI itself, Shadd noted that it had neither a school building nor dormitories. She saw only a small government-run school. While Josiah doesn't mention it in his memoirs, it appears that the government was renting a building on the BAI lands, which operated as a small public school of sorts.

Her criticism was fair. Josiah had raised plenty of money for the BAI, and Scoble had received revenues from renting the sawmill and some of the farmland, but where had the profits gone? Even Scoble couldn't deny the fact that while the institute was languishing, he was enjoying life in the nicest house in town.

Shadd informed her *Provincial Freeman* readers that everyone was preparing for an August 1 dinner celebration, likely in honor of Canada's Emancipation Day. The event would be attended by "great guns," including Frederick Douglass, and John Scoble planned to "divulge a great secret on the August occasion, connected with the 'future' of Dawn Institute." She added that local blacks had already "been told by him that they will not be asked to *approve* the scheme, but only to '*carry it out*.'"[32]

Shadd had heard what Scoble's plan would be: she reported that it was to raise thousands of dollars to construct a new institute building. But whatever his stated plan, she believed the fundraising would be just another way for him to line his pockets.

Shadd scoffed at the idea. To her, the BAI was nothing but a profit center for Josiah and Scoble. She wrote, "The plan itself will furnish another pension-department for its begging agents, at five hundred or a thousand the year, as does another 'institution' in this country."[33]

ANOTHER VIEW

There was another visitor to Dawn in 1854 who wrote a report of what he found, Dr. Robert Burns of Toronto. His piece for the *Canadian Free Press* about his October 20 visit was quickly reprinted in Shadd's *Provincial Freeman.*

Burns first mused that "the land appertaining to the Dawn Institute must now be somewhat valuable," and that it would "give us much pleasure should the Institute be speedily made something beyond a nonentity."[34]

But Burns then gave his readers a quick and highly inaccurate overview of the BAI's history, saying it was officially called the American Educational Institute, and that it had been founded in 1838, paid for by $1,703 from James Canning Fuller, with a mission to settle refugee families on the land. It is not known where he got any of this information.

Burns reported that there was no BAI school and no working sawmill, only the small wooden building used by the government school. He estimated that six to eight people lived on the property, possibly as tenants, and that he was shocked to see the disappearance of the boys' academy and boardinghouse. When William P. Newman and Rev. Samuel H. Davis had been in charge just a few years earlier, sixty students had lived and studied in the two-story brick building. Unfortunately, a storm had torn the roof off, likely in 1852, and rather than restore the building, Scoble had simply allowed the pigs and cows to move in. When the building became too dangerous to remain standing, Scoble tore it down. That was probably in the late summer of 1854, right before the August 1 emancipation celebration.

Burns paints a grim picture of the BAI under Scoble. He went on to mention another two-story wooden house "with doors open, windows all broken," which was supposed to be a girls' dormitory.

Burns's disappointment and disgust at the waste is evident. "My impression is, from all that I have heard and seen, that from 25,000 to

30,000 dollars have from first to last been collected on behalf of the Institution." It is unclear how Burns arrived at this figure; it's an amount equivalent to something like $8 million to $12 million today. But what he was insinuating was that much of it had been channeled into Scoble's pockets, with Josiah as his "Uncle Tom" sidekick.

Burns ended his report by warning readers to oppose Scoble's attempts to incorporate the trust. He called upon John Scoble to issue annual reports on his progress and provide an audited account of the BAI's books immediately.

John Scoble vehemently refused.

SHIFTING GROUND

Perhaps by choice, or perhaps pushed out by Scoble, the government school moved from the BAI lands to the nearby town of Dresden in 1855. It was a subtle shift. The town of Dresden was thriving, even without the help of the BAI. With the loss of the school, there was literally no public good emanating from the institute, and the blame was placed squarely at the feet of John Scoble and Josiah Henson.

Meanwhile, Mary Ann Shadd moved her newspaper to Chatham the following year, where William P. Newman joined her as editor. Together, the pair redoubled their efforts to destroy the reputations of both men.

The *Provincial Freeman* hated what it considered "begging," or fundraising. It believed that asking for money was degrading to blacks and that it put too much financial control into too few hands. Not that it stopped either Newman or Shadd from doing the exact same thing for their personal causes. Josiah simply couldn't win—either he stopped fundraising, or he enabled others—whether Scoble or the warring committee—to retain control over the direction of the struggling school.

In the spring of 1855, James C. Brown, one of the original BAI trustees, went on the offensive, determined to wrest control of the institute from Scoble's hands. On Monday, April 2, Brown held a meeting at the Second Wesleyan Chapel in his hometown of Chatham. There, he leveled all sorts of accusations.

He claimed that eighty of the BAI's three hundred acres had been given to Josiah for "begging services," and that twenty acres had been sold to Hiram Wilson, one of the BAI's original founders. Brown complained about the Boston gift that had been used to build the sawmill and the 25 percent commission that Josiah had allegedly received for his services as a fundraising agent. He railed against the British and Foreign Anti-Slavery Society, and about how John Scoble had seized control; the once prosperous institution, he said, was now defunct, and yet still piling on debts. Brown noted Scoble's ongoing refusal to have the accounts audited and said the man generally directed his affairs with "petty tyranny, confusion, [and] bickering."[35]

Brown certainly had some grounds for his complaints. Evidently John Scoble had, indeed, turned a personal profit from the BAI lands. Despite already having been accused of ruining a grove set aside "for a Methodist Camp Ground and Students Pleasure Grounds," Scoble brazenly hired upward of twenty men to fell trees on the BAI lands just to turn them into wooden barrels. Still, James C. Brown had no way to stop him.

The BAI's original declaration of trust had called for at least six men to sit on the board, and as many as twelve. For years, the board had consisted of James C. Brown as the sole independent trustee and John Scoble holding the other five votes. Brown declared he would try to elect a new board at the next annual meeting and overthrow Scoble if possible.

❧

THE NIGHT OF THE ANNUAL MEETING ARRIVED ON AUGUST 29, 1855. Despite multiple requests from James C. Brown and others, John Scoble repeatedly refused to allow the gathering to meet inside the former government schoolhouse. Scoble informed the crowd that they would now need to consult with him before holding public meetings on the BAI lands, and worse still, that he was "the sole proprietor, in trust, of the Dawn property." If they didn't like it, they would have to sue him in court. Brown's group was furious.[36]

Josiah tried to make peace between the opposing parties, but it wasn't enough. Mary Ann Shadd, who'd never spent a day in slavery in her life, wrote for her own paper, a few weeks later: "Dawn, for one day, at least, was something like a slave plantation. There, the 'master man' [Scoble], declaring that he got his rights in England from the donors, not from the Trustees. . . . There were parties that in the south would be called "nigger drivers"—Josiah Henson, senior, and sons, and Nero Harding. . . . It was humiliating, Sir, to see those old men, Henson and Harding, with feet tottering almost on the brink of the grave, running readily to do the dirty work of their white friend."[37]

The group moved to the nearest house, where James C. Brown moved to elect new trustees for the BAI. The vote was tallied, and six men were elected. Not one was from Dawn. In an attempt to repossess the BAI and get it back on track to fulfill its original purpose, they commissioned Mary Ann Shadd as their fundraising agent. If they could seize control of the BAI, they could evict Scoble. By this point it was clear that Scoble had changed. No longer the fiery abolitionist, he was an entrenched, paternalistic leader of a failed institution who was personally profiting from the trust's buildings, farms, and forests.

Apparently voting Scoble out didn't work, because in mid-October, William P. Newman wrote, in the *Provincial Freeman*, that James C. Brown was looking for funds "to obtain legal advice about Dawn, and to file the bill in Chancery against the original Trustees."[38] Brown also called for another meeting to discuss their next steps toward reclaiming the BAI.

Josiah was now often called "Father Henson." In his article, Newman called him "Daddy Joe." He maintained his five-year-old claim that the funds "the mendicant of Dawn" had raised in England were received under false pretenses, despite the fact that Josiah was later found innocent of the charge and had never had access to the collected funds.

Luckily for Josiah, Shadd and Newman had to put their attacks on hold in July 1856, when the *Provincial Freeman* office was seized for a debt repayment. Newman stopped working with the paper, and it took Shadd until November 25 to get the paper back on its feet and renew her campaign.

A New Love

The third and fourth years passed, and still there was no school. The black settlers at Dawn began to believe what Shadd was saying in her renewed onslaught. They began to talk with Josiah personally, saying they thought he was in league with John Scoble, and that in some way the two of them were making money off the BAI's three hundred acres.

Scoble only made matters worse when he invited his brother-in-law's impoverished family to join him on the BAI lands. Josiah felt bad for the poor family—he fed them often at his house—but the optics were not good. The BAI lands, which were supposed to support a school, were instead racking up debts while enriching two white families, and potentially Josiah himself.

Through all of this, and in the rare quiet moments, Josiah thought of Charlotte. He was still devastated by her loss. Charlotte had been his faithful companion. They'd raised eight children together. In the four years since her death, Josiah had kept company with no one. He assumed he'd be a widower for the rest of his life.

But slowly, Josiah opened himself up to the idea of another companion. Her name was Nancy Braxton. She was a widow and a longtime Sunday school teacher, and she had one son and two daughters. Nancy's mother had been a slave, but she had been such a good laundrywoman that she'd earned enough money to buy her husband's freedom as well as her own. Nancy had been raised by a Quaker lady in Baltimore and was well-educated.

In the autumn of 1856, Josiah went to Boston and visited Nancy several times before finally summoning the courage to ask her to be his wife. Two years later, they married in Boston. Josiah was now sixty-seven. They would remain together for the rest of his life.

The Brothers Henson

Josiah's new marriage brought hope and joy to his life. And yet his mind was often occupied with how to help his older brother John, who was still enslaved in Maryland, to a woman named Jane Elizabeth Beall. Beall was a granddaughter of none other than Adam Robb—the very same tavern owner who had purchased Josiah as a child and later sold him to Isaac Riley for horseshoeing services.[39]

Up to this point, Josiah had been pulled in many different directions. For decades, he had been busy preaching, raising funds for Dawn, and defending his reputation, not to mention providing for a family with eight children. It was during one particular meal in London, at the table of one of the nation's richest men, that his enslaved brother John had flashed powerfully into his mind. Josiah had gotten caught up in the larger abolitionist cause, but he had neglected a problem much closer to home—securing his own brother's freedom.

Before visiting England, Josiah had actually tried several times to rescue his brother. He'd sent a prominent New York abolitionist, William Lawrence Chaplin, to convince his brother to escape, but John was terrified and wouldn't make the journey. Chaplin, known for his abolitionist activities as "General Chaplin," returned a second time, but John still wouldn't go. Chaplin traveled to nearby Washington and attempted to help two other slaves to freedom. Unfortunately, one was owned by Georgia senator Alexander H. Stephens, and the other by another Georgia senator, Robert Augustus Toombs, who would later become a founding father of the Confederacy and its first secretary of state. On August 8, 1850, a posse of six men chased Chaplin's wagon to Silver Spring, Maryland, where they opened fire on the occupants before ramming a fence rail through their wheel spokes, forcing the wagon to stop. Chaplin was beaten badly and thrown into prison, then charged with having "abducted, stolen, taken, and carried out [two fugitive slaves] from the city of Washington." Additional charges were brought against him for supposedly assaulting the men who had arrested him. He had not been armed, however. Since there was a dispute over whether the arrest took place in DC or Maryland, he was apparently jailed in Washington for six weeks, and subsequently imprisoned in Maryland for thirteen.

Rather than let him hang, a group of abolitionists, led by the philanthropist Gerrit Smith, organized the Chaplin Fund Committee to raise money for his bail and defense. The two Georgia slave-owning senators were no doubt pulling strings in the background. Chaplin's bail was set at an appalling $19,000, which would take a modern unskilled laborer more than 150 years to pay off.[40]

Fellow abolitionists raised the bond money. These supporters included a Quaker family, the Hathaways of Farmington, New York, and a father and son, Asa B. Smith and William R. Smith. The Smiths sold their farms to help raise the money, putting themselves in poverty for years to follow. But they managed to win Chaplin's release on Christmas Eve of 1850.

Years passed, meanwhile, and John languished in slavery. He may be the same John Henson who attempted to escape but was jailed as a runaway in Washington, DC, on June 22, 1858, before being returned to Maryland. Josiah had been able to maintain frequent communication with his brother, and although the rescue attempts had failed, Josiah certainly wasn't a man who gave up on anything. So he decided to pursue a more lawful way of securing his brother's release and see if he could purchase him.

The fact that John had already tried to escape gave his owner, Beall, an incentive to sell him; John was in his sixties, past the age where he was valuable to her as a worker. Josiah learned that she would be willing to sell him for $400, which was more than triple the value her family had thought he was worth eleven years earlier. Josiah calculated that he'd need to raise $550 to purchase his brother's release, bring him to Canada, and provide a home for him at Dawn.

Josiah reached out to his antislavery friends in Boston, particularly Amos Lawrence, and they agreed to help him republish an updated story of his life. The book was printed by Harriet Beecher Stowe's publisher, John P. Jewett and Company,* and the new version was decidedly more upmarket than the 1849 paperback. The revised memoir was bound with a purple hardcover and contained an illustration of Josiah and his signa-

---

* Jewett later stated in an 1883 interview in *The Manhattan* that his was the first edition of Josiah Henson's life story, and that he had personally written about a quarter of it. Jewett and Bishop Gilbert Haven had worked, through "tedious cross-examination," to update the book on behalf of their nearly illiterate subject.

ture on the frontispiece, along with an introduction by Harriett Beecher Stowe herself.

It was well known that Josiah had been part of the inspiration for the character of Uncle Tom, and his backers wanted to profit from the connection. The book's new title was *Truth Stranger Than Fiction: Father Henson's Story of His Own Life.*

It might seem strange to release an old book with a new name—Josiah's book was published in at least eight editions during his lifetime—but this was not unusual. Sojourner Truth's narrative went through five editions. Frederick Douglass wrote three versions of his autobiography, with one British version going through nine editions in just two years. Olaudah Equiano's memoir, which was first published in 1789, had gone through thirty-six editions by 1837.

Because of Josiah's heightened popularity, the new book had an advance sale of five thousand copies, but Jewett did little to market the work, and it didn't become particularly well known.[41] Josiah took a bundle of the books on his back and traveled through New England with them, quickly succeeding in raising the funds he needed.

He then hired Charles C. Berry, cashier of the City Bank in Boston, to negotiate the purchase of his brother's freedom. The banker did well. Through his connections in Maryland, Berry was able to secure John Henson's freedom papers for $250—still overpriced—on September 8, 1858. Josiah joyfully sent the ransom money, and John was soon transported to Baltimore. From there he took a boat to Boston and was reunited with his brother after decades apart. Josiah brought John to his home in Canada, where he lived for the next fifteen years.*

---

* After the Emancipation Proclamation, John Henson's eldest son came to Canada to see his father. Josiah wrote, "The meeting would have done President Lincoln's heart good if he had witnessed it." Josiah Henson, *"Uncle Tom's Story of His Life": An Autobiography of the Rev. Josiah Henson,* edited by John Lobb (London: Christian Age Office, 1876), 154. Three years later, James returned and invited John to rejoin his wife and sons in America. James's former owner and her husband had purchased a large dairy farm in New Jersey, but couldn't get used to white servants. She convinced James to bring his family to her farm. James became the dairy superintendent, while John lived as a well-paid servant into his nineties. Although we don't know the circumstances, we do know that Josiah's younger brother, also named James, eventually made his way to Dawn. He was buried in a cemetery on the 9th Concession in Chatham Township.

Despite the ongoing struggle with Scoble, Shadd, and Newman at Dawn, Josiah ended his 1858 memoir on an upbeat note, painting a picture of the progress made by former slaves in their new land:

> I have been requested by many friends in this country to devote a chapter of my book to the fugitive slaves in Canada; to a statement of their present numbers, condition, prospects for the future, etc. At the time of my first visit to Canada, in the year 1830, there were but a few hundred fugitive slaves in both Canadas; there are now not less than thirty-five thousand. At that time they were scattered in all directions, and for the most part miserably poor, subsisting not unfrequently on the roots and herbs of the fields; now many of them own large and valuable farms, and but few can be found in circumstances of destitution or want.

Josiah noted how, when he had arrived in Canada in 1830, there had been no schools or churches for blacks, but now there were plenty of both. He described their farms and the food they grew: "corn, wheat, rye, oats . . . apples, cherries, plums, peaches, quinces, currants, gooseberries, strawberries . . . sweet potatoes . . . tobacco and hemp."[42]

Josiah credited Queen Victoria for their freedom and invited jobless black Americans to find their way north, where the soil was good, their children could be educated, and they would be protected from abuse. As he approached nearly three decades of service to the black people of Canada, he ended his note humbly: "My task is done[;] if what I have written shall inspire a deeper interest in my race, and shall lead to corresponding activity in their behalf I shall feel amply repaid."[43]

OPPOSITION SILENCED

Mary Ann Shadd's early battles with Henry Bibb had taught her the power of the press and its ability to make or break people's lives. Though she had done much to advance the cause of escapees to Canada, she had done much harm as well. Her newspaper's prospectus stated the point of her work best: "It will open its columns to the views of men of different political opinions, reserving the right, as an independent journal, of full expression on all questions or projects affecting the people in a political way; and reserving, also, the right to express emphatic condemnation of all projects."[44]

No one had received more emphatic condemnation than the leaders at Dawn. Shadd's and Newman's tirades against the BAI had wreaked havoc on the institute and its ability to raise funds and operate. But on August 22, 1857, after forty-nine issues and more than three years of constant attacks on Josiah's character, Mary Ann Shadd's *Provincial Freeman* shuttered its doors for good.[45]

⟮⟯

THROUGHOUT THE NEXT YEAR, JOSIAH CONTINUED TO WORK AND advocate on behalf of black people in Canada and beyond. In July 1858, he traveled to the Convention of Colored Citizens of Massachusetts in New Bedford, in celebration of the twenty-fourth anniversary of the liberation of the 800,000 slaves of the British West Indies. Apparently Stowe's *Key to Uncle Tom's Cabin* had done much for Josiah's reputation. William Wells Brown presided over the meeting, and the minutes reported that a "fervent prayer was then offered by Rev. Josiah Henson, of Canada, 'Uncle Tom,' as he is generally known."[46]

Charles Lenox Remond, a black abolitionist, gave a stirring speech about freedom and emancipation. He declared that "colored people would gain nothing by twaddling and temporizing."[47] He was sorry, he said, that so many black people allowed themselves to be led by white men, even considerate ones. He wanted black men to stand up for themselves and fight.

Someone in the crowd yelled that they wanted to hear from Josiah. Remond said he "didn't believe Father Henson could understand our position." He believed Massachusetts blacks were the focus of attention at this celebration, and he didn't want to hear about Canadian liberty. He wanted liberty in America, or nothing else. "We must depend upon our own self-reliance. If we recommend to the slaves in South Carolina to rise in rebellion, it would work greater things than we imagine. If some black Archimedes does not soon arise with his lever, then will there spring up some black William Wallace with his claymore, for the freedom of the colored race."

Remond moved that a committee of five men be appointed to write an address to southern slaves, suggesting they mount an insurrection. He knew his resolution was revolutionary and treasonous, but he wanted to stir up "men who would encourage their brethren at the South to rise with bowie-knife and revolver and musket."

Josiah remembered Nat Turner's Rebellion, which took place in Virginia in 1831. A little less than a year after Josiah's escape, Nat Turner, a slave preacher, and his band had killed up to sixty-five people over a period of three days. Twice as many slaves were killed in retaliation.[48] Turner was hung, and some speculated his body was skinned, beheaded, and quartered. According to a later report, "Turner was skinned to supply such souvenirs as purses, his flesh made into grease, and his bones divided as trophies to be handed down as heirlooms."[49]*

The crowd cried for Father Henson's opinion. Josiah, now almost seventy years old, took the platform and declared that he didn't want to fight any more than he thought Remond actually did. If the time for shooting came, he suspected Remond would be nowhere to be found. Josiah thought the convention should study the West Indies' emancipation and see if there were some lessons to be learned that could help win freedom in America. Failing that, they should find ways to help more people escape north. Josiah conceded that Canada wasn't perfect, by any means, but it was the only place he'd found real freedom for his people. "A good run is better than a bad stand," he declared.

Josiah raised another good point. How would Remond's manifesto be circulated among southern blacks without alerting their white overseers? And how would they fight without weapons or education? Josiah

---

* After nearly 185 years of being sold and handed down as a relic, Nat Turner's skull was delivered to researchers at *National Geographic*. DNA tests are underway to confirm authenticity.

boldly declared that he didn't want to "see three or four thousand men hung before their time," and said he would "oppose any such action, head, neck and shoulders."

Remond replied that he didn't care whether his motion passed or not. He argued that if the manifesto couldn't be circulated in the South, then adopting it couldn't do any harm. As for the claim that many would die, Remond declared that if he had "one hundred relations at the South, he would rather see them die today, than to live in bondage. He would rather stand over their graves, than feel that any pale-faced scoundrel might violate his mother or his sister."[50] Remond said that he only regretted that he didn't have a spear with which to skewer every slaveholder at once, and that he wanted liberty or death. He insisted the insurrection could be accomplished in minutes, and that overthrowing the slavery system could be "instantaneously attained."

The convention put the idea to the vote, and Remond's motion lost.

Even though Josiah had won a temporary victory, a greater war was about to unleash itself in the land of the free and the home of the slave.

THE STRUGGLE CONTINUES

Back in Dresden, yet another meeting was called on January 17, 1859, with James C. Brown, William P. Newman, and Samuel H. Davis in leading roles. Evidently, they'd made little progress on wresting control from Scoble's hands. They now set their sights on the British and Foreign Anti-Slavery Society committee that had formed in London almost a decade earlier to assist Josiah.

First, they wrote a letter to the BFASS in which they repeated their story: the majority of the BAI trustees had signed over their powers to the BFASS committee via Scoble in Toronto on September 12, 1851, provided the BFASS take on the debts and carry out the purposes set forth in the declaration of trust.

"We have waited *seven years* for you to do as you have promised us, through Mr. Scoble," they complained. "The school which we had was broken up, the worship of God was discontinued, and we [are] abused by your Agent, *for the crimes of American tyrants* and the *color of our skin.*"[51]

The group added that Scoble was receiving somewhere between $800 and $1,000 in rents for the BAI lands, but keeping the money for personal use. This was almost certainly true. Scoble's attempts to farm had failed miserably, and Josiah had taken up the BAI's farm tenancy in 1847 and held it for at least three years. In this time, he would have paid rent to Scoble in exchange for the right to clear trees, plant crops, and pasture cattle. Josiah, therefore, was simply guilty by mere association with the hated white man.

⁊ℓ⁊

BY 1859, MORE THAN EIGHT YEARS HAD PASSED SINCE JOHN SCOBLE had promised to rebuild the school. Josiah had no power to force him to act, and neither did anyone else. Luckily, Scoble couldn't claim title to the land, so he had no power to sell it. The BAI had been ground to a stalemate.

Josiah repeatedly tried to bring it up in conversation with Scoble, but Scoble invariably refused to discuss the topic. "Let them growl," he replied.[52]

On November 19, 1859, Samuel Davis chaired another meeting at the Baptist Church in Dresden to talk about the institute and how they might be able to unjam the gridlock. The only way they could get rid of Scoble was to bring a lawsuit. In order to do that, they needed money to fund it. Mary Ann Shadd had been unable to raise the funds they needed, and their call to the various black settlements had also failed. They needed a better way to raise funds.

SHOTS FIRED

In November 1860, the nation elected Abraham Lincoln as president of the United States. But it was a country divided. Lincoln was seen as "anti-southern," and it was only a matter of time before the outbreak of war.

Slavery was not the only cause of the Civil War. Religion played a role—southern "Christianity" versus northern humanism and transcendentalism—as did cultural and political differences. The South favored states' rights, whereas the North preferred more centralization. As in most wars, money and power lay near the root. But although many in the modern South choose to underplay or forget it, the issue of slavery—along with its societal, religious, cultural, and economic implications—was the fulcrum on which all else turned.

On December 20, 1860, the slave state of South Carolina seceded from the Union. In February 1861, the Confederate States of America was formally established, with Jefferson Davis as its president and Montgomery, Alabama, as its capital. Their motto was "Under God, our Vindicator," and the unofficial anthem was "God Save the South."

By the time Lincoln was inaugurated on March 4, 1861, six more states—Mississippi, Florida, Alabama, Georgia, Louisiana, and Texas—had joined the Confederacy. Each state's written declaration made it clear that slavery was the main point of contention, with Mississippi making it emphatically clear: "Our position is thoroughly identified with the institution of slavery—the greatest material interest of the world. . . . [A] blow at slavery is a blow at commerce and civilization."

Less than one month later, at 4:30 a.m. on April 12, 1861, Confederate forces, under General Pierre Gustave Toutant Beauregard (the "Little Napoleon"), fired a ten-inch mortar at Union-held Fort Sumter in Charleston, South Carolina. It was the first shot of the Civil War.

Three days later, Lincoln called for 75,000 volunteers to suppress the rebellion. Several slave states refused to send troops against their neighboring slave states, and by May 20, four more states—Virginia, Arkansas, Tennessee, and North Carolina—had joined the Confederacy.

By the time Robert E. Lee surrendered to Ulysses S. Grant at the Battle of Appomattox nearly four years later, upward of 750,000 Americans lay dead across the nation's fields and forests. Among them were as many as 80,000 slaves. Potentially more than half of the fallen had died from the outbreaks of yellow fever, pneumonia, and smallpox that had plagued camps in both the North and the South.

Black soldiers captured by Confederate troops faced far harsher treatment than white soldiers as prisoners of war—the Confederate Congress even threatened to enslave all black POWs. Nevertheless, approximately 10 percent of the Union Army was made up of black soldiers. Roughly 179,000 black men served in the US Army, and another 19,000 served in the Navy, along with nearly 80 commissioned officers and thousands more in noncombat support functions. By the end of the war, 16 black soldiers had been awarded the Medal of Honor for their bravery.[53]

But prejudice certainly still existed in the North. Black soldiers were usually placed in segregated units headed by white officers. They were paid less than their white counterparts, and they had to pay for their own uniforms. What other choice did they have? Many simply needed jobs. Many more proudly enlisted to fight for the freedom of their friends and families.

Even though, because of the British Foreign Enlistment Act of 1819, it was against the law for British subjects to encourage others to serve, it was up to aging men like Josiah to convince young black men to join the fight and help free their four million enslaved brethren.

⟡⟡⟡

SEVENTY-ONE-YEAR-OLD JOSIAH REGRETTED THAT HE WAS TOO OLD to fight. As he wrote, "My sword had been turned into a ploughshare. . . . If I could have carried a gun, I would have gone personally, but I thought it was my duty to talk to the people." Josiah told them "that the young and able-bodied ought to go into the field like men, that they should stand up to the rack, and help the government."[54]

This was no slave-led insurrection. This was a civil war, funded by the federal government. When the American Civil War broke out, free black men in Canada began to dream of continental emancipation. They had been trying to liberate their American brethren for years, and this was their best chance at freedom for all.

There were rewards for enlisting early. The "bounty system" was a program of cash bonuses to entice enlistees into the army, and it worked very well. Between 1861 and 1865, the government paid out nearly $750 million in recruitment bonuses. In July 1861, Congress authorized a $100 bounty for three years of service, and on March 3, 1863, expanded the bounty to $300 for three years' service and $400 for five years' service. At a time when average annual incomes ranged from $300 to $1,000, these amounts were significant.[55]

At least two members of Josiah's family enlisted, including his oldest son, Tom, who moved to California and signed onto a man-of-war in San Francisco. Josiah counseled other men around Dawn, in general terms, to do the same. He casually mentioned that if any of them wanted to go enlist early in order to receive the enlistment bounty offered, he would personally provide for their families until they could send the bonus back to them.

This encouragement bordered on the illegal under the Foreign Enlistment Act, which forbade any subject of the British Empire—including those in Canada—from enlisting or recruiting fellow citizens to fight for a foreign power.[56] But men like Josiah had been raised in America, and some had great affinity for the nation of their birth. Often, remnants of their families remained enslaved in the United States. Canada was their home, but their allegiance was continental.

The bounty system was rife with defects, the largest being the ability to "bounty jump." The widespread practice saw men enlist, collect their bonus, desert the army, reenlist, and collect another bonus. Some men would move from recruitment station to recruitment station, while others would simply change their clothes, shave their beards, and return to the same registrar using a different name.

An entire industry of bounty brokers soon emerged, and these speculators often pocketed a sizable portion of an enlistee's bonus. Some bounty brokers even resorted to recruiting non-able-bodied men and receiving their bonus before their shortcomings were discovered and the men were discharged.

A number of people from the Dawn area went south to enlist. Sadly, some of them lost their bounty money to "sharpers." Sharpers were truly despicable con men—they targeted freshly enlisted soldiers in an effort to relieve them of their freshly pocketed bounties, often by getting them drunk and robbing them, by pickpocketing them, by cheating while gambling, or by running any number of scams and frauds.

Josiah proposed to travel with a second group of Canadians so that they wouldn't have the same thing happen to them. One black man, named John Alexander, decided to join Josiah's company. He was a poor man, with a wife and children, and the opportunity to have them fed while he went to earn a living fighting for the North seemed worth the risk. While he was gone, Josiah had clothing and meat sent to Alexander's family.

Josiah and his group traveled to the border and crossed into the United States, but at some point on the journey, Alexander seems to have deserted the pack. When Josiah arrived in Massachusetts, he received a telegram from his wife, Nancy, telling him to "remain in Boston and not return."[57]

John Alexander had returned to Dawn and falsely declared that Josiah had "tried to induce him and others to enlist." Alexander testified to the statement before a magistrate, and Nancy warned her husband that he would be arrested as soon as he arrived home. If the charge was proven true, Josiah would spend seven years in prison.

At first Josiah thought about staying in Boston until the excitement had subsided. Perhaps he could wait out the war entirely. But then he remembered his purpose for having made the trip in the first place. Josiah believed he was helping men enlist in what he believed was a righteous war. He believed that black people should take part in the great struggle for freedom. Josiah told one of his companions, after receiving the letter, "God helping me, I will not run away when I have done no wrong."

The aging Josiah returned to Dawn and rode in a wagon straight to his front door. He wanted others to know that he wasn't ashamed to be seen. He arrived home on a Thursday afternoon at about 4:00 p.m., and his family tearfully begged him to get away from Dawn. Josiah insisted that he would remain and see his name cleared.

Early the next morning, before 7:00 a.m., a local constable, William Nellis, walked up the lane. Josiah was talking with his son-in-law when he saw his old friend approach.

"Good morning, Mr. Henson," the constable said pleasantly. "Have you any potatoes to sell?"

"Good morning," Josiah answered. "Yes, sir, I have some."

"I should like to buy a few if you can spare any."

"How many do you want?"

"Ten or fifteen bushels."

"I can spare one hundred bushels."

"Oh, I do not want so many."

"Very well," Josiah said. "I suppose it is only one good black potato about my size that you want, and you can have it if you will come and get it."

The constable stepped forward and put his hand on Josiah's shoulder. "Mr. Henson, you are my prisoner in the name of the Queen." He handed him a writ.

"All right, Bill," Josiah said. "Let me have a bit of breakfast, and then you can have me."

The two men went into the house. Nancy and his children were crying. Josiah invited the constable to eat, but he declined, saying he had eaten breakfast. They talked for half an hour. Josiah then stood and grabbed his hat. "I am ready," he said. "How are we going? The writ says you must take me."

"If you will have your horse and wagon prepared, I'll pay for it."

"I will do no such a thing," Josiah said. "You must take me, and if you have no other way, go get a wheelbarrow, for I will not walk with you."

The constable argued with his friend for an hour or two, until it was approaching noon. Finally Josiah stopped toying with the man. "You can go your way when you like," he said. "And you may tell the squire I will soon be there."

Josiah arrived at the courthouse that Friday afternoon to discover that the magistrates wouldn't let him make a statement of defense or even hire a lawyer to plead his case. One of the magistrates was prejudiced against Josiah because of his position in the lawsuit against the BAI trustees, but the other magistrate, Squire Terrace, was his friend. It was the pair's job to interpret the law, but because they couldn't agree, the case was referred to another judge.

The third judge also couldn't decide on the case. He suggested they consult the county attorney.

The county attorney was a man from nearby Chatham, a Mr. Mc-Lean. He was an old friend of Josiah's—Josiah had worked for his grandfather. McLean was known for keeping his word and doing his duty.

"I am surprised to find these charges against Mr. Henson," McLean said. "He is a common-sense man, and knows the laws better than the majority of the people. There must be a screw loose somewhere in this affair. If what John Alexander has declared on oath be true, nothing will prevent Mr. Henson from seven years' imprisonment in Kingston under the Foreign Enlistment Act, which does not allow a man to entice or persuade another to enlist in the army." He looked at Josiah. "Mr. Henson, give me your version of the case."

Josiah recounted the whole story, and didn't try to dodge the facts. He admitted he'd given John Alexander's wife some food and clothing, and said, "I would give them to any one, white or black, if I had them to give, and the individual needed them." He added that he hadn't expected Alexander to turn his generosity against him, for Josiah intuited that the only "proof" they had was his gift to Alexander's family, which Alexander called bribery to get him to enlist.

"We all know Mr. Henson's character," McLean ruled. "He is an honest, upright, Christian man. . . . [W]hat is the character of his accuser?"

McLean deferred his decision until Monday morning, and sent people to make inquiries into the truthfulness of Josiah's accuser.

On Saturday afternoon, Constable Nellis allowed Josiah to return home under house arrest. That evening, a man who had heard about the case came to Josiah's house.

"There is a man loading his boat up the river," he said. "He comes from the same district where John Alexander lived before he prowled about Dresden . . . says Alexander is a thief, that he stole a lot of clothes from a line in a yard there." He went on to explain that the man loading his boat, named Mr. Smith, believed there was an arrest warrant pending to Alexander, but that Alexander had fled before his arrest.

Josiah asked the constable for permission to see Terrace. The magistrate listened as he relayed the facts.

"Go home and be quiet over Sunday," the judge said. "Monday morning before the sun rises I will be at the river, and if I can find that Smith . . . I will have him in court on Monday morning by nine o'clock."

Josiah stayed home all day Sunday, grateful to God for providing a way out. His family worried that the judge wouldn't find Smith, and that Josiah would go to prison for potentially the rest of his life. Though Josiah's fate hung in the balance, he was certain all would end well.

Early on Monday morning, Terrace walked the riverbank until he spotted a boat about half a mile off.

"Is there a man named Smith on that boat?" he yelled.

"I'm the man, sir."

"Come ashore, I want to speak to you."

Smith told the magistrate that he had worked with Alexander, that he was "a mean, lying thief, and [that] he could prove it."

Terrace immediately subpoenaed the man to appear in court at nine.

At 9:00 a.m. on Monday morning, John Alexander sat in the courtroom with a triumphant look on his face. Terrace called the witness.

"You have worked with John Alexander," the attorney said. "Is he a trustworthy man? Has he a good, reliable character?"

"He is one of the greatest rogues out[side] of prison," Smith answered.

Alexander tried to interrupt him, but Smith looked him square in the face and said, "You know if you stepped your foot where you used to work with me, you'd be hustled off to prison, where you ought to go if you got your desserts."

"What do you say?" Squire McDonald asked. "Is the man a rogue . . . has he no character?"

"He has none, sir," Smith replied. He explained again how Alexander had dodged arrest for his crimes in another county.

"Well," McDonald said, "if John Alexander has no character, Mr. Henson has his acquittal."

Josiah's friends and family cheered.

Josiah sent word to Alexander that their part of the world was too small for the both of them, and that if he saw the man again, he might be tempted to shoot him. Alexander sent friends to ask for his forgiveness, and Josiah told them Alexander would need to admit his meanness in the presence of three of Josiah's friends.

John Alexander, to his credit, apologized to Josiah and his entire family for endangering Josiah's life.

"It was about the meanest thing you could do to defame me in my absence," Josiah said. He explained that his character was one of his most prized possessions. But Alexander was clearly shaken, and Josiah felt conciliatory. "I forgive you," he said. "Go and sin no more."

EMANCIPATION OVERTURNED

Abraham Lincoln had long deliberated over the issue of slavery. As a wartime president, his goal was to reunite the country. As he considered emancipation, he struggled to carefully balance the weighty loads of public opinion, diplomatic pressure, military abilities, and his responsibility to the Constitution. It was a moral issue at its core, but Lincoln was still a politician eyeing reelection.

Although Lincoln considered compensated emancipation as a form of southern appeasement, others began to take matters into their own hands. As slaves crossed north of Union military lines, two generals declared emancipation. In late August 1861, General John C. Frémont started freeing slaves in Missouri; the following May, General David Hunter copied the action in parts of South Carolina, Georgia, and Florida.

Lincoln overrode both his generals, arguing that only the president had the power to declare such an edict. In truth, he feared that these radical actions might push Missouri and other proslavery Union states toward the Confederate cause. He asked Frémont to rescind his orders, and when the general refused, Lincoln publicly revoked the proclamation. He relieved Frémont of his duties on November 2, 1861.

⁓∾⁓

NORTHERN WRITERS USED THE PRESS TO PUT ENORMOUS PRESSURE on President Lincoln and his Congress. Stowe published prolifically in the *New York Independent* during 1861 and 1862, one of the city's leading newspapers. She primarily wrote letters to the editor, frequently employing scripture references and biblical phrasing to elicit strong emotional and religious responses from her readers. She was well informed, and her incisive critiques of the government struck a nerve. She poked and prodded, cajoled and persuaded, and lobbied for altruistic and immediate action against slavery.

As Lincoln delayed taking action, Stowe grew more frustrated and her writing took on a harder edge. She wrote to the *Independent* in August 1861 declaring, "We consider this war is a great Anti-Slavery War, not in form, but in fact: not in proclamation, but in the intense conviction and purpose of each of the contending parties, and still more in the inevitable overruling indications of divine Providence."[58]

On July 31, 1862, Stowe wrote, "The time has come when the nation has a RIGHT to demand, and the President of the United States a right to decree, their freedom; and there should go up petitions from all the land that he should do it. How many plagues must come on us before we will hear the evident voice, 'Let this people go, that they may serve me.'"[59]

Though President Lincoln had begun to set his course, the public did not yet know it, and the finest writers in the nation put increasing public pressure on him to do the right thing. But it would take far longer than the northern abolitionists hoped for him to respond to their pleas.

OVERDUE AND UNDERWHELMING REVELATION

For the past three or four years, Josiah had rented a portion of the BAI lands from John Scoble. As time wore on, the conflicts between the two men grew. They disagreed about rent payments, and Josiah pressed for property improvements; then Scoble wanted more money for his services as manager.

It had taken nine years for Josiah to come to the full realization that John Scoble was not the heroic abolitionist he'd envisioned him to be. In December 1861, he sat the Englishman down for a serious conversation on Scoble's plans for the institution.[60]

"The people about here are beginning to talk hard about you and myself," Josiah said. "I do not want to let them have any cause to think ill of us. If you will be so kind as to give me some intimation when you propose to commence the school-buildings I can satisfy them."

"When I get ready," Scoble replied curtly. "When I please."

"It is quite unfortunate for me," Josiah replied meekly. "For my honour is impeached, as I have always defended you."

"What's your honour to me? I don't care what they say. I did not come here for the coloured people to dictate to me."

"If you really do not intend to build us a school, you ought to leave the farm, and let us manage for ourselves," Josiah replied.

This angered Scoble. "Pay me what I have expended during the many years I have tried to make this place meet its expenses, and I will go at once."

Their relationship had been strained for several years, but suddenly the scales fell from Josiah's eyes and he saw through the man's motives. Scoble had no plans to build a school for black students. He had no plans to make the BAI a financially sustainable enterprise. Scoble had used Josiah for rent and influence in order to support his own family and in-laws. Josiah called the British abolitionist on his ruse and demanded he make changes immediately, or he would sue him for nonperformance of his duties as the man entrusted with the BAI.

John Scoble had had enough. He put his son in charge of the BAI premises and promptly left for Toronto to file a pair of lawsuits against Josiah. It was one thing to ward off attacks from Mary Ann Shadd, William P. Newman, and James C. Brown, however, but no one could withstand a fight from Josiah Henson. Josiah was seventy-two years of age, and the old man had yet to be bested by anyone.

⁂

JOSIAH HAD TO MOVE QUICKLY. HE PERSONALLY OWNED THE GRIST-mill on the BAI property, but he no longer held the lease to the land it was on. If he didn't remove it before the lawsuit got underway, he would almost certainly have problems with Scoble's son. The last thing Josiah wanted was for the gristmill to end up in the same position as the sawmill.

Josiah devised an ingenious plan. He sold the mill to a local Dresden businessman, William Wright, the Irishman who had developed Fairport just east of the town. Wright, along with Josiah's son-in-law, who was the miller, got twenty men together on a Sunday evening, and as soon as midnight struck, they carefully and quietly took the whole thing apart.

Josiah gleefully wrote that "by ten o'clock on Monday morning the mill had vanished, as if by magic, from its old resting-place, and by noon it was carried off, in ten or twelve teams that were in readiness, to Dresden." The men rebuilt the gristmill on a lot owned by Wright.[61]

The joke around town was that the gristmill had been spirited away by ghosts. One reporter wrote: "We cannot account for the strange behaviour of the spirits, but it is surmised that the Rev. Josiah Henson and Mr. Wright [may have been] employed as mediums." The gristmill remained in Dresden, in "splendid working order," for at least another fifteen years.

⁂

JOSIAH HAD TRUSTED SCOBLE AND PATIENTLY WAITED FOR HIM TO act for almost a decade. The lawsuit was the final straw, and Josiah was now back on his own, separated from his disappointing longtime partner. If the BAI was to be revived, and reopened as a school to train freed blacks, it would be up to him.

Josiah glumly reported in his memoir that he asked for help from the other settlers at Dawn: "I went to the coloured people and told them, sadly, that I had been greatly deceived, that we should never have a school until we gained possession of the property, and that if I had a power of attorney to act for them I would consult an able lawyer, and ascertain what could be done."

A group of black men got together, likely including James C. Brown and Samuel Davis, and deputized Josiah to explore options. Josiah immediately went to London, Ontario, and hired two experienced lawyers to take their case. They advised Josiah to stay in the background, as he had clear conflicts of interest, and to find a front man who was closely related to the BAI.

Josiah approached James C. Brown later that same night and personally pledged his entire life savings if Brown would bring the suit. Josiah would mortgage himself to the point of bankruptcy, if necessary, in order to win the fight for the BAI.

The *Brown v. Scoble* lawsuit would soon commence.[62]

A PUBLIC CHALLENGE

Horace Greeley, founder and editor of the influential *New-York Tribune*, was a man ahead of his time. He promoted temperance, opposed capital punishment, and fought against land monopolies. He zealously opposed slavery. Greeley wrote an editorial in the *Tribune* on Wednesday, August 20, 1862, titled "The Prayer of Twenty Millions." It was an open letter to Abraham Lincoln, with Greeley posing as the spokesperson for the twenty million northerners still loyal to the president.[63]

Greeley opened by saying that Lincoln should "EXECUTE THE LAWS." In the scathing piece, he accused the president of being "strangely and disastrously remiss" in his duty to enforce the Confiscation Acts, which allowed the Union to free any slaves it captured from Confederate territory.

Greeley further blasted Lincoln for annulling Frémont's proclamation, and encouraged the president to realize that there could be no liberty while slavery remained. The "Union cause," he wrote, "is now suffering immensely, from a mistaken deference to rebel slavery."

Greeley reiterated his hope that the president would proclaim emancipation and ended by warning that without the help of black "scouts, guides, spies, cooks, teamsters, diggers and choppers . . . we cannot conquer Ten Millions of People united in solid phalanx against us, powerfully aided by Northern sympathizers and European allies."

Two days later, Abraham Lincoln responded to Greeley's article with a letter of his own. He tried to defend himself and correct errors and suppositions, and he forgave the accusatory tone, waiving it "in deference to an old friend, whose heart I have always supposed to be right."

The president cut straight to the quick: he wanted to save and restore the Union above everything else, regardless of whether slavery continued or ceased.

Lincoln continued: "My paramount object, in this struggle is to save the Union, and is not either to save or destroy Slavery. If I could save the Union without freeing any slave I would do it. . . . What I do about slavery and the colored race, I do because I believe it helps to save the Union and what I forbear I forbear because I do not believe it would help to save the Union."

He concluded: "I shall do less whenever I shall believe what I am doing hurts the cause, and I shall do more whenever I shall believe doing more will help the cause. . . . I shall adopt new views so fast as they shall appear to be true views."

Needless to say, the letter Lincoln intended to please everyone pleased no one.

❧

HARRIET BEECHER STOWE WAS ALSO FURIOUS THAT LINCOLN HAD overruled and fired Frémont, and she, too, had started calling for immediate emancipation by presidential proclamation. When Stowe read Lincoln's response to Greeley's plea, she countered with a biting biblical-themed parody in the *New York Independent* on September 11, 1862, rewriting Lincoln's words to reflect the priorities of "the King of kings": "My paramount object in this struggle is to set at liberty them that are bruised, and not either to save or destroy the Union. What I do in favor of the Union, I do because it helps to free the oppressed; what I forbear, I forbear because it does not help to free the oppressed. I shall do less for the Union whenever it would hurt the cause of the slave, and more when I believe it would help the cause of the slave."[64] Stowe and others kept hammering away at Lincoln, and they would soon see nation-shifting results.

WHISPERS OF LIBERTY

Eleven days after Stowe's parody appeared in the *New York Independent*, Abraham Lincoln released a copy of the preliminary Emancipation Proclamation. It was September 22, 1862. This early version included compensation for slave owners and resettlement of emancipated slaves. Both provisions were dropped from the final proclamation. Lincoln announced that he would sign the proclamation exactly one hundred days later, on the first of January.

Stowe and her fellow abolitionists were not confident that Lincoln would fulfill his promise. How could they ensure that political pressure from the South, and from slavery-approving states in the Union, wouldn't prevent Lincoln from following through on his commitment? Stowe's brother Henry was especially skeptical, saying, "It's far easier to slide down on the bannisters than to go up the stairs."[65]

❦

HARRIET BEECHER STOWE PROVED TO BE A SAVVY POLITICAL PRO-moter. She regularly approached northern politicians with her ideas, including US senator Charles Sumner, Chief Justice Salmon P. Chase, and one-time presidential candidate John Charles Frémont.

Finally, tired of Lincoln's slowness to proclaim an immediate emancipation, Stowe decided to personally approach the president. She wrote to her publisher on November 14, 1862, "I am going to Washington to see the heads of department myself and to satisfy myself that I may refer to the Emancipation Proclamation as a reality and a substance not to fizzle out at the little end of the hour. . . . I start for Washington tomorrow morning—and mean to have a talk with 'Father Abraham' himself."[66]

On Tuesday, November 25, 1862, ten years after the publication of *Uncle Tom's Cabin*, Harriet Beecher Stowe met with the president in Washington, DC. She had taken along her daughter Hattie and her sister, Isabella Beecher Hooker.

Though there is no document or diary entry detailing all that was said in the meeting or meetings Harriet had with the president in late November 1862, it seems to have been a very jovial affair. Harriet wrote to her husband, Calvin, that she had a "really funny interview with the President." The biography of Stowe written decades later by her son and grandson reported that

> Mrs. Stowe, in telling of her interview with Mr. Lincoln . . . dwelt particularly on the rustic pleasantry with which that great man received her. She was introduced into a cosy room where the President had been seated before an open fire, for the day was damp and chilly. It was Mr. Seward who introduced her, and Mr. Lincoln rose awkwardly from his chair, saying, "Why, Mrs. Stowe, right glad to see you!" Then with a humorous twinkle in his eye, he said, "So you're the little woman who wrote the book that made this great war! Sit down, please," he added, as he seated himself once more before the fire, meditatively warming his immense hands over the smouldering embers by first extending the palms, and then turning his wrists so that the grateful warmth reached the backs of his hands. The first thing he said was, "I do love an open fire. . . ." "Mr. Lincoln," said Mrs. Stowe, "I want to ask you about your views on emancipation." It was on that subject that the conversation turned.[67]*

---

* Stowe's daughter Hattie wrote to her twin sister, Eliza, that "it was a very droll time that we had at the White House I assure you. . . . I will only say now that it was all very funny—and we were ready to explode with laughter all the while." Once the women returned to their

Stowe's meeting with the president evidently changed her opinion of him.* She wrote to her publisher, on November 27, "It seems to be the opinion here not only that the president will stand up to his Proclamation but that the Border states will accede to his proposition for Emancipation—I have noted the thing as a glorious expectancy!"[68]

WOMEN AT WAR

Harriet Beecher Stowe was simultaneously fighting the war against slavery on another front. It had been nine and a half years since the women of Great Britain had presented her with twenty-six massive, leather-bound books filled with 563,000 signatures, begging their American sisters to pursue the immediate abolition of slavery. But the demand for American cotton continued, and that demand had driven the growth of slavery.

Although the times had changed, the insatiability of human consumption had not. The British had abandoned slavery across their own empire, and yet they were still heavily dependent on southern cotton, and as the Civil War progressed, Stowe observed the proslavery sympathies of Great Britain rising back to the surface.

But Stowe also realized that women could turn the tide. Women could win the war.

She decided to remind her British sisters of their own words. In Washington, she sat down on November 27, 1862, and wrote an article for the *Atlantic Monthly* titled "A Reply to 'The Affectionate and Christian Address of Many Thousands of Women of Great Britain and Ireland to Their Sisters the Women of the United States of America.'"[69]

---

rooms, they apparently "screamed and held our sides while we relieved ourselves of the pent up laughter." Quoted in Elizabeth Brown Pryor, *Six Encounters with Lincoln: A President Confronts Democracy and Its Demons* (New York: Penguin, 2017), 215.

* Stowe would go on to publish a warm report on Lincoln noting his "dry, weary, patient pain." Her article also contains Lincoln's chilling premonition, "Whichever way it ends . . . I have the impression that I sha'n't last long after it's over." Quoted in Harold K. Bush, *Lincoln in His Own Time: A Biographical Chronicle of His Life, Drawn from Recollections, Interviews, and Memoirs from Family, Friends, and Associates* (Iowa City: University of Iowa Press, 2011), 111.

Stowe wrote plainly and to the point: "It is an unaccountable fact, and one which we entreat you seriously to ponder, that the party which has brought the cause of freedom thus far on its way, during the past eventful year, has found little or no support in England. Sadder than this, the party which makes slavery the chief corner-stone of its edifice finds in England its strongest defenders."

Stowe encouraged British women to get on board with the Union cause, lest American progressives leave England behind. "We loved England; we respected, revered her; we were bound to her by ties of blood and race. Alas! must all these declarations be written in the past tense?"

Stowe pointed out that France and the rest of continent immediately saw the justice of the Union cause, and England was the European exception. She called out the English Navy for considering lending their boats to the Confederacy, and skewered the British Evangelical Alliance and the British Christian newspapers for refusing to side with "the liberating party."

Finally, Stowe invoked God's blessing on her endeavor and invited British women to join the cause of abolition: "Mark our words! If we succeed, the children of these very men who are now fighting us will rise up to call us blessed. . . . We appeal to you, then, as sisters, as wives, and as mothers, to raise your voices to your fellow-citizens and your prayers to God for the removal of this affliction and disgrace from the Christian world."[70]

Although France and Britain remained officially neutral, elites in both nations tended to favor the Confederacy. Slavery was immensely profitable, making it attractive even for nations that had already banned it domestically. Just as we capitalize on the low wages in poor countries today for our clothing, France and Britain enjoyed their steady shipments of inexpensive American cotton, Caribbean sugar, Brazilian coffee, and other slave imports, such as tobacco and grain, in the 1800s. Just as we today sell guns to African, Middle Eastern, and South American warlords, Britain's industrialists were all too happy to sell munitions to the South, enough so that Lincoln had to commission 500 ships to form a 3,500-mile-long blockade to prevent them from arming the enemy to the teeth.[71]

A New Year

> I break your bonds and masterships,
> And I unchain the slave:
> Free be his heart and hand henceforth,
> As wind and wandering wave.

—Ralph Waldo Emerson, "Boston Hymn," 1862

At around 2:00 p.m. on the first day of the New Year in 1863, President Abraham Lincoln walked into the study in the White House—then called the Executive Mansion. He picked up a steel pen and dipped it into a two-chamber inkwell filled with purple-black iron gall ink. His hand trembled. He had just shaken hands for three straight hours with the attendees at a party, and he didn't want anyone to think that his signature was shaky because he was still uncertain about his action.[72]

Lincoln steadied his hand and signed his final version of the Emancipation Proclamation. He had finally come to the conclusion that it was not only a military necessity, but also an act of supreme justice. Later in the day, he reportedly said, "I never, in my life, felt more certain that I was doing right than I do in signing this paper. If my name ever goes into history it will be for this act, and my whole soul is in it." With the stroke of a pen, three million slaves were unbound from their legal chains.

The news echoed through the telegraph wires from Washington, DC, spreading like a shockwave through the nation. Crowds that had waited all day for the news erupted with excitement. Lincoln had done it. Henry Ward Beecher declared, "The Proclamation may not free a single slave, but it gives liberty a moral recognition."[73]

Harriet Beecher Stowe attended a New Year's Day concert at the Boston Music Hall. The three-thousand-person event was studded with a sparkling galaxy of literary luminaries, including John Greenleaf Whittier, Oliver Wendell Holmes, Frederick Douglass, William Lloyd Garrison, and Henry Wadsworth Longfellow. Henry David Thoreau, who had written and railed and spent time in prison in righteous civil disobedience against the slavery-approving nation, had died just a few months earlier and was unable to see the fruits of his labor.

Ralph Waldo Emerson surprised the audience with a poem he had written for the occasion, entitled "Boston Hymn."[74] According to the music critic John Sullivan Dwight, "an electric thrill" tore through the crowd as the poem was read. It became famous almost immediately and was later adopted as the anthem of an all-black regiment in South Carolina.

When news of the Emancipation Proclamation broke over the wires, the city of Boston burst into pandemonium. The music hall crowd started chanting, "Harriet Beecher Stowe! Harriet Beecher Stowe! Harriet Beecher Stowe!"

❧

UNCLE TOM'S CABIN FOREVER CHANGED HOW AMERICANS VIEWED slavery. Stowe's conversational writing style inspired people in a way that political speeches could not. It personalized the arguments about slavery and helped Americans determine what kind of country they wanted to create. *Uncle Tom's Cabin* demanded that America deliver on her promise of freedom and equality for all.

Some historians think it's unlikely that Lincoln ever read *Uncle Tom's Cabin*, and the president himself admitted he avoided novels. But it is impossible to believe that Lincoln was not at least familiar with Stowe's work. Is it conceivable that, at a pivotal moment in history, Lincoln could have avoided reading America's most popular and divisive book? As the novelist and political essayist George Sand wrote from France, it was "no longer permissible to those who can read not to have read it."[75]

Although slavery likely would have eventually ended even without Stowe's novel, the simple fact remains that without *Uncle Tom's Cabin*, there may not have been a President Abraham Lincoln. The Republican Party, of which Lincoln was the leader, had distributed 100,000 copies of *Uncle Tom's Cabin* during the election campaigns of 1860 as a way to stir up abolitionist support for the party. Lincoln received almost no support from the South, and slavery was the hot-button issue of the election. Without the abolitionist press and *Uncle Tom's Cabin* in Lincoln's corner, there's no telling whether John C. Breckinridge's Democrats might not have won the day. As Radical Republican leader and US senator Charles Sumner declared, "Had there been no *Uncle Tom's Cabin*, there would have been no Lincoln in the White House." And without Lincoln, there may have been no reuniting of the United States of America.

According to the Library of Congress's circulation records, President Lincoln borrowed *The Key to Uncle Tom's Cabin* on June 16, 1862, and returned it forty-three days later, on July 29. The dates correspond exactly to the time during which he drafted his "Proclamation of Emancipation."

We may never know the degree to which Harriet Beecher Stowe influenced Abraham Lincoln himself. But it is clear that the northern writer used her celebrity platform to powerfully sway public opinion toward emancipation. And during the critical time when Lincoln was crafting the Emancipation Proclamation, he had Stowe's *Key* near at hand.

∽≈∾

LINCOLN'S EMANCIPATION PROCLAMATION DECLARED THAT ALL slaves in states that were "in rebellion against the United States" were to be "thenceforward, and forever free," and that the government and the military would recognize and maintain their freedom. He added an incredibly personal touch to an otherwise legal-heavy document, encouraging the newly freed slaves to abstain from violence, except in self-defense, and to "labor faithfully for reasonable wages." He then offered them work in the US Army.

The proclamation, like most policy documents and laws, was not, by any means, perfect. Because it only addressed states in the Confederacy, it completely exempted many areas of the country, including forty-eight counties in Virginia, twelve parishes in Louisiana, and all of Tennessee, along with the Union states, including Josiah's home state of Maryland.

Frederick Douglass called it "the first step on the part of the nation in its departure from the [bondage] of the ages."[76]

Douglass and Lincoln both understood that the proclamation was only a temporary military measure—only Congress, in fact, could permanently abolish slavery in the whole United States. But it was a brilliant tactical move nonetheless. Lincoln's decision likely kept England and France from intervening for the Confederacy to retain the economic benefits of slave-subsidized cotton. The proclamation deprived the South of a massive valuable slave labor force. Lincoln himself declared it a "military necessity." It allowed more than 180,000 former slaves and free black men to fight for and serve the Union Army. As the Civil War dragged on for two more years, nearly half of them would die in combat.

Without black freedom, America as we know it simply would not exist.

FREEDOM IN MARYLAND

Though Josiah's home state of Maryland remained a part of the Union and later dubbed itself the "Free State," at the time it was in no hurry to give up slavery. Since Maryland was excluded from the Emancipation Proclamation, the state didn't budge for nearly two years, during which time many Maryland slaves escaped north or to Washington, DC, or joined the Union Army. When Maryland did finally get around to holding a referendum to abolish slavery, on November 1, 1864, it passed by a margin of just 0.006 percent. Out of the nearly 60,000 ballots cast, the scales were tipped in favor of freedom by just 375 votes—and then only after the absentee ballots of Union soldiers were added.[77]

❧

FIVE DAYS AFTER ROBERT E. LEE'S SURRENDER TO ULYSSES S. GRANT, at around 10:15 p.m. on the evening of Good Friday, the twenty-six-year-old Maryland-born stage actor and southern sympathizer John

Wilkes Booth walked into Ford's Theatre in Washington, DC, raised his Philadelphia Derringer pistol, and shot President Abraham Lincoln in the back of the head from a distance of less than four feet.*

The creator of the Emancipation Proclamation would die nine hours later, at 7:22 a.m. on Saturday, April 15, 1865, in a house across the street from the theater.

Last Train to Springfield

Lincoln's funeral procession left Washington and passed through 7 states and 444 communities on its 13-day, 1,654-mile journey. More than 7 million people observed some part of the procession. It remains the largest non-televised funeral in American history.

With few exceptions, the crowds were segregated by race in nearly every city Lincoln's body passed through. It arrived in Springfield, Illinois, on May 3, 1865, where two African American ministers, Rev. Henry Brown and Rev. William C. Trevan, led Lincoln's cortege to the burial site. Lincoln's barber of twenty-four years, William de Fleurville, declined to join the front of the funeral procession, but instead chose to walk in the rear, where Springfield's African American delegation had been positioned.

The Great Emancipator was gone.

The Battle Is Ended

Less than one week after Lincoln's burial, and exactly one month after General Robert E. Lee's surrender, on May 9, 1865, the new president, Andrew Johnson, officially declared the end of the Civil War. Confederate president Jefferson Davis was captured the following day, evidently disguised in his wife's overcoat and shawl.[78]

---

* Three days earlier, the well-known actor had attended a speech at the White House. Afterward, he said to coconspirator Lewis Powell, "That means nigger citizenship. Now, by God, I'll put him through. That is the last speech he will ever give."

We cannot underestimate the importance of the Civil War in the erad-ication of slavery. In 1850, the future of American slavery seemed bright. One US census superintendent estimated that the slave population would reach 10.6 million by the year 1910, and an Alabama politician hoped for 31 million by the following decade.[79] In 1856, the *Southern Literary Messenger* dreamed of the year 1950 and predicted that the American slave population by then would top 100 million. The following year, the *Charleston Mercury* declared that "the wants of white men must triumph over the negro's absurd claim to liberty."[80] Clearly, southern plantation society would not die willingly. South Carolina slave owner and sena-tor James Henry Hammond insisted that "sugar, rice, tobacco, coffee . . . can never be produced as articles of wide extended commerce, except by slave labour."[81] Slavery was outrageously profitable, even by today's most egregious capitalistic standards. Without the introduction of modern in-dustrial agricultural equipment—and the Union boot that snapped the Confederacy's neck—we might still own slaves today.

FIVE-FIFTHS

In an act long overdue for the land of liberty, President Johnson's new government proposed an amendment to the US Constitution. The Con-stitution had been amended only twelve times before, and the Thirteenth Amendment took dozens of forms before it was passed.

The amendment was passed by the Senate on April 8, 1864, and moved on to the House, where, on January 31, 1865, it passed by a margin of just seven votes. The required number of states ratified the amendment on December 6, 1865, and twelve days later, Secretary of State William H. Seward proclaimed its adoption. The Thirteenth Amendment's wording was short but groundbreaking: "Neither slavery nor involuntary servitude, except as a punishment for crime whereof the party shall have been duly convicted, shall exist within the United States, or any place subject to their jurisdiction. Congress shall have power to enforce this article by appropriate legislation."

After centuries of cruel enslavement in the United States of America, the institution of slavery was officially abolished throughout the nation. Four million black people were now free, finally considered fully human—five-fifths—in the eyes of the federal government.

The Underground Railroad—and the fugitive settlement at Dawn—were no longer necessary.

RESOLUTION

The case of *Scoble v. Brown* over the management of the BAI dragged on for seven years. In 1863, Scoble's shrewd Toronto lawyer requested that the court appoint a receiver to reimburse his client for certain expenses and legal costs, and for some reason, the court accepted the suggestion. Unfortunately, the BAI property no longer produced sufficient revenue to cover the costs, and it fell into receivership. William Wright's son-in-law, Alex Trerice, served as the court-appointed receiver for the next five years.

On the other side, Josiah continued to foot the bill for James C. Brown in hopes of redeeming the BAI. Josiah later wrote: "In the beginning I paid two hundred dollars, and borrowed money from time to time by mortgaging, first one house and lot, then three houses and lots, then re-mortgaged them, then sold several lots to pay the mortgages, then re-mortgaged, and was constantly called upon to pay disbursements to the lawyers."[82]

The lawsuit was long and wearying, and Josiah eventually ran out of credit. The Toronto lawyer offered to settle if his expenses were paid. It had been a long and hard battle, and all sides agreed.

On March 24, 1868, the newspaper reported that "after a determined fight of seven years' duration in which the better nature of Mr. Henson was most creditably shown, and in which he sunk much of his means," a decree was granted by which Scoble's control ceased.[83]

After sixteen long and contentious years, John Scoble left Dawn for good. The court appointed a new board, which consisted of James C.

Brown, among others, and incorporated the property with a new name: the Wilberforce Institute.*

THE LAST AUCTION

The new trustees used their power to sell the BAI lands, with plans to use the profits to endow an institute in Chatham. They sectioned the land into lots, with one and a half acres set aside for a market and another six for a cemetery. The board transacted a number of private sales at different times, and then held a public auction on January 13, 1871. A large number of people from Dawn, Dresden, and Fairport snapped up plots of land. In total, the BAI properties sold for nearly $40,000. The trustees paid off the debts from the Scoble era of $8,000 and had more than $30,000 left over.†

WILBERFORCE NORTH

In 1872, nearby Dresden incorporated as a village, and in 1873 the Wilberforce Institute built a four-room brick schoolhouse for $3,500. On March 29, 1873, the institute received a royal assent to merge with another school to form the Wilberforce Educational Institute of Chatham, Ontario. The new school was exclusively for black students and offered courses at all levels, from elementary school to university.[84]

❧

---

* The new school was named after William Wilberforce, the English politician who led the movement to end the British slave trade for twenty years.

† Thirty thousand dollars in 1871 would have a real price of $608,000 today. An unskilled worker would need to earn $4 million to earn the modern equivalent of $30,000, or $8 million using production worker compensation. Thirty thousand dollars had the economic status of $9.24 million today and the economic power of $72.9 million. In other words, in 1871 it was a massive sum.

JAMES C. BROWN WAS LAUDED FOR HIS TENACITY IN WINNING THE lawsuit, but with John Scoble gone, Josiah bore the brunt of responsibility for the BAI's failure. To be sure, Josiah did not play his cards well. He blamed many of his early faults on the system of slavery, but he changed little in later life. William King, leader of the Elgin Settlement just twenty-six miles south of Dawn, wrote, years later, that "Henson was more than a match for anyone that ever tried to curb his authority, or to call him to an account."[85]

Josiah had been unable to provide the stable leadership that Dawn needed. He had many wonderful qualities, but flaws as well, and those flaws would cause him no small measure of harm in his life. He lacked the critical thinking skills and foresight that could have allowed him to run the school efficiently. He didn't question anyone who flattered or encouraged him, and Scoble had taken advantage of it.

At the end of the day, virtually all of the criticism leveled at Josiah came from three people: Shadd, Newman, and Brown, and their motivations and agendas were decidedly Garrisonian American Baptist from the outset. Once Scoble got involved, there was little hope for Josiah's reputation to survive unscathed, as he clearly sided with the wrong man. But while Newman and Shadd did much to nourish doubts about Josiah's aptitude, they went too far by maligning his character, and none of their investigations produced anything more than ambiguous fault-finding. Despite being accused constantly, and being called before committees and hearings to defend himself, and despite the unending newspaper vitriol from Newman and Shadd, no one ever brought forth any actual proof of wrongdoing on Josiah's part. He hadn't become a wealthy duke or industrial baron. He didn't have fancy clothes or carriages. Nancy and his daughters weren't adorned in jewels. No doubt jealousy played a large role, however; nor can we rule out the massive confusion that abounded in simply defining Dawn versus the BAI, or ignore the war for resources that existed between the black colonies. James C. Brown was a Chatham man and insisted that the BAI should be owned by "the colored people of Canada" in general, instead of by the people of Dawn specifically. In the end, Brown succeeded when the BAI's wealth was transferred to the new Wilberforce Institute in his hometown of Chatham.

Speaking about Scoble and Josiah, *The Anti-Slavery Reporter* wrote: "Their honours, their exercise of authority, their emoluments, awakened jealousies around; and these stimulated murmuring, and refactoriness, and intrigues. . . . Under these circumstances, what could be expected but the result that followed?"

In fairness to Josiah, the controversy that grew around him wasn't over Henson himself so much as over what he represented. Those who hated *Uncle Tom's Cabin*—either because it seemed anti-South or degrading to blacks—disliked Josiah because of his fictional connection. Among abolitionists, Josiah found it impossible to win everyone's approval, as the warring camps remained at odds. He was also caught in a denominational battle between the American Baptists and the British Congregationalists.

The British American Institute was completely and utterly financially unsustainable from day one. It's absolutely remarkable and greatly to Josiah's credit that it lasted as long as it did and was able to serve as many people as it had. It was impossible for the school to pay for itself by having students work three or four hours each day. In the early years, their labor was absorbed just in clearing the land, and all other financial support needed to be raised from outside sources. Hiram Wilson had to spend much of his time fundraising overseas, and the original board didn't have the capacity to take up the slack. When the board members did help out, they had to be paid for their time, which required even more money to be raised.

The Anti-Slavery Reporter summed it up well: "In looking at the actual state of matters we need scarcely wonder at the result. To raise an institution of learning here were 300 acres of wild land in a remote and unsettled part of the country. The men to work the bush farm and carry out the plan were a few escaped slaves."[86]

Still, while scorned by some, he was loved by more. Josiah is one of the best representations of both human frailty and human greatness in history. If he was self-serving in some ways, he certainly did far more to help those around him than most. Josiah had raised untold sums of money for the community, yet he never had an official say in how the money would be spent. He was never a trustee, and there's little evidence that he was ever anything more than a fundraising agent who occasionally served on the BAI's executive committee. The BAI was always run by white men.

Hiram Wilson was a dreamer who picked fights with others. Samuel H. Davis was biased toward the American Baptists. John Scoble was selfish and polarizing toward the black settlers. The BAI failed as a result of poor management, religious sectarianism, and black factionalism. Dawn failed, in part, because of a lack of unity.

Despite his lack of official involvement, Josiah served as the patriarch of Dawn and as a spokesman for Canada's growing black population. He used both roles as a way to raise funds for his mission. Historians must conclude that his motives, for the most part, were appropriate for the needs of Dawn, the BAI, and his own family. His opponents were wrong. Josiah was a larger-than-life personality who was caught in a maelstrom of abolitionist ideologies, warring denominations, petty jealousies, serious rivalries, racism, paternalism, overwhelming need, and a chronic cash-flow problem.

Josiah's work at the BAI was done, even undone. The younger generations went to seek their fortunes in the newly emancipated United States. Josiah continued on his own path, doing the task to which he had been called.

So what did he think of all this? How did Josiah feel about the constant slander, the unproven accusations, and the ongoing character assassination? If he felt it, he never mentioned it. Josiah simply went about his business, working hard and plowing the profits back into his community. He knew his mission in life—to spread abolitionist ideas and the Christian faith, to educate young people, and to help those in need—and he didn't stop for anyone or anything. Josiah spoke and preached often, sometimes three times on Sundays, with the aim of spreading the gospel and changing public sentiment about black people. His aim was to make blacks educationally and economically equal to whites in order to break down prejudice and gain their respect.

As with any refugee camp or workers' collective, the Dawn Settlement was bound to collapse in the long run. In fact, all the black settlements in Canada disappeared in time. The needs of the communities were too great, the available resources too few. Moreover, after the Emancipation Proclamation, many former slaves simply returned to America as free citizens of a nation reborn. Dawn and the BAI had served its purpose, in a sense, and then it simply faded away.

The attempt had been laudable. As *The Voice of the Fugitive* wrote of Josiah: "The executive talent which could collect, organize and control a colony of runaway slaves and shape out of such hopeless material a virtuous and self-respecting community can hardly be inferior to that which fills with the highest credit the first places of our nation."

The land had provided decades of food. The forest had provided the lumber that had sheltered five hundred souls. The BAI had educated hundreds of black, white, and native students. The Dawn Settlement had provided jobs for many and served as an inspirational focal point for the abolitionist movement. Finally, the BAI had ended with the modern equivalent of millions in assets to its name, making way for a new and necessary work that better fit the needs of the time. It had fulfilled people's needs as well as it could for more than a decade, closed its doors when it was no longer needed, and donated its assets to help start a new endeavor.

Hiram Wilson had had a dream. The dream never would have gotten off the ground without James Canning Fuller and his British Quaker donors. Credit must also be given to Amos Lawrence and his Boston philanthropists, along with British and American donors, for patiently sustaining the work for a decade. James C. Fuller should be applauded for leading the lawsuit. Even William P. Newman, Samuel H. Davis, and John Scoble deserve some sliver of credit for Dawn's successes, simply because they cared enough to be involved.

And then there was Josiah Henson. He shared Hiram's dream. He found the ideal spot to settle. He continually used his fame to raise money on behalf of the community. He risked his life to rescue slaves, and he traveled the world to spread the message about their cause. He raised the funds to build the gristmill, and he boldly repatriated it when it was threatened with destruction. He borrowed the funds to build the sawmill, and he raised the funds to pay that money back. When it came to the final showdown with Scoble, who funded the lawsuit? Mary Ann Shadd failed to raise the funds, as did James C. Brown with his call to the other black settlements. Samuel H. Davis's committee of seven was unable to raise the money as well. Josiah not only succeeded, but he served as Dawn's patriarch for more than twenty-five years. Though he was not perfect, by any means, he had shouldered more of the labor, more of the debts, and more of the worries than anyone.

And, in the end, he was left with less than anyone.

Josiah, nearing ninety years old, was near bankruptcy. His landholdings and life savings had been decimated, and his home and farm were leveraged to the hilt. He may have owed upward of $8,000—it could take the average worker ten years to pay off such a debt. He described feeling as if a heavy weight "was pressing down my spirits and embarrassing my declining years when I could not labour as formerly."[87] After all the good he'd done throughout his long life, he faced this last challenge: if he couldn't find a way to pay off his debts, he could lose his home and the family farm.

TEN

HOMECOMING

The righteous shall flourish like the palm tree:
he shall grow like a cedar in Lebanon.
Those that be planted in the House of the Lord
shall flourish in the courts of our God.
They shall still bring forth fruit in old age . . .

—PSALM 92:12–14 (KJV)

REV. THOMAS HUGHES, THE SECRETARY OF THE COLONIAL AND Continental Missionary Church Society in Canada and a long-time missionary, had an idea. He had been a friend of Josiah's for nearly seventeen years, and he knew about Josiah's sacrifices for the BAI and his crippled finances. He proposed that Josiah, despite his old age, make one final visit to London. He assured him that his old friends would rally to help.

Hughes[*] wrote an article about Josiah's mission to London in the annual report of the Colonial and Continental Missionary Church Society:

---

[*] Rev. Hughes died on April 11, 1876, three months before Josiah left Canada. Josiah later wrote: "It was a sad day to me. . . . I was summoned to his dying bedside. His last moments were peaceful, and his faith to the last was triumphant. He died as he had lived, a genuine Christian."

Josiah Henson (Mrs. Stowe's "Uncle Tom"), who, I think you are aware, resides near Dresden, proposes starting in a week or two for England. His principal object will be to try to raise money to clear off a heavy mortgage he had to give on his farm in order to meet the costs of the long lawsuit over the Dawn Institute property, and which but for him would have been entirely lost. Mr. Henson bore the whole expense of that suit, and when the case was settled it was found that the trustees, appointed by the Court of Chancery, had no power to refund him out of the estate. The proceeds of the sale of the Dawn property, nearly 30,000 dollars, constitute the greater part of the endowment of the Wilberforce Educational Institute. You will be pleased to learn that this institute is now in active operation, and if only wisely managed in the future will be a great blessing, in an educational point of view, to the coloured people of Canada. A voyage to England is no light undertaking for a man of Henson's extreme age, he being now eighty-seven. Though he is not by any means the man he was when in England twenty-five years ago, yet he still possesses extraordinary energy both of body and mind, and knowing, as I do, his circumstances, and the hardship of his case, I sincerely hope he may be successful.

As word spread that Josiah was intending to visit England, Hughes encouraged many of Josiah's friends to write testimonials. With Hughes's help, Josiah received letters of commendation from a missionary, a society secretary, a judge, a sheriff, a mayor, an archdeacon, and a justice of the peace. Their introductions were kind and warm, and spoke of his "sterling Christian character." They informed the British that Josiah "occupied a foremost place in all movements for the advancement of his people," and was "a great blessing to his coloured brethren in Canada." More than anything, Josiah's life simply spoke for itself: "for the last forty-five years; that he has ever borne the highest character in this community, and is worthy of the confidence of the public."[1]

Armed with glowing letters of commendation, Josiah and Nancy made their way from Dawn to Boston.

REUNION

By the time Josiah arrived in the late summer of 1876, it had been twenty-five years since he had last been in London, and he was delighted to be back in a city of such happy memories. Many of his friends had passed away, but some remained. Thomas Church, author of *Gospel Victories*, and his family gladly welcomed Josiah as they had in 1851. Samuel Morley and George Sturge remembered him fondly. Sturge assured Josiah he would send him back to Canada with a light heart, and Josiah quipped he would then be "heavy with gratitude."

Josiah made some new friends in London, including Dr. James Macaulay, editor of the *Religious Tract Society* and the popular monthly magazine *Sunday at Home*, who wrote an article in the October issue entitled "Uncle Tom" to stir up churches to support Josiah in his quest to pay off the lawsuit debts.

Another new friend was Professor Fowler,* who studied the pseudo-science of the time, phrenology—based on the belief that the characteristics of human skulls indicate character and mental ability.[2] Dr. Fowler made an analysis of Josiah's head, and Josiah joked that he guessed his old master had beaten out all his brains, but Fowler remarked that perhaps Josiah's "skull was so thick, the blows did not penetrate."[3]

Josiah's portrait, along with Fowler's amusing analysis, were published in *The Christian Age*, a weekly newspaper with a circulation of eighty thousand:

> The organisation of "Uncle Tom" is as remarkable as his life and labours have been. . . . The strength of his social nature centres in love to his wife and children. . . . No white man has a greater sense of liberty, love of freedom, manliness of feeling, and independence of mind, joined to a degree of firmness, perseverance, and determination of mind, not exceeded by a Cromwell or a Wellington, than Uncle Tom. . . .

---

* This was probably Orson Squire Fowler, who was a friend of Harriet Beecher Stowe's brother, but may have been Orson's brother, Lorenzo Niles Fowler.

He has by organisation, as well as by grace, a strong feeling of devotion, worship, and sense of dependence. As a Christian, some of his strongest religious feelings are his love of prayer and thankfulness. . . . He is liable to forget his own interests when he can make himself useful to others. In his mind, "faith without works is dead." He does not expect an answer to his prayers without he makes an effort in the right direction.

He has a vast amount of dry humour. . . . He is a great lover of simple truths; acts and speaks just as he feels, and thinks instinctively. . . . Though in his eighty-eighth year, he appears to be at least fifteen years younger, for he is firm in step, erect in form, disposed to wait on himself, and prefers to walk rather than ride; is positive in his manner of speaking, social in his disposition, emotional in his feelings, tender in his sympathies, distinct in his intellectual operations, humorous in his conversation, and apt in his illustrations.

I have been much gratified in making the acquaintance of "Uncle Tom," and hope the friends of the coloured race in England will send him back to Canada with sufficient means to enable him to live in comfort the remainder of his days.

Quite the report, considering the professor only looked at his head. Fowler would not be the only showman to join the Josiah Henson promotional committee.

THE PITCH MAN

Another man who befriended Josiah was John Lobb, the youthful managing editor of *The Christian Age*. Lobb was unbelievably (perhaps embarrassingly) good at marketing, having recently grown his paper's circulation from five thousand to eighty thousand. Morley and Sturge asked for Lobb's help in marketing the "real Uncle Tom," and Lobb seized on the opportunity with gusto in August 1876. He was well-connected with most of the evangelical ministers in London, and he took on the role of managing Josiah's speaking schedule.

Soon Lobb was the unofficial chairman of the fundraising effort to relieve Josiah of his lawsuit debts. The master marketer started a collection called "Uncle Tom's Fund," and shuttled Josiah around on a whirlwind book tour. Money began to pour in. Soon both men became the talk of England.

Considering his age—eighty-seven—Josiah's speaking schedule was impressive. It comprised ninety events in quick succession, with church crowds often numbering into the thousands. Josiah spoke at art galleries, city halls, and private dinner parties. He spoke to packed halls, chapels, and schoolrooms. He addressed the employees of George Williams, founder of the YMCA, and spoke twice at the famed Brighton Pavilion, a former royal residence. Josiah toured Vice-Admiral Horatio Nelson's 104-gun flagship HMS *Victory*, entertained 500 children at George Müller's orphanage, and handed out half-pennies to the 250 boys in C. H. Spurgeon's Stockwell orphanage.

Josiah felt obligated to repay Lobb for his help and unwittingly overpaid him, assigning the sole copyright of his memoir to the magazine editor.

Lobb swiftly created a "revised and enlarged" London edition of Josiah's memoirs, hardbound in green and gold. He kept Harriet Beecher Stowe's preface, but added several photos, an index, and an introduction by the abolitionists George Sturge and Samuel Morley. The title of the new edition, published in 1876, was *"Uncle Tom's Story of His Life": An Autobiography of the Rev. Josiah Henson*, with Lobb's name appearing just as big as Josiah's. The pitchman made Josiah promise that this new version would be the "only authorized edition."[4]

It was the first edition that directly connected Josiah with the character of Uncle Tom, and the book sold 30,000 copies in its first six weeks. It went on to sell 96,000 copies total. It is unlikely that Josiah received any of the profits from the so-called authorized edition of his life story.

The culmination of Josiah's visit was a massive farewell meeting at the Metropolitan Tabernacle, the largest church of its day, whose pastor was the legendary C. H. Spurgeon. Lobb marketed the event in *The Times*, the *Daily News*, and every other London paper he could think of, then dutifully reported that nearly six thousand people had been present for the raucous affair. Spurgeon started with a devotional, then Lobb worked the crowd into a frenzy with a rousing introduction. When Josiah took the stage, it brought down the house.

The ever-angling editor was able to open many doors for Josiah, including that of the very woman who represented freedom to a former slave such as himself.

On the day prior to meeting Josiah in person, Queen Victoria read Lobb's "autobiography" of Josiah's life and then wrote in her journal: "Reading in that most interesting book the Life of Mr. Josiah Henson, a fugitive slave & the original of Mrs. B. Stowe's 'Uncle Tom's Cabin.' He is now in his 88th year, & his sufferings, energy, patient endurance, & his anxiety for the good of his suffering brethren, are admirable."[5]

Josiah mentions Queen Victoria several times in his memoirs, and it is very obvious that he is in awe of her. The royal Victoria, the very embodiment of Britannia, was a living symbol of emancipation and freedom to him. She was the regent who ruled the empire whose colony had been his home and haven for nearly fifty years.

On Monday, March 5, 1877, Josiah, Nancy, and John Lobb rode to Windsor Castle to meet the queen. The savvy Lobb made sure *The Times* reported on the meeting right away:

> On Monday, March the 5th, the Rev. Josiah Henson, the hero of Mrs. Stowe's story of "Uncle Tom's Cabin," left London on a visit to her Majesty at Windsor Castle. . . . Her Majesty expressed pleasurable surprise at the coloured clergyman's strikingly hale and hearty looks, considering his great age. He was born, it will be remembered, on June 15, 1789. Her Majesty was also pleased to say that for many years she had been well acquainted with his history, and presented him with her photograph, signed "Victoria Reg., 1877," and mounted in a handsome ormolu frame. Mr. Henson thanked her Majesty on his own behalf for the great honour conferred upon himself, as well as on behalf of his coloured brethren in Canada and other portions of her Majesty's dominions—for her august protection when they were poor fugitive slaves, and for the unspeakable blessings they had at all times enjoyed under her rule.[6]

Lobb managed to get the *Birmingham Daily Mail* to run an even longer story the following day:

Windsor welcomed a visitor yesterday around whose name and history clusters an exceptional interest. He has done nothing, in the ordinary meaning of the phrase, to win fame. He has produced no work of genius, performed no feat of statesmanship, discovered no new lands. He has not devastated countries with conquest, or colonised them with venturous enterprise. He has done nothing but suffer. He was a slave in the United States when slavery was at the high tide of its cruelty and oppression. He has felt the lash of man-trafficking monsters in human form. He has seen husbands and wives ruthlessly separated for purposes too base to be recalled without a hot tinge of indignation. The Rev. Josiah Henson is a person of rare and special interest, inasmuch as he was the original Uncle Tom of Mrs. Stowe's remarkable novel of slave-life in the Southern States. Who that is over thirty years of age does not remember the deep impression made on the public when that heart-lacerating story made its appearance on this side of the Atlantic? How many thousands of honest British eyes, albeit not used to the melting mood, were wet with the record of poor, patient, noble Tom's sufferings? Who has not laughed over the humour of Topsy's denseness, and wept over the inexpressible pathos of little Eva's death-bed? Who has not flushed with a righteous anger at the merciless cruelties of Simon Legree, and been thrilled with sympathy for Eliza in her wild flight over the broken ice? No story was ever written that had a more iniquitous wrong to redress; no story was ever written that so deeply stirred the hearts and consciences of the English and American people. "Uncle Tom's Cabin" was the death-blow to slavery as an American institution.[7]

As for Queen Victoria, she wrote in her journal later that day: "After luncheon saw, in the Corridor [at Windsor Castle] this most remarkable old man, Josiah Henson, who was during 4[1] years a slave, enduring great sufferings & cruelty & endowed with wonderful courage, energy & patience."[8]

For Josiah, the audience with Queen Victoria was a high point in an already extraordinary life. It no doubt validated his decades of service as a citizen of Her Majesty's colony, and reminded him of his gratitude toward the empire that had offered him freedom. Many years later, after Josiah passed away, his gravestone would be topped with a stone replica of Victoria's crown, a symbol of his undying love for the monarch who represented the freedom he'd dreamed about for forty long years.

A Fond Farewell

Following their visit to Windsor Castle, the Hensons traveled north to Scotland. Josiah accepted as many speaking invitations as his strength would allow and was met by warm crowds across the country. The Scots, in particular, were very generous with the Hensons—even James Adams Wenley, the treasurer and general manager of the Bank of Scotland, made a donation.

John Lobb, more than any other man, made sure to impress upon the public that Josiah was the living Uncle Tom. Josiah appears to have been uncomfortable with the moniker to an extent, and despite how often he was described in the newspapers or introduced at live events as such, he never personally claimed to be Uncle Tom. If anything, he went out of his way to inform the audiences that he was, indeed, his own man. It was a game of push and pull, with Lobb desiring to give his potential book-buying audiences the opportunity to see the real Uncle Tom in the flesh, and Josiah wanting simply to share his story as a means of raising support for his mission.

Josiah addressed this issue with his usual charm in his final appearance in Britain on April 25, 1877:

There has been so much said and written about me, so much read about me, and so many things thought about me, that I did not know that I could do better than come and let you see me.

It has been spread abroad that "'Uncle Tom' is coming," and that is what has brought you here. Now allow me to say that my name is not

Tom, and never was Tom, and that I do not want to have any other name inserted in the newspapers for me than my own. My name is Josiah Henson, always was, and always will be. I never change my colours. I would not if I could, and I could not if I would.*

John Lobb's "Uncle Tom's Fund" raised over £3,000 in less than nine months. Lobb would go on to earn much more because of Josiah's book, of course.

Josiah and Nancy sailed home from Liverpool on April 27, 1877, on board the Cunard line's *China* steamship. They had earned enough to clear all their mortgages and make themselves comfortable in their old age, with several souvenirs to boot. Josiah's favorites were his signed photo of Queen Victoria, a gold watch and chain from tea magnate Frederick John Horniman, a German music box from his wife, and an elegant gold watch, chain, and locket from their Scottish friends in Edinburgh.[9]

After the Hensons arrived in Boston, they went directly home to Dresden, where they stayed for the summer and fall with their children and friends.

While Josiah enjoyed the warm months back in Canada, John Lobb kept as busy as ever on the other side of the Atlantic. No one did more to stoke the association between Josiah Henson and Uncle Tom, and no one profited from it more richly.

Soon Josiah's story was the most popular American slave narrative in Europe. In 1877, translations of his memoir appeared in Danish, Welsh, and two Swedish editions. Dutch and French were added the following year, with a German version for both Germany and US German readers. A Norwegian translation surfaced in 1879, and according to Lobb, the

---

* Josiah's natural inclination when speaking was to use humor. Though some have incorrectly assumed his humor to be prideful or cocky, the content of his talks consistently suggest that he knew how to implement humor as a way to engage audiences and draw people into his far greater and more important message. Consider one of his more brilliant lines, which reveals a greater truth: "Some have asked me 'if those who have been accustomed to a hot climate at the south, do not find the cold Canadian winters long and unpleasant?' I have only one reply to make to that query, *'that cool freedom is far better than hot oppression.'*" Josiah Henson, *"Uncle Tom's Story of His Life": An Autobiography of the Rev. Josiah Henson*, edited by John Lobb (London: Christian Age Office, 1876), 191 (emphasis in original).

narrative had been translated into twelve languages, though only these seven have been found so far.

Later in 1877, Lobb wrote—without Josiah's help—*The Young People's Illustrated Edition of "Uncle Tom's" Story of His Life*. The Earl of Shaftesbury wrote the preface, and Lobb included "Uncle Tom's Address to the Young People of Great Britain," which Josiah probably did not dictate. Lobb's versions sold more than 250,000 copies, but neither Josiah nor his family saw much, if any, profit from these sales.[10]

A RETURN TO ISAAC RILEY'S

As winter approached, Josiah felt an inexpressible longing come over him. Perhaps it was because he was getting older and sensed there wasn't much time left for him. Whatever the reason, he desperately wanted to see his boyhood home in Maryland. Josiah and Nancy set out for the East Coast of the United States in December 1877 and stayed for several months with her family in Baltimore.

On March 3, the Hensons traveled to Washington, where Josiah visited many of his old haunts from his days as Isaac Riley's market man.

Furnished with an introduction from Frederick Douglass, Josiah and Nancy paid a visit to the White House. President Rutherford B. Hayes entertained Josiah in his office while the First Lady showed Nancy around the house. Hayes and Josiah chatted about Josiah's British trip, and Hayes invited him to pay another visit if he was ever in the capital.

From Washington, Josiah and Nancy traveled twelve miles by wagon to his old home in Montgomery County, Maryland. Almost fifty years had passed since he'd last seen the place. He no doubt thought of the day he had turned his back on Isaac as he left to collect his family in Kentucky and march his way to freedom.

Josiah didn't expect Isaac to still be alive; nor did he know what had become of Matilda, Isaac's grasping wife. But he almost unconsciously expected to see the old place nearly as he'd left it. He still pictured a lush plantation, with a crowd of busy slaves planting seeds, plowing the land, and harvesting the valuable crops. He envisioned the big house, well-furnished and housing a luxurious and lazy family. He pictured the outdoor kitchen, where the black cook and her maids had prepared meals for the family. He imagined the barns and storehouses packed with plenty, the cellars filled with cider and apple brandy and fruit. Clearer than all of that, he pictured the little village of huts where he had lived, which had been so full of life and pain and sorrow.

As Josiah reached the plantation, he realized the great change that had come over the land of the slave masters. The property was no longer the rich farm of his boyhood memory. It was little more than wilderness, desolate and barren. The once fertile fields that had waved with corn and rye and oats and barley were now overgrown with trees and underbrush and weeds. The fences had fallen, or been hauled off for firewood, and the orchards were worn and dead.

The lane to the big house was overgrown with grass, and Josiah saw the house standing alone, without a barn or stable or shed to keep it company. The place was so worn down that the windows rattled as the Hensons' carriage pulled up in front.

A black boy came out at the sound of the wheels and stared at the Hensons with his mouth wide open.

"Does Mrs. Riley live here?" Josiah asked.[11]

"Yes, sir."

"Is she at home?"

"Yes, sir."

"Can she be seen?"

The boy explained she was sick, and hadn't been out of bed all day.

"Well," Josiah said. "I have come a long distance on purpose to see her."

"I'll ask," the boy said. He turned and vanished into the house. Josiah soon heard a whining voice ask, "Who is he?"

"Dunno!" the boy replied. "He's a black gemman."

"And he wants to see me? Well, tell him to come in."

Josiah and Nancy went in, and sure enough, there was Matilda Riley. Instead of a young, blossoming woman of twenty, she was a poor and frightened seventy-year-old invalid. Josiah looked around the room. Matilda's bed was in the old sitting room, which was the first place that felt familiar to him. The old corner cupboard, where Isaac used to keep his brandy, was just as it was fifty years ago. The room was the same, but the furniture was dilapidated, and the floor was completely bare.

Josiah went up to her and bowed.

"How do you do, madam?" he said.[12]

"I am poorly," Matilda complained, "Poorly. How do you do?"

"I am well, thank you."

"I—I don't seem to know you," Matilda said. She looked hard at Josiah, trying to recall the old face before her.

"Is that so?" Josiah teased. "You have seen me many a time."

Matilda thought for a moment, and suddenly it sprang to her mind.

"Can it be Si?" she asked.

"Yes, madam."

"Not Si Henson!—surely, surely, it can never be!"

"Yes, madam."

Matilda Riley burst into tears "Si, your master is dead and gone!"

Isaac Riley had died almost thirty years earlier, on July 5, 1850, around the same time Josiah had been planning to head to the World's Fair, and just two months after the passing of the Fugitive Slave Act. After losing Josiah's prudent financial management, the drunken Isaac Riley had died nearly impoverished. Yet he had somehow managed to cling to the Old Georgetown Road property, close to three hundred acres,* along with five slaves, four of them children.

"No, madam," Josiah replied. "My master is alive."

"I mean Mr. Riley. If only he was here you would be good friends now; I know you would. You were always a good man, Si. I never blamed you for running away. Oh! Si, don't you wish you could see your old master again?"

Josiah tried to say yes, and shed a tear with her, but he "couldn't get up a real honest cry," so he gave up. Matilda inspected Josiah more closely.

---

* Local legend identifies the property as the "scene of many activities of the Southern army. . . . [T]hey were camped on the grounds on their way to Washington." If true, it adds to the pattern of Montgomery County's white slaveholders being southern sympathizers during the Civil War.

"Why, Si, you are a gentleman!"

"I always was, madam."

"Yes, but you are rich! What have you brought me?"

"Nothing," Josiah said. "I came to see if you had anything to give me!"

"Oh, no. We are poor; poor, Si. We do all our own work, my daughter and granddaughters; and we don't have much to eat even."

Nancy interrupted. "Why didn't you keep some of your slaves to do your work?"

"Oh, well, Mr. Riley bought lots of niggers after you went away, Si, but some died, and he sold some, and Linkum set the rest free, so I couldn't keep 'em."

"But couldn't you keep them by paying them?" Nancy asked.

Old Matilda was shocked by the question.

"Oh! they wasn't worth paying," she said. "I never could pay niggers for work, so I let 'em all go."

Matilda quickly changed the subject, peppering Josiah with questions about the names of the officers her husband had fought under during the War of 1812. Matilda's son-in-law joined the conversation, and Josiah's memory spit out names and dates as the son-in-law jotted them all down.

Josiah soon learned that Matilda was trying to get an army pension, but didn't have all the information necessary until that moment. Josiah supplied as much information as he recalled. Matilda believed God had sent him to provide for her.

Eventually, Josiah asked the most important question on his mind—the location of his mother's grave. Matilda knew the spot well and directed her son-in-law to show it to him.

The slave graveyard was no more than a little collection of dirt mounds raised slightly higher than the surrounding level. But it was enough to show the final resting place of many who had escaped this life of sorrow. There, a little removed from the others, was Celia's grave.

Josiah bowed his head to the ground, hid his face in the long grass, and wept.

⸙

Josiah returned to Dawn to live out his days with Nancy and his children and grandchildren. He was a free man, in a free country, in a cabin built by his own hands, on a fertile farm, and free from mortgages and debts of any kind. He used some of his newfound wealth to continue to breed and invest in fine horses.*

Although the term "Dawn" had faded, according to the 1880 Kent County Directory, nearby Dresden was now a "thriving incorporated village" with a population of nearly two thousand people. The directory noted that "for a town without railway facilities its growth has been something remarkable." It had a hub and spoke factory, a large sawmill, a woolen mill, two foundries, three flour mills, a tannery, several carriage and wagon shops, a weekly newspaper, a bank, four hotels, billiards, and "churches of all the leading denominations, and good educational facilities." The town had daily stagecoaches to Chatham, and in the summer a steamer made three weekly trips to Detroit. The directory contains a list of shoemakers, furniture craftsmen, blacksmiths, grocers, masons, machinists, gunsmiths, brickmakers, physicians, tailors, engineers, sailors, gardeners, veterinarians, butchers, teamsters, bartenders, confectioners, wood dealers, painters, jewelers, bakers, barristers, preachers, and laborers, plus a cheesemaker, a druggist, and a fruit-tree agent.[13]

The BAI was gone, but many of the businessmen are listed as colored. Josiah Henson is listed as a farmer in the southwestern part of the village. Dawn had been a beautiful idea, a vision of a place where all men could live and work in harmony, peace, and freedom. Although the name had changed, the dream was still becoming a reality.

By 1881, Josiah had seven living children. His eldest son, Tom, had gone to California, but Josiah hadn't heard from him since he had enlisted in the Civil War. Josiah was immensely proud of his second son, Isaac, who had been educated in London with the help of his British friends. Isaac married and became an ordained Wesleyan minister; he

---

* The current Dresden racetrack sits incredibly close to the former Henson farm, and though unconfirmed, there is speculation that Josiah may have had a hand in starring it.

preached for about fifteen years before his death at age thirty-seven. Isaac was universally beloved.

Josiah's third son, Josiah Jr., worked on the family farm until he married at age twenty-two and moved to Michigan, where he bought land near an antislavery college. He worked as a shoemaker during the winter, and as a lather and plasterer when the weather warmed. Like his father, Josiah Jr. was an avid horticulturalist; he cultivated a large variety of fruit trees. Josiah was proud to note in his memoir that his son's property was worth "several thousand dollars," giving him the modern economic power of a millionaire.

Josiah's fourth son, Peter, stayed with Josiah and took over the family farm. His four daughters all married, and he noted proudly that "all of them can read and write well."*

⤜⤛

NINETY-TWO-YEAR-OLD JOSIAH PREACHED WHAT WAS LIKELY HIS last sermon at Park Street Baptist Church in Hamilton, Ontario, on Thursday, January 12, 1882. The *Hamilton Evening Times* reported on the event the following day. The evening's chairman had introduced him as Uncle Tom, and Josiah had confidently assured the congregation that it was true.

The *Times* reporter mentioned Josiah's crippled arms, observed that he seemed "somewhat feeble," and noted that his daughter was in attendance with him. Josiah "cracked plenty of jokes in his lecture," including one where he called Adam Robb "a bad man, and a *Scotchman*," joking that "the truth had to be told."

---

* Despite his advanced age, Josiah continued to preach and serve his local community. Although Lobb's editions continued to sell well in England, the book still hadn't made a splash in Canada, and Josiah took it upon himself to arrange the first Canadian edition of his story. He enlisted the support of Eben Tourjée, the director of the New England Conservatory of Music in Boston, to publish and advertise the work, as a way to raise funds to do his community "a final service by building a substantial church for the colored people of his home, Dresden, Canada." The work was printed in London, Ontario, by Schuyler, Smith, and Company, in 1881, and Josiah made sure to drop "Uncle Tom" from the title. It was *his* autobiography.

In addition to mistaking his own age and declaring himself to be a fictitious character, Josiah's speech seemed uncharacteristically disturbed. He had always been an articulate orator, but the article reported that "his remarks were not so well connected, nor his ideas expressed in such correct language as one bears at some lectures."*

Two and half hours into his talk, Josiah joked he was halfway through. The newspaper reported that "the Chairman went away then in order to catch the last train for Dundas, and Mr. Henson soon closed his lecture."

It all smacks of dementia. Josiah had always been clear that he was not a fictional character, and it is unlikely that he ever fully adopted his legend. Ninety-two years of hard life had clearly taken its toll. It seems that Josiah's aging brain had stirred and mixed up dates, facts, and locations.[14]

⚏

THREE DAYS BEFORE HIS DEATH, JOSIAH SIGNED HIS LAST WILL AND testament. Despite earning a good living from his land, his sawmill, the gristmill, book sales, horse breeding, and perhaps thousands of speaking engagements, he was not rich. He had spent the majority of his earnings on building Dawn and the BAI, freeing other slaves, and settling lawsuits in an effort to rescue the institute. No doubt Josiah would have earned far more money in his closing years if he hadn't surrendered his copyright to John Lobb, or if John Scoble had succeeded in the job he had promised to carry out.

---

* The newspaper stated that Josiah had been born in Charles County, Virginia, on the Potomac River, when in fact he had been born in Charles County, Maryland. Josiah said that he had loved his master, and that after traveling to Kentucky he had returned to Virginia. Neither of these things were even remotely true. Josiah's hazy memory then returned to his childhood. He recalled that the kindly Dr. Josiah McPherson had drowned in the Spring-branch River. This is unlikely. There is a Cool Spring Branch on the Potomac River in Montgomery County, but it's more than fifty miles from where McPherson lived. The stream in question is located near Rockville, Maryland, where Josiah was enslaved on Isaac Riley's plantation for decades. Indeed, Josiah's memory appears to have been slipping for a while. When asked in Glasgow on Friday, April 20, 1877, the name of the Scottish captain who had helped him to safety, he had replied that, to the best of his recollection, the man's name was John Burns or Burnet. He had called the man Captain Burnham in his 1849 memoir.

According to historian Robin Winks, "Henson left virtually nothing to his family, and his son Peter apparently sold the little landed property that he possessed. Two aged daughters who moved to Flint, Michigan, and a grandson, Beecher Stowe Henson, later said that nothing remained save his papers, which disappeared, and a few relics."[15]

Though we don't know, exactly, how much remained of his estate, we do know that Josiah appointed four trustees to settle it—Charles Livingston, Anthony Johnston, Walter Hawkins, and William Price. They were instructed to sell virtually everything and split the proceeds among his heirs.

His wife, Nancy, received "all the household furniture and effects—one cow, one of the black mares and the buggy and harness."[16] She also received an annual income for as long as she remained unmarried.

Josiah gave his daughter Julia Ann Wheeler 2.5 acres of land, while two of his other daughters, Matilda Clay and Mrs. Thomas, received $200 each. Josiah Jr. and four grandsons each received $100 cash. Josiah's son Peter received a golden watch and chain as well as half the proceeds from the sale of Josiah's horse, a "Hambletonian stallion called *John.*"

A generous patron to the very end, Josiah also left $100 cash to the British Episcopal Methodist Church of Dresden.

All told, Josiah left an estate worth at least several hundred thousand dollars in today's terms. While certainly it was an impressive sum for a man who didn't learn to read until his forties, and never learned to write, the relatively small total is a testament to the fact that Josiah used his earnings to help his fellow man. According to family tradition, Josiah's only prized possessions were his gold watch and his signed portrait of Queen Victoria.

GOODBYE, FRIEND

On May 5, 1883, Josiah Henson entered everlasting freedom at the age of ninety-three years, ten months, and twenty days. The *New York Times* reported his death the following day:

DRESDEN, Ontario, May 5.—The Rev. Josiah Henson,
the original of Mrs. Stowe's "Uncle Tom," died to-day in his
ninety-fourth year.

His funeral was one of the largest in Dresden's history. Ministers from all denominations came to pay tribute. Bells rang from the churches, and most of the businesses closed for the service. Black musicians from Chatham performed hymns, and fifty wagons followed his casket in a nearly two-mile procession to the graveside.[17]

One of the hymns sung was the negro spiritual "Steal Away, Steal Away to Jesus."*

Steal away, steal away, steal away to Jesus
Steal away, steal away home
I ain't got long to stay here

My Lord, He calls me
He calls me by the thunder
The trumpet sounds within-a my soul
I ain't got long to stay here

Green trees are bending
Po' sinner stand a-trembling
The trumpet sounds within-a my soul
I ain't got long to stay here

Three lodges performed the Masonic burial service according to their order's rituals. Nine preachers prayed and paid their respects. The family buried their patriarch in the family plot, in one of his beloved fields, while thousands of black and white attendees bore witness to his earthly departure.

Josiah's true dawn had finally come.

---

* The song was written by none other than Wallace Willis, the Choctaw freedman who also penned "Swing Low, Sweet Chariot."

EPILOGUE

> While our nation has made great advances in
> equality, the obstacles that remain for too many
> Americans demand we carry forward Harriet
> Beecher Stowe's legacy of building understanding
> and pursuing justice and opportunity for all.
>
> —BARACK OBAMA

Mid to Late 1883

Upon learning of Josiah Henson's passing, the Masons of the Committee on Foreign Correspondence for the Prince Hall Grand Lodge of Louisiana wrote of their brother: "We seem again to hear his strong advocacy of Methodism, as opposed to our father's views of the Baptist faith; and we are proud to state as our firm belief, that he was a Christian in the full sense of the term. A minister properly endowed, and a thorough gentleman by nature; though scant in modern talent, he was weighted down with tact. . . . Again we hear as it were his flashes of merriment, nature's gift to his ever-ready witticisms. . . . [H]e is not lost! He is only gone before."[1]

January 23, 1891

The *Washington Post* reported that a Boston publisher claimed he still sold thirty thousand copies of *Uncle Tom's Cabin* every year. The *Post* happily reported that "the book seems to have outlived the bloodhounds and cheap actors."[2]

But although the novel may have outlived its commercial exploitation, the derogatory connotation assigned to its lead character only grew with time. Despite the fact that "Uncle Tom" is actually a fictitious Christian martyr who protected two sexually abused women from their rapist master, the racist blackface minstrel shows ensured that the term would live on in infamy as a demeaning epithet for an "aww shucks" type of black man who kowtows to his white superiors, or even sells out his fellow black people for the favor of his white boss. That the use of the term "Uncle Tom" exists to this day as a racial slur, based on the minstrel shows, suggests that we must still confront the legacy of race relations in America.

July 5, 1905

Exactly fifty-five years after Isaac Riley's death, on July 5, 1905, the Niagara Movement began with a meeting at a hotel on Waverly Beach, Fort Erie, just south of Josiah Henson's Canadian landing site. That meeting laid the foundation for the founding of the National Association for the Advancement of Colored People (NAACP) five years later.

April 6, 1909

On April 6, 1909, Matthew Henson, as Admiral Robert Peary's right-hand man, became the first person to plant a flag on the North Pole. Family lore holds that Matthew is one of Josiah Henson's great-grandnephews. DNA testing will likely be needed for the long-held family tradition to be proved true.

1903–1927

Many film adaptations of *Uncle Tom's Cabin* were produced between 1903 and 1927, including at least nine during the silent era.

Black-faced minstrel shows were performed in Canada from at least the 1860s, with "Tom shows" reaching rural communities five or six times each decade in the 1880s. Ironically, similar groups performed in Dresden—half a mile from Josiah's grave—in 1919 and 1923.

1948

Josiah's house was used as a chicken coop for many years before owner William Chapple turned it into a museum in 1948. The BAI cemetery was restored by the Ontario Historic Sites Board; the Henson family cemetery still stands to this day.[3]

May 7, 1949

Despite Canada's image as a nation free of racism, black people in Canada were openly denied service, jobs, insurance, mortgages, and medical treatment into the 1950s, and Josiah's hometown was no exception.[4] Three of Dresden's five restaurants refused to serve black customers. A descendant of former slaves started a campaign that led to a referendum in which the citizens of Dresden were asked, "Do you approve of the council passing a bylaw licensing restaurants in Dresden and restraining the owner or owners from refusing service regardless of race, colour or creed?" The results: 108 people voted that restaurant owners should serve everyone, while 517 voted against the measure.

1952

The Wilberforce Educational Institute continued to operate as a school for nearly eight decades. It closed shortly after the turn of the century when a government-funded public high school became available.

The building fell into disuse for several years before a black carpenter, George Grand, began using it to train young men as cabinet makers. He held the training at that location for about thirty years. During World War II, the building was used for first and second graders, but that school was shut down again in 1946. There were plans to resurrect the space as a senior citizens' home and Bible school, but the building was instead demolished in 1952. The institute's magnificent wooden barn remains in the backyard of a private home to this day.

May 5, 1963

To mark the eightieth anniversary of Josiah's passing, a six-mile motorcade of more than two thousand Masons—black and white, Canadian and American—gathered at Josiah's graveside in Dresden to honor their brother. Josiah's gravestone prominently bears the Masonic square and compass, a testament to their fraternity. Grand Master Garfield W. Parker wrote of the occasion: "As a result of the understanding, patience, and humility of [Josiah Henson], the world has recognized our rights to claim full benefits of democracy."

September 16, 1983

On September 16, 1983, Josiah became the first black man to have his portrait printed on a Canadian stamp.[5] His face appeared on more than fourteen million thirty-two-cent stamps.

Today

The village of Dresden is still home to hundreds of descendants of slaves, men and women who first settled around the BAI as fugitives in Josiah Henson's time. Dawn's soil still produces a strong crop each year on lands first cleared by these settlers, including Josiah himself.

Over two hundred of Josiah's descendants are still alive today. Hensons have fought in wars, survived Nazi POW camps, become pastors and preachers, and made films in Hollywood.[6]

As if in a physical testament to the belief that all men are equal, today the Henson family contains all shades of skin color, from nearly black to white-skinned blondes. They are students and teachers, therapists and

CEOs, factory workers and artists, ministers and engineers. Dozens work or volunteer with human rights, racial reconciliation, and social justice initiatives. Josiah's descendants—from newborns to retirees—still meet for their annual Henson family reunion in Michigan. Family names include Peter, Isaac, Tom, Beecher, Stowe, and Josiah.

> **It is for freedom that Christ has set us free.**
> **Stand firm, then, and do not let yourselves**
> **be burdened again by a yoke of slavery.**
>
> **—Galatians 5:1 (KJV)**

Josiah's story has something for everyone. If you are looking for truth, you will find it. If you are looking for scandal, you will find it. If you are looking for resistance, you will find it. Josiah defies national boundaries, and he fits no category. He refuses to be the victim, or the political puppet; nor can he play the faultless hero. He will not be boxed in—perhaps precisely because he spent so much time in confinement.

When reflecting back on Josiah's story as a whole, it is easy to see, indeed, that Josiah used his freedom well, as he had promised to do. Not only did he provide for a large family, and hand down important values to subsequent generations, but he shouldered the debts of Dawn and the BAI time and again. He helped the poor. He supported churches. He paid for his brother's freedom. He spent decades rescuing others, preaching, and educating and training others despite overwhelming odds and opposition.

Rather than simply settle into a comfortable and safe life in a new nation, Josiah understood his deep responsibility to his fellow man. Though certainly not high-born, he possessed a certain dignity, a regal noblesse oblige, a deep and abiding moral obligation to act with honor, kindness, and generosity. Josiah Henson is a hero whose life speaks of a deep love of humanity and invites us to follow in his steps.

⁓⁓⁓

THERE LINGERS A TEMPTATION TO MAKE A TENUOUS CONNECTION between Josiah Henson and the end of slavery. If he was the inspiration for *Uncle Tom's Cabin*, and the novel sparked the Civil War, and the war led to emancipation, then did not Josiah's story lead to freedom for the slaves?

Of course, no one person, no one story, no one book sparked the Civil War. But Josiah's story represents one of *millions* of similar stories. He just happened to be one of the very few "lucky" ones who, by courage and chance, managed to live to tell his tale.

While Josiah's life story is perhaps more dramatic than some, it certainly isn't the most harrowing. People suffered and died by the millions, and less than a few hundred ever had the chance to tell their stories in ink. If Josiah had died as a boy, or been killed by Bryce Litton, or sold south, we would never have heard his story, and Stowe would have found a different model, perhaps, and her novel may have had different details, but would have been just as powerful.

It wasn't Josiah's story that started the Civil War—it was the story of Josiah's people. Few individuals received the attention that Josiah did, but his life serves as one of a million representations of the brutal reality of slavery. Josiah didn't cause the Civil War. *Uncle Tom's Cabin* didn't cause the Civil War. And John Brown's raid at Harpers Ferry didn't cause the Civil War, either. Emancipation was won by four million enslaved people because of the resilient human desire for justice, equality, and liberty for all. We share Josiah's story in remembrance of all those whose stories are lost.

✶

JOSIAH'S LIFE ALSO REMINDS US THAT DESPITE ALL THAT HAS BEEN stolen from them, black people have thrived through centuries of hardship and cruelty, from the transatlantic passage to the slave era, from Jim Crow to modern mass incarceration.

Indeed, America has yet to fully abolish slavery, as the Thirteenth Amendment still allows the state itself to underpay or not pay convicted persons, which is precisely what has happened to black prisoners at alarming rates since the end of Reconstruction. As W. E. B. Du Bois wrote, "Negroes have emerged from slavery into a serfdom of poverty and restricted rights."[7]

Neither have we seen the global end of slavery and indentured servitude. Indeed, the "peculiar institution" still exists in nations such as Mauritania. Six modern nations (India, China, Pakistan, Uzbekistan, North Korea, and Russia) each enslave more than one million people, and sixteen nations still use forced or child labor to produce cotton. Du Bois is also prescient on this point: "Most men today cannot conceive of a freedom that does not involve somebody's slavery."[8]

What will happen to people of color in years to come? Will we see violent uprisings and rebellions against the establishment that continues to press them low? Will we see entire swaths of the country carved up as free cities and free states? Will we see African American investment in Africa, or perhaps a new wave of repatriation and resettlement? What new nations will be born?

And what new ways will be invented to keep black people down? Surely mass incarceration will eventually be unwound, but perhaps only to be replaced by widespread control of movement via bracelet or chip monitoring. Will voter suppression continue? Will the Republic awaken to the fact that it is not yet a true democracy?

This we know: Control is lucrative. Repression is profitable. Today we have more enslaved people than at any point in human history. They make our clothes, harvest our coffee, and extract our minerals. They are the unseen slaves upon whose backs we continue to profit.

Will we ever learn?

Will the people of Africa ever be free?

The enduring belief that the "South will rise again" suggests a deep flaw in the southern psyche. The Confederate flag is to many Americans what the Nazi flag is to many Jews, yet a profound lack of sympathy toward people of color continues unabated. Oh for understanding! May we pray and work toward a greater union as a species.

What will become of us?

When will we see the African as equal and fully human?

Will we ever all be free?

The whole story has yet to be written. To paraphrase feminist re-former Fredrika Bremer, the fate of the African is the romance of our history.[9]

~~~

I OPENED THIS BOOK WITH A QUOTE FROM FREDERICK DOUGLASS: "When we get a little farther away from the conflict, some brave and truth-loving man, with all the facts before him . . . will gather from here and there the scattered fragments . . . and give to those who shall come after us an impartial history of this the grandest moral conflict of the century."

To be clear, I am not that man. Though I love truth, wish to be brave, and stand far from the conflict, all the facts of Josiah Henson's life, and of the story of slavery, are still not before me. They have been buried, lost, hidden, and stolen. Even a correspondent for *The Anti-Slavery Reporter* who visited the British American Institute on March 28, 1856, opened his report by saying, "The difficulty of obtaining facts in regard to the past history of these is much greater than I anticipated, and even yet my information is very imperfect."[10]

History is the ultimate mystery. We hold the fragments of millions of shattered lives. Josiah's story, though roughly intact, is still full of holes and contradictions and questions and mysteries, not least of which is his actual birthdate. But the lessons of his life hold true. His narrative, despite its flaws, tells us of an uneducated slave who tried to use his freedom well, to steward his wealth on behalf of others, and to serve his fellow man—regardless of color—for the entirety of his life.

~~~

AND WHAT OF UNCLE TOM AND HIS CABIN?

There is no cabin. It is no more real than the Tara plantation in *Gone with the Wind*.

Nor is Josiah Henson "Uncle Tom." The fact that he was one of the many people who inspired the fictional character isn't the most important thing about his life. It is his unwavering faith, his love of humanity, and his commitment to nonviolence and education that sets him apart. Josiah stands as one who survives and thrives despite a lifetime of attack. He fights with his mind. He speaks with his voice. He gives with his heart.

No, Josiah Henson is not the "real Uncle Tom." The man we remember is a real human being. He was a living embodiment of the best we can hope to achieve, if we are willing to selflessly serve our fellow man 'til the last of our breaths. Josiah Henson's life symbolizes the definitive triumph of the human spirit over the impossible cruelty of slavery. His legacy of honor, nonviolence, and selfless generosity will live on in the hearts of millions.

His name is Josiah Henson.

And that is more than enough.

A CLARION CALL

I WROTE THIS BOOK IN THREE COUNTRIES—CANADA, THE UNITED States, and the United Kingdom. One of the many things I appreciate about the British is their reverence for history. You cannot walk a mile in London—the City That Remembers—without passing a dozen black plaques and a hundred blue circles that point out the great deeds of the historical figures who went before. Josiah Henson touched our planet, and the time has come to commemorate his contribution to our common good.

Accordingly, I have started taking steps to establish the Josiah Henson Foundation. There is much work to be done.

To start, the Uncle Tom's Cabin Historic Site in Dresden simply must be renamed. The Josiah Henson Homestead or the Josiah Henson National Historic Site sound about right.

Josiah's dream was to have a place where people in great need could receive a great education. Wouldn't it be wonderful if some great philanthropists endowed a Dawn College or Henson University on Josiah's very own farmland? Furthermore, Canada does not have a National Underground Railroad Museum, and I believe the still-undeveloped BAI lands would make a wonderfully adequate spot for one.

In Canada, we have yet to see a man of African descent adorn our currency, despite the fact that nearly one-fifth of Canadians are members of a visible minority. I often recall how Josiah was just $100 from freedom before Isaac Riley tricked him, changing the figures on the contract. Just $100 was the difference between slavery and freedom. What about the "Henson Hundred"? With Josiah's image on our $100 bill, we would have a physical reminder of freedom and how precious a thing it is. Americans have their Benjamins, and we could have our Hensons.

The busiest highway in the world is Southwestern Ontario's Highway 401. Perhaps a portion, if not the entirety, could be named Henson Highway, after the man who traversed that very corridor.

Canada could also consider designating June 15, Josiah's birthday, as Josiah Henson Day, the Canadian equivalent of Martin Luther King Jr. Day. On this day, we could further affirm our embrace of human equality and racial reconciliation.

Lastly, in Canada, it would be lovely to mark Henson's Landing with a plaque and park at the foot of Lavinia Street on the Niagara River, in celebration of all those whose first steps of freedom fell at the exact same spot.

On the American side of the border, we would do well to preserve the Josiah Henson Birthplace Site at La Grange in Maryland and support the work in Montgomery County to restore the Isaac Riley plantation. Although I doubt Amos Riley's descendants are willing to part with the Kentucky plantation, we could at least straighten the tilting historical marker that stands on the edge of their property.

Similar to "Henson's Landing" in Canada, it would be lovely to see a plaque and park to mark "Henson Harbor," the spot in the former village of Venice, west Sandusky, from which Josiah caught his boat to freedom.

At Rockport, Indiana, the spot where Josiah first touched the free state, and where a young Abraham Lincoln first witnessed slavery, could be renamed the Henson-Lincoln Landing. We would do well to place a monument there of the two men together, arm in arm.

Internationally, we must all work to redeem the racist term "Uncle Tom." It is within our power to change its meaning, so that future generations will equate it with "Superman." We must also do an internal check on ourselves and our own views of slavery. I'm ashamed to admit that, before being introduced to Josiah Henson, I didn't realize how poorly my own country (Canada) treated African Americans, or how widely the remnants of racism and slavery lay scattered. It is easy to dismiss slavery as a thing of the past, but its evident ripple effects continue to this very day. It is profoundly naïve to think the Civil War is ancient history—it is conceivable that there are people alive today whose grandparents were slaves.

One last idea, if the reader will indulge me. In 1834, after British slavery had ended and British slave owners were forced to free their slaves, Parliament paid them a total of £20 million—perhaps $20 billion today—as compensation for their loss of property. The Church of England's Codrington Plantations received £8,823. 8s. 9d in compensation (an income value of around $10 million today) for their 411 slaves. The slaves themselves, of course, were never paid.

I believe the descendants of the African slave trade deserve reparations for the vast injustices perpetuated against their peoples. Make no mistake, this was a war of culture wherein vastly stronger forces enslaved weaker people groups for incalculable profits.

Slaves were forced to build, rebuild, and serve in the White House; they played an important role in constructing the US Capitol Building as well.[1] Perhaps we should rename it the Black House. The simple fact is that America, and much of the Western world, was built on slavery. According to *Harper's Magazine*, while the United States waged its 246 Years' War against the African tribes and nations, the land of liberty stole an estimated $100 trillion in forced labor between 1619 and 1865.[2]

Yet the Land of the Free imported less than 5 percent of all African slaves. While JPMorgan Chase and Barclays grew filthy rich by financing the trade in America, the profits of slavery built everything from the haunting squares of Savannah to the rotting canals of Amsterdam and the Codrington Library at All Souls College in Oxford.

The United States, along with the other nations, including the United Kingdom, the Netherlands, France, Spain, and especially Portugal, owe a great debt to the descendants of the survivors of the African holocaust. Reparations must be made. It is my belief that all plantations—including the several hundred acres of her ancestor's Virginia plantation that currently profits one of my own relatives—should be seized and forfeited to black causes such as the United Negro College Fund.

I am compelled to stand with Ralph Waldo Emerson, who called for reparations in a stanza of his 1863 poem "Boston Hymn," which he read in the presence of Harriet Beecher Stowe on the day of the Emancipation Proclamation:

> *Pay ransom to the owner,*
> *And fill the bag to the brim.*
> *Who is the owner? The slave is the owner,*
> *And ever was. Pay him.*

If nations are unwilling to stand accountable for the deeds of their past, I see little hope for us avoiding repeat events in the future. If nations prove unwilling to settle the score, perhaps they could start funds to establish and endow schools like Josiah's, so at least the African people can find equal footing in order to prepare for future sieges.

We must abolish human trafficking and sex slavery immediately. We must stop arming warlords and dictators. We must halt the environmental degradation that is ruining Africa's coastline. We must crush our demand for cheap clothing and electronics, gold and diamonds, and all goods produced by child labor.[3] We must come to grips with the fact that we have simply outsourced our slavery to parts unknown. We must crush the corruption of governmental and capitalist collusion that, for the period between 1970 and 2008, illegally siphoned between $854 billion and $1.8 trillion from Africa—more than enough to feed all her citizens—into offshore accounts in London, New York, and Zurich.[4] Let us, at least, allow Africans access to the knowledge to protect themselves.

But, of course, I am a writer with no other discernible skills, and none of this can be accomplished alone. Each of these endeavors will require a huge team and several champions to be accomplished. This is a call to all people of goodwill to join in the work of the Josiah Henson Foundation and to give time, invest money, make introductions, and spread the word.

With your help, Dawn shall rise again.

ACKNOWLEDGMENTS

My thanks start with my wife, Michelle, for introducing me to Josiah Henson in that roundabout way. I hope we can share many more fruitful and committed decades together, like Josiah and Charlotte, through happiness and hardship alike.

I must express great gratitude to Alex and Renie Elsaesser. I wrote many early drafts in their centuries-old barn conversion, and to them I'm grateful for providing such a hallowed hall in which to work.

Elizabeth Stein edited a winning proposal, Beth Fisher Adams once again ensured my submitted draft was actually readable, and Katherine H. Streckfus's work was nothing less than a great gift. My work is by many degrees better for having such capable editors aboard.

Jennifer Gates and Jane von Mehren, my literary agents at Aevitas Creative Management, took on a young author with high hopes and helped them become a reality.

Colleen Lawrie grew up just minutes from Port Tobacco and had never heard of Josiah Henson, but she seized upon the story with an immediate and sustained passion. My gratitude extends to her especially, along with Jaime Leifer, Lindsay Fradkoff, Miguel Cervantes, Brooke Parsons, Katherine Haigler, Melissa Raymond, Michelle Welsh-Horst, and the rest of the team at PublicAffairs, plus Lauren Peters-Collaer, whose cover design was breathtaking from its very first draft.

I am also grateful to Andrea Cohen Barrack, Beth Puddicombe, Ibrahima Gueye, Edwige Jean-Pierre, Loida Ignacio, Ruby Weber, David Murray, Omar Omar, and the rest of the Ontario Trillium Foundation for their support in helping bring Josiah's story to a wider audience through live events.

My appreciation extends to the National Endowment for the Humanities and the Gladys Krieble Delmas Foundation for supporting the Documenting the American South project of the University Library of the University of North Carolina at Chapel Hill, especially for the project's electronic publication of four of Josiah Henson's original texts.

An author could spend a small eternity on the Library of Congress's website, which I did, and I'm grateful to the library's kind staff for their assistance.

Thanks to one of my lawyers, Robert Lanteigne, and Amanda Fudge at the Waterloo Region Law Library, for tracking down details on several 150-year-old lawsuits.

I also owe thanks to the many researchers, librarians, archivists, historians, and archaeologists whom I've had the pleasure of meeting: Professor Julia Ann King, Gary A. Adams, Isaac Settle, Jamie Glavic, Jamie Kuhns, Alex J. Flick, Sondra Millner, Rachel M. Kennedy, Karen Milligan, Samantha Meredith, Chantelle Rodrigues, Sabina Beauchard, Anna Clutterbuck-Cook, Maira Liriano, Cassandra Michaud, Joey Lampl, Shirl Spicer, Mike Nardolilli, Sarah Hedlund, Pat Andersen, and Leslie Thomas-Smith. A special thanks to Cindy Robichaud and the Kent Branch of the Ontario Genealogical Society, along with the Black Mecca Museum in Chatham and the Chatham-Kent Public Library for their wealth of information. I also must thank several other libraries, including the Guelph Public Library in Ontario, the Boston Public Library and the Marlborough Public Library in Massachusetts, and the New York Public Library, particularly its Schomburg Center.

I am grateful to Michael J. Sullivan for the hours of laughter and conversation, and for opening up his magnificent barn for several sleepovers while I conducted research in Maryland.

A very special thanks to the immensely kind Beth Burgess at the Harriet Beecher Stowe Center for taking me into the vaults and showing me the petition signatures of 563,000 women who were as passionate about ending slavery then as Beth is about preserving Stowe's legacy now. I am especially grateful that she allowed me the thrilling experience of holding (with white gloves, of course) a document signed by Josiah Henson's own hand.

I am humbled by Mr. and Mrs. Kevin Wilson, the Wills Family, and George and Cynthia Hawes, who all graciously allowed me to step foot on private properties once trod by Josiah himself.

An especially warm thanks is reserved for Steven Cook and Brenda Lambkin at the Uncle Tom's Cabin Historic Site in Dresden, for giving me the freedom to roam Josiah Henson's homestead at will, as well as for sharing their deep passion with me.

I'm grateful for many of the people who gave me their time in the form of an interview, including University of Maryland's Dr. Cheryl La-Roche, Erin Greenwald at the Historic New Orleans Collection (whose *Purchased Lives* exhibition I cannot recommend highly enough), Kathy Olsen at the Owensboro Museum of Science and History, Dr. Michael Battle at the National Underground Railroad Freedom Center, John Franklin at the Smithsonian's National Museum of African American History and Culture, Janice Wilson at the Charles County Branch of the NAACP, and Lisa Macleman at Montgomery Parks, who kindly allowed me to interview her twice.

I am profoundly grateful for the hospitality of friends who played host along my journey, including Chris and Katherine Rader near Washington, DC, my dear aunt-in-law Anneli McCulley near Boston, and especially the ever-generous Keith and Rosie Ketchum near London, in whose astoundingly welcoming home I have penned thousands of words.

I'm incalculably indebted to Ari and Lea Uotila for the countless sleepovers in your spare room, days of work in your spare office, and ceaseless support of my projects.

Thanks to Pastor Bob, for his constant encouragement and confident prayers, as well as the prayers, love, and support of my own parents, Gord and Karen Brock.

I extend my deep appreciation to the members of the Henson family who so kindly welcomed me into their homes—and fed me so deliciously at the Michigan family reunion. Thanks to those who volunteered to share with me, including Kristel Anthony, Darryl Beard, Marie Booker Woodard, and Ron Dean, plus Michelle Roberts for making introductions, and Stephanie Johnson for joining our board and providing an exceptional and profoundly moving interview. To my dear friend and brother, Rev. Terrence Vick, a special thanks for being a willing and passionate spokesperson for the Henson family.

I'm deeply indebted to the Reverend Father Josiah Henson himself, for providing me with an intimately personal example of justice without violence, generosity without question, and faith without compromise. I hope this humble biography honors your memory and furthers your legacy.

NOTES

CHAPTER 1. PORT TOBACCO

1. Josiah Henson, *The Life of Josiah Henson, Formerly a Slave, Now an Inhabitant of Canada, as Narrated by Himself* (Boston: Arthur D. Phelps, 1849), 19.

2. Rebecca J. Webster, Alex J. Flick, Julia A. King, and Scott M. Strickland, "In Search of Josiah Henson's Birthplace: Archaeological Investigations at La Grange Near Port Tobacco, Maryland," St. Mary's College of Maryland, 2017.

3. Ibid.

4. The event is recounted in "A Loyal Negro Whipped to Death," a letter from a US Army general that was published in the *New York Times* on February 4, 1862, www.nytimes.com/1862/02/04/news/a-loyal-negro-whipped-to-death.html.

5. George P. Rawick, *From Sundown to Sunup: The Making of the Black Community* (Westport, CT: Greenwood, 1973).

6. John Newton, *The Posthumous Works of the Late Rev. John Newton* (Philadelphia: W. W. Woodward, 1809), 237.

7. Josiah Henson, *Truth Stranger Than Fiction: Father Henson's Story of His Own Life* (Boston: John P. Jewett and Company, 1858), 7.

8. Irwin Unger and David Reimers, eds., *The Slavery Experience in the United States* (New York: Holt, Rinehart and Winston, 1970), 64.

9. Ibid. It was called the *Zong* massacre. See https://en.wikipedia.org/wiki/Zong_massacre.

10. See "25 Curious Facts About Slavery in Brazil," Black Women of Brazil, n.d., https://blackwomenofbrazil.co/2013/12/29/25-curious-facts-about-slavery-in-brazil.

11. Henson, *Life of Josiah Henson, Formerly a Slave*, 18.

12. Ibid.

13. William Lloyd Garrison, *The Letters of William Lloyd Garrison: From Disunionism to the Brink of War, 1850-1860* (Cambridge, MA: Harvard University Press, 1971), 177.

14. Malcolm Bell Jr., *Major Butler's Legacy: Five Generations of a Slaveholding Family* (Athens: University of Georgia Press, 1987); Dorothy Schneider and Carl J. Schneider, *Slavery in America* (New York: Facts on File, 2007), 75.

15. Benjamin Lloyd, *The Primitive Hymns, Spiritual Songs, and Sacred Poems* (Greenville, AL: n.p., 1858), 473.

16. Josiah Henson, *"Uncle Tom's Story of His Life": An Autobiography of the Rev. Josiah Henson*, edited by John Lobb (London: Christian Age Office, 1876), 19–20.

17. Information about Robb from Bryan Prince, *A Shadow on the Household: One Enslaved Family's Incredible Struggle for Freedom* (Toronto: Emblem, 2009).

18. John Milner Associates, *Historic Structure Report for The Riley House / Josiah Henson Site*, Maryland–National Capital Park and Planning Commission, Montgomery County Department of Parks, June 2008, https://doczz.net/doc/5069369/the-riley-house—josiah-henson-site.

19. Henson, *"Uncle Tom's Story of His Life,"* 20.

CHAPTER 2. THE WOUNDED LEADER

1. Josiah Henson, *"Uncle Tom's Story of His Life": An Autobiography of the Rev. Josiah Henson*, edited by John Lobb (London: Christian Age Office, 1876), 20.

2. Curtis Bunn, "10 Slave Codes That Were Designed to Oppress and Humiliate Black People," *Atlanta Black Star*, December 22, 2014, http://atlantablackstar.com/2014/12/22/10-slave-codes-that-were-designed-to-oppress-and-humiliate-black-people/10; Ned Sublette and Constance Sublette, *American Slave Coast: A History of the Slave-Breeding Industry* (Chicago: Chicago Review Press, 2015).

3. Henson, *"Uncle Tom's Story of His Life,"* 188.

4. Ibid.

5. Ibid., 189.

6. Ibid.

7. "William Watkins (b. circa 1803–d. circa 1858): Educator and Minister, Baltimore City, Maryland," Archives of Maryland, Biographical Series, MSA SC 5496-002535, http://msa.maryland.gov/megafile/msa/speccol/sc5400/sc5496/002500/002535/html/002535bio.html.

8. "Quotes," Frederick Douglass Heritage Official Website, www.frederick-douglass-heritage.org/quotes.

9. Henson, *"Uncle Tom's Story of His Life,"* 190.

10. *State Papers and Publick Documents of the United States, from the Accession of George Washington to the Presidency* (Boston: Thomas B. Wait, 1819), 457.

11. John W. Blassingame, *Slave Testimony: Two Centuries of Letters, Speeches, Interviews, and Autobiographies* (Baton Rouge: Louisiana State University Press, 1977), 250.

12. Federal Writers' Project: Slave Narrative Project, vol. 11, North Carolina, Part 1, Adams-Hunter, www.loc.gov/resource/mesn.111/?sp=143.

13. Josiah Henson, *The Life of Josiah Henson, Formerly a Slave, Now an Inhabitant of Canada, as Narrated by Himself* (Boston: Arthur D. Phelps, 1849), 10.

14. Josiah Henson, *Truth Stranger Than Fiction: Father Henson's Story of His Own Life* (Boston: John P. Jewett and Company, 1858), 66.

15. Source for this account is Henson, *"Uncle Tom's Story of His Life,"* 25–33.

16. "History of the College," All Souls College, University of Oxford, www.asc.ox.ac.uk/history-of-the-college; Source docs behind https://en.wikipedia.org/wiki/Codrington_Library; see also source documents at "USPG," Wikipedia's article on the United Society Partners in the Gospel, at https://en.wikipedia.org/wiki/USPG.

17. Albert J. Raboteau, "The Secret Religion of the Slaves," *Christianity Today*, 1992, www.christianitytoday.com/history/issues/issue-33/secret-religion-of-slaves.html.

18. Henson, *"Uncle Tom's Story of His Life,"* 36.

19. See "Brice Reuben Letton (1782–1860)," WikiTree, n.d., www.wikitree.com/wiki/Letton-59; "The Litton Family: Life on a Colonial Farm," Meadow Hall Elementary School, n.d., www.montgomeryschoolsmd.org/schools/meadowhalles/history/Lytton2.aspx; "The Litton House and Lands," Meadow Hill Elementary School, n.d., www.montgomeryschoolsmd.org/schools/meadowhalles/history/lytton3.aspx.

20. For accounts of this attack, see Henson, *Life of Josiah Henson, Formerly a Slave*, 15–19, and Henson, *"Uncle Tom's Story of His Life,"* 39.

21. Henson, *Truth Stranger Than Fiction*, 39.

22. Henson, *Life of Josiah Henson, Formerly a Slave*, 37.

23. My source for the trial is Henson, *Truth Stranger Than Fiction*, 38.

24. See John Milner Associates, *Historic Structure Report for The Riley House / Josiah Henson Site*, Maryland–National Capital Park and Planning Commission, Montgomery County Department of Parks, June 2008, https://doczz.net/doc/5069369/the-riley-house—josiah-henson-site.

CHAPTER 3. KENTUCKY BOUND

1. See family records at Family Search, www.familysearch.org/ark:/61903/1:1:X8ZL-Z9Q.

2. On the land disputes between Arnold Windsor and Isaac Riley, see "Part I: Developmental History," in John Milner Associates, *Historic Structure Report for The Riley House / Josiah Henson Site*, Maryland–National Capital Park and Planning Commission, Montgomery County Department of Parks, June 2008, https://doczz.net/doc/5069369/the-riley-house—josiah-henson-site.

3. Conversation from Josiah Henson, *Truth Stranger Than Fiction: Father Henson's Story of His Own Life* (Boston: John P. Jewett and Company, 1858), 45–47.

4. William Wells Brown, *Narrative of William W. Brown, A Fugitive Slave, Written by Himself* (1847), in Brown, *From Fugitive Slave to Free Man: The Autobiographies of William Wells Brown*, edited by William L. Andrews (Columbia: University of Missouri Press, 2003), 32.

5. Moses Roper, *A Narrative of the Adventures and Escape of Moses Roper, from American Slavery* (Philadelphia: Matthew and Gunn, 1838).

6. Henson, *Truth Stranger Than Fiction*, 50.

CHAPTER 4. DOUBLE CROSS

1. Acreage calculations by Gary Adams, AICP (American Institute of Certified Planners), Preservation Alliance of Owensboro-Daviess County.

2. Albert J. Raboteau, *Slave Religion: The "Invisible Institution" in the Antebellum South* (Oxford: Oxford University Press, 2004).

3. Ibid., 215.

4. Ibid., 217.

5. Ibid., 220.

6. William W. Brown, *The Narrative of William W. Brown, a Fugitive Slave* (New York: Dover, 2003), 52.

7. Josiah Henson, *Truth Stranger Than Fiction: Father Henson's Story of His Own Life* (Boston: John P. Jewett and Company, 1858), 61.

8. The man was likely Benjamin Ogden. See Lewis Collins, J. A. James, and U. P. James, *Historical Sketches of Kentucky*, vol. 1 (Methodist Episcopal Church, 1847; reprinted 1968), 447, www.rootsweb.ancestry.com/~kygenweb/kybiog/caldwell/ogden.b.txt.

9. Conversation from Josiah Henson, *The Life of Josiah Henson, Formerly a Slave, Now an Inhabitant of Canada, as Narrated by Himself* (Boston: Arthur D. Phelps, 1849), 28–29.

10. For this account, see Henson, *Truth Stranger Than Fiction*, 63.

11. Ibid., 67.

12. Josiah's interactions with Frank Middleton in this section are from Henson, *Life of Josiah Henson, Formerly a Slave*, 32.

13. Conversation from Henson, *Truth Stranger Than Fiction*, 72.

CHAPTER 5. MURDER AND PROVIDENCE

1. Josiah's discovery of Isaac Riley's treachery with his manumission papers is recounted in Josiah Henson, *Truth Stranger Than Fiction: Father Henson's Story of His Own Life* (Boston: John P. Jewett and Company, 1858), 74.

2. This account appears in ibid., 76.

3. Frederick Douglass, *Narrative of the Life of Frederick Douglass, an American Slave, Written by Himself* (Cambridge, MA: Harvard University Press, 2009), 70.

4. Henson, *Truth Stranger Than Fiction*, 87.

5. The source for this section is Josiah Henson, *The Life of Josiah Henson, Formerly a Slave, Now an Inhabitant of Canada, as Narrated by Himself* (Boston: Arthur D. Phelps, 1849), 44–46.

6. Alton Telegraph, n.d., in William Wells Brown, *Narrative of William W. Brown, A Fugitive Slave, Written by Himself* (1847), in Brown, *From Fugitive Slave to Free Man: The Autobiographies of William Wells Brown*, edited by William L. Andrews (Columbia: University of Missouri Press, 2003), 91.

7. *St. Louis Republican*, September 15, 1844, in Brown, *Narrative*, 92.

8. Josiah Henson, *"Uncle Tom's Story of His Life": An Autobiography of the Rev. Josiah Henson*, edited by John Lobb (London: Christian Age Office, 1876), 162.

9. Ibid., 75.

CHAPTER 6. THE GREAT ESCAPE

1. Josiah Henson, *Truth Stranger Than Fiction: Father Henson's Story of His Own Life* (Boston: John P. Jewett and Company, 1858), 100.

2. Will Ferguson, *Beauty Tips from Moose Jaw: Travels in Search of Canada* (Toronto: Vintage Canada, 2010), 199–200.

3. Quotations in this section are from Henson, *Truth Stranger Than Fiction*, 104.

4. For the account of the Henson family's departure, see Henson, *Truth Stranger Than Fiction*, 107–108.

5. For this exchange, see ibid., 108.

6. See "Lincoln Landing," n.d., Roadside America, www.roadsideamerica .com/story/24359; "Ontario's Historical Plaques," n.d., www.ontarioplaques.com /Plaques/Plaque_Niagara74.html; Benjamin P. Thomas, *Abraham Lincoln: A Biography* (Carbondale: Southern Illinois University Press, 2008 [1952]), 24; Darrel E. Bigham, "Lincoln and His World: The Early Years, Birth to Illinois Legislature, by Richard Lawrence Miller," *Journal of the Abraham Lincoln Association* 29, no. 1 (2008): 71–75, https://quod.lib.umich.edu/j/jala/2629860.0029.108/—lincoln-and-his-world-the -early-years-birth-to-illinois?rgn=main;view=fulltext; William McKinley, *Life and Speeches of William McKinley*, edited by J. S. Ogilvie (New York: J. S. Ogilvie, 1896), 214.

7. The source for this account is Josiah Henson, *"Uncle Tom's Story of His Life": An Autobiography of the Rev. Josiah Henson*, edited by John Lobb (London: Christian Age Office, 1876), 89.

8. On the First Nations, see "Underground Railroad," *Dictionary of American History*, Encyclopedia.com, 2003, www.encyclopedia.com/history/united-states

-and-canada/us-history/underground-railroad; "Fugitives from Slavery," Ohio History Central, Ohio History Connection, www.ohiohistorycentral.org/w/Fugitives_from _Slavery; David A. Love, "Native American Roots in Black America Run Deep," Grio, November 22, 2012, http://thegrio.com/2012/11/22/native-american-roots -in-black-america-run-deep; Bill Gould, "Delmarva Native Americans and the Earliest Underground Railroad," Native Americans of the State of Delaware, October 26, 2007, http://nativeamericansofdelawarestate.com/Delmarva_Indians _&_Underground_Railroad.htm; "Conference Between Governor Burnet and the Indians," Early Recognized Treaties with American Indian Nations, American Indians Treaties Portal, http://treatiesportal.unl.edu/earlytreaties/treaty.00001.html; "Further Propositions of the Gov of Virginia Made to the Five Nations of Indians," New York Colonial Manuscripts, http://treatiesportal.unl.edu/earlytreaties/images /images.html?n=674&ref=treaty.00001.

9. In contrast, 58 percent of black Americans have at least 12.5 percent white ancestry.

10. Quoted in Sylviane A. Diouf, *Slavery's Exiles: The Story of the American Maroons* (New York: New York University Press, 2016), 24.

11. Quoted in Benjamin Drew, *A North-side View of Slavery: The Refugee; or, The Narratives of Fugitive Slaves in Canada, Related by Themselves, with an Account of the History and Condition of the Colored Population of Upper Canada* (Boston: John P. Jewett and Company, 1856), 192.

12. Source for the conversations in this section is Henson, *Truth Stranger Than Fiction*, 121–122.

13. This account is based on ibid., 125.

14. Josiah Henson, *The Life of Josiah Henson, Formerly a Slave, Now an Inhabitant of Canada, as Narrated by Himself* (Boston: Arthur D. Phelps, 1849), 94.

15. Henson, *Truth Stranger Than Fiction*, 126.

16. See William H. Siener and Thomas A. Chambers, "Crossing to Freedom: Harriet Tubman and John A. Roebling's Suspension Bridge," Western New York Heritage, n.d., www.wnyheritage.org/content/crossing_to_freedom_harriet_tubman_and_john _a_roeblings_suspensi/index.html.

17. For coordinates and distance from Black Rock to Fort Erie for the ferry across the Niagara, see "Coordinate Distance Calculator," http://boulter.com/gps/distance /?from=42.916272%2C+-78.909609&to=42.916209%2C+-78.901487&units=m. On Black Rock ferry, see Charles D. Norton, "The Old Black Rock Ferry: Read Before the Society, December 14, 1863," Maritime History of the Great Lakes, www .maritimehistoryofthegreatlakes.ca/Documents/BlackRockFerry/default.asp?ID =c1; "Broderick Park: Underground Railroad Station in Buffalo, New York," University at Buffalo, Archaeology Survey, Department of Anthropology, http://

archaeologicalsurvey.buffalo.edu/outreach/broderick-park; Jeff Z. Klein, "Heritage Moments: Fugitive Slave Fights for a Family's Freedom," WBFO Buffalo 88.7, November 23, 2015, http://news.wbfo.org/post/heritage-moments-fugitive -slave-fights-familys-freedom.

18. Conversation from Henson, *Truth Stranger Than Fiction*, 126.

19. "Broderick Park."

20. Source for this section is Henson, *Truth Stranger Than Fiction*, 127.

21. Glenn Walker, "Ferried to Freedom, Black History," Underground Railroad Research, Digital Collections, Monroe Fordham Regional History Center, Archives and Special Collections Department, E. H. Butler Library, State University of New York–Buffalo State, http://digitalcommons.buffalostate.edu/cgi/viewcontent. cgi?article=1003&context=ur-research.

Chapter 7. The Struggle for Light

1. Exodus 2:22.

2. Josiah Henson, *The Life of Josiah Henson, Formerly a Slave, Now an Inhabitant of Canada, as Narrated by Himself* (Boston: Arthur D. Phelps, 1849), 197.

3. For Josiah reading with Tom, see ibid., 63–64.

4. Josiah Henson, *"Uncle Tom's Story of His Life": An Autobiography of the Rev. Josiah Henson*, edited by John Lobb (London: Christian Age Office, 1876), 67.

5. Brion Gysin, *Back in No Time: The Brion Gysin Reader* (Middletown, CT: Wesleyan University Press, 2015), 46.

6. Detroit had a population of only 2,222 in 1830. See "Boomtown Detroit (1820–1860)," Detroit Historical Society, https://detroithistorical.org/learn /timeline-detroit/boomtown-detroit-1820-1860.

7. On land grants at that time and conditions being set, see Gysin, *Back in No Time*, 47.

8. Josiah Henson, *Truth Stranger Than Fiction: Father Henson's Story of His Own Life* (Boston: John P. Jewett and Company, 1858), 145.

9. Ibid., 146.

10. On William Still, see "William Still Historical Marker," Explore PA History, http://explorepahistory.com/hmarker.php?markerId=1-A-3EB; "William Still and the Pennsylvania Vigilance Committee," Historical Society of Pennsylvania, https://hsp.org/balch-institute/calendar/william-still-the-pennsylvania-vigilance-committee; "Vigilant Committee of Pennsylvania Records: 1839–1844," Collection 1121, Historical Society of Pennsylvania, www2.hsp.org/collections/manuscripts/v /vigilant1121.htm; "Underground Railroad: The William Still Story," PBS, www .pbs.org/black-culture/shows/list/underground-railroad/home.

11. See Christopher Klein, "Who Received the Reward for John Wilkes Booth's Capture?" History.com, April 16, 2015, www.history.com/news/ask-history/who -received-the-reward-for-john-wilkes-booths-capture.

12. Kate Clifford Larson, "Myths and Facts About Harriet Tubman, and Selected Quotes and Misquotes," Bound for the Promised Land: Harriet Tubman. Portrait of an American Hero, www.harriettubmanbiography.com/harriet-tubman -myths-and-facts.html.

13. "FAQ," Harriet Tubman Historical Society," www.harriet-tubman.org /facts-kids.

14. "Hunters' Lodges," *Encyclopaedia Britannica*, www.britannica.com/topic/ Hunters-Lodges.

15. Henson, *"Uncle Tom's Story of His Life,"* 176; Rev. J. W. Loguen, *The Rev. J. W. Loguen, as a Slave and as a Freeman: A Narrative of Real Life* (Syracuse, NY: J. G. K. Truair, 1859), 345; Adrienne Shadd, *The Journey from Tollgate to Parkway: African Canadians in Hamilton* (Toronto: Dundurn, 2010), 108.

16. Fort Malden sources: Shaun McLaughlin, *The Patriot War Along the Michigan-Canada Border: Raiders and Rebels* (Charleston, SC: History Press, 2013); "Rebellions of 1837–38," Canadian Encyclopedia, Historica Canada, n.d., www .thecanadianencyclopedia.ca/en/article/rebellions-of-1837. On African American militia service, see "Uncle Tom Fights for Canada," Raiders and Rebels, August 1, 2011, www.raidersandrebels.com/2011/08/uncle-tom-fights-for-canada.html; McLaughlin, *Patriot War*.

17. "Hardy, Sutherland, Theller, Roberts: The Four Stooges Go to War," Raiders and Rebels, February 22, 2010, www.raidersandrebels.com/2010/02/handy-sutherland -theller-roberts-four.html.

18. Daniel Palmer, *The McKee Treaty of 1790: British-Aboriginal Diplomacy in the Great Lakes* (master's thesis, University of Saskatchewan, 2017), 93, https:// ecommons.usask.ca/bitstream/handle/10388/8168/PALMER-THESIS-2017.pdf ?sequence=1; "McKee Purchase Treaty," Internet Archive, http://archive.org/stream /mckeepurchasetre00land/mckeepurchasetre00land_djvu.txt; "McKee's Purchase," Ontario's Historical Plaques, www.ontarioplaques.com/Plaques/Plaque_Chatham Kent29.html.

19. 1883 Kent County Almanac, available at http://vitacollections.ca/ckpl /2676482/data.

20. "Dawn Settlement Tour," Explore Dresden, http://dresden.ca/wp-content /uploads/2015/01/DawnI-WebTour.pdf.

21. Letter from Hiram Wilson at "British American Institute, September 30, 1843," The Letters of Hiram Wilson, https://hiramwilson.wordpress.com/2013/03 /28/british-american-institute-september-30-1843.

22. "T. H.," "The Dawn Institute Canada West," *Anti-Slavery Reporter*, May 1, 1856.

23. "Category Archives: 1843," Letters of Hiram Wilson, https://hiramwilson .wordpress.com/category/1843.

24. Victor Lauriston, *Romantic Kent: More Than Three Centuries of History, 1626–1952* (Chatham, Ontario: Corporation of the County of Kent, 1952).

25. "The Elgin Settlement," Buxton National Historic Site and Museum, www .buxtonmuseum.com/history/virtual-elgin-settlement.html; Oscar Reiss, *Blacks in Colonial America* (Jefferson, NC: McFarland, 1997), 156.

26. Fred Landon, *Ontario's African-Canadian Heritage: Collected Writings by Fred Landon, 1918–1967*, edited by Karolyn Smardz Frost, Bryan Walls, Hilary Bates Neary, and Frederick H. Armstrong (Toronto: Natural Heritage Books, 2009), 93.

27. "Dawn Settlement Tour," Explore Dresden, http://dresden.ca/wp-content /uploads/2015/01/DawnI-WebTour.pdf.

28. On William P. Newman, see "Josiah Henson," Waterloo Region Generations, http://generations.region.waterloo.on.ca/getperson.php?personID=I119988&tree =generations; Linda Brown-Kubisch, *The Queen's Bush Settlement: Black Pioneers, 1839–1865* (Toronto: Natural Heritage Books, 2004), 266; William Cheek and Aimee Lee Cheek, *John Mercer Langston and the Fight for Black Freedom, 1829–65* (Urbana: University of Illinois Press, 1996), 120; "Francis Newman," Newman Family Tree, www.newman-family-tree.net/francis-newman.html; Newman documents at London Anti-Slavery Research Project, www.huronantislaveryhistory.ca/newman.html.

29. On Newman's report, see R. E. Gillett, *The Oberlin Evangelist*, vols. 7–8 (Oberlin, OH: James M. Fitch, 1845), 180.

30. Samuel Longfellow, ed., *Life of Henry Wadsworth Longfellow*, vol. 1 (Boston: Houghton Mifflin, 1891), 47–48.

31. Longfellow sources: Christoph Irmscher, *Public Poet, Private Man: Henry Wadsworth Longfellow at 200* (Amherst: University of Massachusetts Press, 2009), 116–117; "Josiah Henson," Longfellow's House Washington Headquarters, www .nps.gov/long/learn/historyculture/josiah-henson.htm; Samuel Longfellow, ed., *Life of Henry Wadsworth Longfellow*, vol. 2 (Boston: Ticknor and Company, 1886), 48.

32. Henson, *"Uncle Tom's Story of His Life,"* 174.

33. Ibid., 175.

34. Jane H. Pease and William Henry Pease, *Bound with Them in Chains: A Biographical History of the Antislavery Movement* (Westport, CT: Greenwood Press, 1972), 131.

35. On Josiah Henson and Masonry, see "Josiah Henson," Grand Lodge of British Columbia and Yukon, http://freemasonry.bcy.ca/biography/henson_j/henson_j .html; "Scottish Rite Freemasonry," Celestial Lodge #80 F&AM PHA, shared photo of Josiah Henson, posted March 12, 2016, www.facebook.com/permalink .php?story_fbid=1148018048565695&id=141434429224067; "Masons," African Canadian Community, Windsor Mosaic, www.windsor-communities.com

/african-organ-masons.php; Cheryl Janifer LaRoche, *Free Black Communities and the Underground Railroad: The Geography of Resistance* (Urbana: University of Illinois Press, 2013); Grand Lodge, A.F. & A.M., of Canada in the Province of Ontario, *Newsletter of the Committee on Masonic Education* 9, no. 4 (1990), http://home .golden.net/~djjcameron/9.4.pdf; Dumas Malone, ed., *Dictionary of American Biography*, vol. 8 (New York: Charles Scribner's Sons, 1932), 564–565; C. L. Murphy, *Postage Stamps and Freemasonry* (New York: Carleton Press, 1988), 142–143; W. S. Wallace and W. A. McKay, eds., *Macmillan Dictionary of Canadian Biography*, 4th ed. (Toronto: Macmillan, 1978), 354; R. W. Winks, *The Blacks in Canada: A History* (New Haven, CT: Yale University Press, 1971), 181–195; "International Prince Hall Day: Freedom Fighters" program, Dresden, Ontario, 1972.

36. La Roche, *Free Black Communities*, 152.

37. Josiah Henson, *An Autobiography of the Rev. Josiah Henson (Mrs. Harriet Beecher Stowe's "Uncle Tom") from 1789 to 1877*, with a preface by Harriet Beecher Stowe, edited by John Lobb, revised and enlarged (London: Christian Age Office, 1878).

38. "What Was the Three-Fifths Compromise?," Laws, http://constitution.laws .com/three-fifths-compromise.

39. La Roche, *Free Black Communities*, 6.

40. On fugitive slave law, see "New Struggles in Canada After the Underground Railroad," Canadian Museum for Human Rights, February 12, 2015, https:// humanrights.ca/blog/new-struggles-canada-after-underground-railroad; LaRoche, *Free Black Communities*, 118–122, 158; Benjamin Brawley, "From *A Short History of the American Negro*" (New York: Macmillan, 1924), at Uncle Tom's Cabin and American Culture: A Multimedia Archive, Institute for Advanced Technology in the Humanities, Special Collections, Alderman Library, University of Virginia (UTC/ IATH hereafter), http://utc.iath.virginia.edu/africam/afesbbat.html.

41. Daniel Alexander Payne, *Recollections of Seventy Years*, edited by C. S. Smith (Nashville, TN: A.M.E. Sunday School Union, 1888), http://docsouth.unc.edu /church/payne70/payne.html?highlight=WyJGb3J0IFN1bXRlciJd.

42. Mary Kelley, "'Feeling Right': Harriet Beecher Stowe, *Uncle Tom's Cabin*, and the Power of Sympathy," UTC/IATH, 2007, http://utc.iath.virginia.edu/interpret /exhibits/kelley/kelley.html.

43. Joan D. Hedrick, *Harriet Beecher Stowe: A Life* (Oxford: Oxford University Press, 1994), 207.

44. Henson, *Truth Stranger Than Fiction*, 178.

45. "Transcription: AHN Newman's Letter to Douglass," New Research on Old Connections: William Newman and the Black Abolitionist Movement, https:// williampnewman.wordpress.com.

CHAPTER 8. THE GREAT EXHIBITION

1. On the World's Fair, see "Crystal Palace: Building, London, United Kingdom," *Encyclopaedia Britannica*, n.d., www.britannica.com/topic/Crystal-Palace -building-London; "World's Fairs," Gale, World History in Context, n.d., http:// ic.galegroup.com/ic/whic/ReferenceDetailsPage/DocumentToolsPortletWindow ?displayGroupName=Reference&jsid=7c80cac443c70bc64f049166655025d5 &action=2&catId=&documentId=GALE%7CCX3446900895&u=mlin_s_martha &zid=6d28932e81a63a4d3eb14c7fe71291fb; Liza Picard, "The Great Exhibition," British Library, October 14, 2009, www.bl.uk/victorian-britain/articles/the -great-exhibition; "Location and Ground Plan of the Great Exhibition," Great Exhibition 1851 Blogspot, November 2, 2011, http://greatexhibition1851.blogspot.com /2011/11/location-and-ground-plan-of-great.html; "The Great Exhibition," Victoria and Albert Museum, www.vam.ac.uk/page/g/great-exhibition; John R. Gold and Margaret M. Gold, *Cities of Culture: Staging International Festivals and the Urban Agenda, 1851–2000* (New York: Routledge, 2016 [2005]); "The Crystal Palace," The White Files, n.d., http://whitefiles.org/b3_q/1_architecture/zqla/qla7/7_xtlplc .htm; "Crystal Palace," Grace's Guide to British Industrial History, www.graces guide.co.uk/Crystal_Palace; Gili Merin, "AD Classics: The Crystal Palace / Joseph Paxton," *Arch Daily*, July 5, 2013, www.archdaily.com/397949/ad-classic-the-crystal -palace-joseph-paxton; "Crystal Palace," BBC, www.bbc.co.uk/london/content/articles /2004/07/27/history_feature.shtml; "The Crystal Palace," Victoria and Albert Museum, www.vam.ac.uk/content/articles/t/the-crystal-palace; Peter Berlyn and Charles Fowler, *The Crystal Palace: Its Architectural History and Constructive Marvels* (London: James Gilbert, 1851), http://gwydir.demon.co.uk/PG/Crystal/Palace.htm; Randy Alfred, "Aug. 3, 1803: Crystal Palace Architect Born," *Wired*, July 31, 2009, www.wired.com/2009/07/dayintech_0803; "Joseph Paxton," Los Angeles Institute of Architecture and Design, www.greatbuildings.com/architects/Joseph_Paxton .html; www.punch.co.uk/about; "*Punch* (magazine)," Wikipedia, https://en.wikipedia .org/wiki/Punch_(magazine); "America at the Great Exhibition," The Great Exhibition 1851, November 13, 2011, http://greatexhibition1851.blogspot.co.uk/2011/11 /america-at-great-exhibition.html; Menachem Wecker, "The Scandalous Story Behind the Provocative 19th-Century Sculpture 'Greek Slave,'" *Smithsonian*, July 24, 2015, www.smithsonianmag.com/smithsonian-institution/scandalous-story-behind -provocative-sculpture-greek-slave-19th-century-audiences-180956029; *Official Catalogue of the Great Exhibition* (London: Spicer Brothers, 1851); https://ia902606 .us.archive.org/34/items/officialcatalog06unkngoog/officialcatalog06unkngoog.pdf; *Official Catalogue of the Great Exhibition*, Second Corrected and Improved Version

(London: Spicer Brothers, 1851), 169; "About Us," Royal Commission for the Exhibition of 1851, www.royalcommission1851.org/about-us.

2. Martin Delany, "Frederick Douglass' Paper," April 29, 1853, UTC/IATH, http://utc.iath.virginia.edu/africam/afar03ot.html.

3. Josiah Henson, *"Uncle Tom's Story of His Life": An Autobiography of the Rev. Josiah Henson*, edited by John Lobb (London: Christian Age Office, 1876), 132.

4. Ibid., 142.

5. "The Great Exhibition: Queen Victoria's Journal," Victoria and Albert Museum, www.vam.ac.uk/content/articles/g/great-exhibition-queen-victorias-journal.

6. Thomas F. Army Jr., *Engineering Victory: How Technology Won the Civil War* (Baltimore: Johns Hopkins University Press, 2016); B. Zorina Khan, *The Democratization of Invention: Patents and Copyrights in American Economic Development, 1790–1920* (Cambridge: Cambridge University Press, 2005); Eric Chiu, "The New York Crystal Palace: The Birth of a Building," A Treasure of World's Fair Art and Architecture, University of Maryland Libraries Digital Collections, n.d., http://digital.lib.umd.edu/worldsfairs/record?pid=umd:989; *Sheldon & Co.'s Business or Advertising Directory: Containing the Cards, Circulars, and Advertisements of the Cities of New-York, Boston, Philadelphia, Baltimore, Etc.* (Boston: John F. Trow and Company, 1845), 5.

7. Henson, *"Uncle Tom's Story of His Life,"* 137.

8. Charles Frederick Holder, ed., *The Californian Illustrated Magazine: December 1892 to May 1893*, vol. 3 (San Francisco: Californian Publishing Company, 1893), 577.

9. Conversation from Henson, *"Uncle Tom's Story of His Life,"* 137.

10. Ibid., 139.

11. See the first article on the newspaper page archived at INK-ODW Newspaper Collection, *The Voice of the Fugitive*, June 1, 1851, http://ink.scholarsportal.info/viewer/cecil/focus/ink/newspapers/vf/reel1/000311-x0-y0-z1-r0-0-0?q=%22josiah%20henson%22.

12. "Henson, Josiah," *Anti-Slavery Reporter*, June 2, 1851, http://research.udmercy.edu/digital_collections/baa/Henson_11608spe.pdf.

13. Henson, *"Uncle Tom's Story of His Life,"* 133.

14. "Scoble, John," Dictionary of Canadian Biography, www.biographi.ca/en/bio/scoble_john_9E.html.

15. Josiah Henson, *Truth Stranger Than Fiction: Father Henson's Story of His Own Life* (Boston: John P. Jewett and Company, 1858), 185.

16. Henson, *"Uncle Tom's Story of His Life,"* 165.

17. *Provincial Freeman*, October 8, 1851.

18. "Biographical Sketches: Uncle Tom," *The School Newspaper*, 1876–1877, 39, available at https://books.google.com/books?id=75EFAAAAQAAJ.

19. The Boston review appears in *Littell's Living Age* 34 (1852): 61, available at https://books.google.ca/books?id=hwNGAQAAMAAJ.

20. On *Uncle Tom's Cabin*, see "American Reviews of Uncle Tom's Cabin," UTC/IATH, http://utc.iath.virginia.edu/reviews/rehp.html; "Sample Notices: 1851–1865," UTC/IATH, http://utc.iath.virginia.edu/notices/nohp.html; "What They Think in England of 'Uncle Tom's Cabin,'" *New York Independent*, November 11, 1852, UTC/IATH, http://utc.iath.virginia.edu/reviews/read12bt.html; "Uncle Tom's Cabin," *New York Independent*, May 20, 1852, UTC/IATH, http://utc.iath .virginia.edu/reviews/read12at.html; "Uncle Tom's Cabin," *The Independent*, May 13 1852, UTC/IATH, http://utc.iath.virginia.edu/notices/noar12dt.html; *New York Times*, May 14, 1852, UTC/IATH, http://utc.iath.virginia.edu/notices/noar05dt .html; "Uncle Tom's Cabin," *The Liberator*, June 11, 1852, UTC/IATH, http://utc .iath.virginia.edu/notices/noar02at.html; "Uncle Tom's Cabin," *National Anti-Slavery Standard*, July 15, 1852, UTC/IATH, http://utc.iath.virginia.edu/notices/noar08ct .html; *New York Times*, January 4, 1853, UTC/IATH, http://utc.iath.virginia.edu /notices/noar05st.html.

21. *The Independent*, May 13, 1852, UTC/IATH, http://utc.iath.virginia.edu /notices/noar12dt.html.

22. *New York Times*, May 14, 1852, UTC/IATH, http://utc.iath.virginia.edu /notices/noar05dt.html.

23. *National Anti-Slavery Standard*, July 15, 1852, UTC/IATH, http://utc.iath .virginia.edu/notices/noar08ct.html.

24. *Washington Post*, September 3, 1879, UTC/IATH, http://utc.iath.virginia .edu/articles/n2ar19act.html.

25. *Davenport Independent*, quoted in "What They Think in England, of "Uncle Tom's Cabin," *New York Independent*, November 11, 1852, UTC/IATH, http://utc .iath.virginia.edu/reviews/read12bt.html.

26. "Sutherland, Robert (c. 1830–1878)," Queen's Encyclopedia, Queen's University, www.queensu.ca/encyclopedia/s/sutherland-robert.

27. Henson, *"Uncle Tom's Story of His Life,"* 141.

28. Henson, *Truth Stranger Than Fiction*, 201.

29. Henson, *"Uncle Tom's Story of His Life,"* 166.

30. R. J. Hinton, *Brief Biographies: English Radical Leaders* (New York: G. P. Putnam's Sons, 1875); Edwin Hodder, *Life of Samuel Morley* (London: Hodder and Stoughton, 1887); "Mr. Samuel Morley," Commons and Lords Hansard archives, http://hansard.millbanksystems.com/people/mr-samuel-morley.

31. Robin W. Winks, *The Blacks in Canada: A History*, 2nd ed. (Montreal: McGill-Queen's University Press, 1997).

32. Henson, *"Uncle Tom's Story of His Life,"* 206.

33. Ibid., 207.

34. Ibid, 166.

35. Ibid, 167.

CHAPTER 9. THE REAL UNCLE TOM

1. Josiah Henson, *An Autobiography of the Rev. Josiah Henson (Mrs. Harriet Beecher Stowe's "Uncle Tom") from 1789 to 1877*, with a preface by Harriet Beecher Stowe, edited by John Lobb, revised and enlarged (London: Christian Age Office, 1878), 224.

2. Harriet Beecher Stowe, "Preface," in *Uncle Tom's Cabin* (Boston: John P. Jewett and Company, 1852), available at UTC/IATH, http://utc.iath.virginia.edu /uncletom/uteshbsbt.html.

3. *Richmond Daily Dispatch*, August 25, 1852, www.newspapers.com/newspage /79776180.

4. *De Bow's Southern and Western Review*, March 1853, UTC/IATH, http://utc .iath.virginia.edu/proslav/prno30gt.html.

5. Mary H. Eastman, *Aunt Phillis's Cabin: Or, Southern Life As It Is* (Philadelphia: Lippincott, Grambo, 1852).

6. *Souther v. the Commonwealth of Virginia*: "Person Page—682," Souther Family Association, http://rdsouther.com/p682.htm; "Souther v. Commonwealth," Casetext, https://casetext.com/case/souther-v-commonwealth.

7. *Richmond Daily Dispatch*, May 18, 1853, UTC/IATH, http://utc.iath.virginia .edu/proslav/prar170art.html.

8. A razor strop was used to polish blades, such as razors, knives, and other tools. See *Daily Picayune*, June 15, 1853, UTC/IATH, http://utc.iath.virginia.edu/proslav /prar97akt.html.

9. Published by Boston's John P. Jewett and Company.

10. "Southern Slavery and Its Assailants," in *De Bow's Review* 15 (1853): 486, available at https://books.google.ca/books?id=Mv0cAAAAIAAJ.

11. "A Key to Uncle Tom's Cabin," *Southern Literary Messenger* 19, no. 6 (1853): 321, available at https://books.google.ca/books?id=bZBFAQAAMAAJ.

12. Irwin Unger and David Reimers, *The Slavery Experience in the United States* (New York: Holt, Rinehart and Winston, 1970).

13. "Comic Almanacs," UTC/IATH, http://utc.iath.virginia.edu/minstrel/gall mitxtf.html.

14. Harriet Beecher Stowe, *The Key to Uncle Tom's Cabin* (Boston: John P. Jewett and Company, 1854).

15. Ibid.

16. Joan D. Hedrick, *Harriet Beecher Stowe: A Life* (Oxford: Oxford University Press, 1994), 237.

17. Frederick Douglass, "Appendix," in *Life of an American Slave* (Boston: Anti-

Slavery Office, 1845), available at UTC/IATH, http://utc.iath.virginia.edu/abolitn /abaufda14t.html.

18. Martin Delany, "Uncle Tom," *Frederick Douglass' Paper*, April 29, 1853, UTC/IATH, http://utc.iath.virginia.edu/africam/afar03ot.html.

19. Ibid.

20. Josiah Henson, *"Uncle Tom's Story of His Life": An Autobiography of the Rev. Josiah Henson*, edited by John Lobb (London: Christian Age Office, 1876), 157–158.

21. Ibid., 174.

22. Letter from A. A. Lawrence to John Scoble, March 30, 1851.

23. Letter from S. A. Eliot, December 21, 1852, Massachusetts Historical Society (http://masshist.org/).

24. Henson, *"Uncle Tom's Story of His Life"*.

25. Ibid.

26. On William Whipper, see Boulou Ebanda de B'béri, Nina Reid-Maroney, and Handel Kashope Wright, eds., *The Promised Land: History and Historiography of the Black Experience in Chatham-Kent's Settlements and Beyond* (Toronto: University of Toronto Press, 2014), 80; "William Whipper," Charles H. Wright Museum of African American History, http://ugrr.thewright.org/media/Pdf/Whipper _William_People_UGRR_Final_1.pdf; "William Whipper: Father of Non Violence Resistance," Original People, November 14, 2012, http://originalpeople.org /william-whipper-father-of-non-violence-resistance100-years-before-gandhi-or -dr-king; "William Whipper," Wikipedia, https://en.wikipedia.org/wiki/William _Whipper.

27. For Shadd references, see Martha Schoolman and Jared Hickman, eds., *Abolitionist Places* (New York: Routledge, 2013); "Mary Ann Shadd," Historica Canada, www.thecanadianencyclopedia.ca/en/article/mary-ann-shadd; "King, William," Dictionary of Canadian Biography, www.biographi.ca/en/bio/king_william _12E.html; Adrienne Shadd, "Mary Ann Shadd Cary: Abolitionist," Library and Archives Canada, www.collectionscanada.gc.ca/northern-star/033005-2201-e.html.

28. "Proceedings for the North American Convention Held in Toronto, Canada, 1851," Colored Conventions, http://coloredconventions.org/items/show/324.

29. "Black Settlement in Ontario," Ontario Heritage Trust, www.heritage trust.on.ca/en/index.php/pages/our-stories/slavery-to-freedom/history/black -settlement-in-ontario.

30. Henson, *"Uncle Tom's Story of His Life,"* 201.

31. Ibid., 168.

32. Shadd writing for her own *Provincial Freeman* on July 22, 1854.

33. Ibid.

34. Dr. Robert Burns of Toronto, letter reprinted in the *Provincial Freeman* on November 4, 1854, about his October 20 visit to Dawn.

35. *Provincial Freeman*, April 7, 1855. J. C. Brown lectured on April 2 at the Wesleyan Chapel.

36. *Provincial Freeman*, August 29, 1855.

37. *Provincial Freeman*, September 13, 1855.

38. *Provincial Freeman*, October 20, 1855.

39. Diane D. Broadhurst, "An Examination of Slaves and Slavery in the Beall Family Household," Montgomery County Historical Society Library, n.d. Vertical File.

40. On Chaplin, see "Gen William L. Chaplin," Find a Grave, www.findagrave.com/cgi-bin/fg.cgi?page=gr&GRid=71095418; "William L. Chaplin Arrested!," Waymarking, www.waymarking.com/waymarks/WM3V71_William_L_Chaplin_Arrested_Silver_Spring_MD; "William L. Chaplin Arrested!," Historical Marker Database, www.hmdb.org/Marker.asp?marker=3969; "Image 12 of the Case of William L. Chaplin," Library of Congress, www.loc.gov/resource/llst.041/?sp=12; "The Case of William L. Chaplin," Library of Congress, www.loc.gov/resource/llst.041/?st=gallery&c=160; "William L. Chaplin," Wikipedia, https://en.wikipedia.org/wiki/William_L._Chaplin.

41. Charles T. Davis and Henry Louis Gates Jr., eds., *The Slave's Narrative* (Oxford: Oxford University Press, 1991), xvi.

42. Josiah Henson, *Truth Stranger Than Fiction: Father Henson's Story of His Own Life* (Boston: John P. Jewett and Company, 1858), 210.

43. Ibid., 212.

44. "Provincial Freeman," Accessible Archives, www.accessible-archives.com/collections/african-american-newspapers/provincial-freeman.

45. Ibid.

46. "Convention of the Colored Citizens of Massachusetts, August 1, 1858," Colored Conventions, http://ccp.lib.udel.edu/scripto/revision/264/2139/0/6412.

47. Ibid.

48. Christopher Klein, "10 Things You May Not Know About Nat Turner's Rebellion," History.com, May 24, 2016, www.history.com/news/history-lists/10-things-you-may-not-know-about-nat-turners-rebellion; mira1217, "The Execution of Nat Turner," Life of the Nation—an Early 19th C. Journalism Project," November 15, 2013, https://ush1unit2assessment.wordpress.com/2013/11/15/the-execution-fo-nat-turner; Daina Ramey Berry, "Nat Turner's Skull and My Student's Purse of Skin," *New York Times*, October 18, 2016, www.nytimes.com/2016/10/18/opinion/nat-turners-skull-and-my-students-purse-of-skin.html; Justin Fornal, "Exclusive: Inside the Quest to Return Nat Turner's Skull to His Family," *National Geographic*, October 7, 2016, http://news.nationalgeographic.com/2016/10/nat-turner-skull-slave-rebellion-uprising.

49. Jeffrey L. Kirchmeier, *Imprisoned by the Past: Warren McCleskey and the American Death Penalty* (Oxford: Oxford University Press, 2015), 54.

50. "Free Blacks Address the Enslaved: Resist, Run Away, . . . Revolt?," National Humanities Center Resource Toolbox, The Making of African American Identity, vol. 1, 1500–1865, http://nationalhumanitiescenter.org/pds/maai/enslavement/text7 /freeblacksaddress.pdf.

51. *Chatham Weekly Planet*, February 17, 1859.

52. Henson, *"Uncle Tom's Story of His Life,"* 168.

53. On African Americans in the Civil War, see "Black Soldiers in the U.S. Military During the Civil War," National Archives, Educator Resources, www .archives.gov/education/lessons/blacks-civil-war; "Deaths of Blacks During Civil War Pondered," Cotton Bowl Conspiracy, April 23, 2012, https://southcarolina 1670.wordpress.com/2012/04/23/deaths-of-blacks-during-civil-war-pondered; "The First Shot of the Civil War," Eyewitness to History, www.eyewitnesstohistory .com/sumter.htm.

54. Henson, *"Uncle Tom's Story of His Life,"* 177.

55. On bounty brokers, see "Bounty System," *Encyclopaedia Britannica*, www.bri tannica.com/event/Bounty-System; "Bounty Jumper," Wikipedia, https://en.wikipedia .org/wiki/Bounty_jumper; William C. Moffat Jr., "Soldiers Pay," Cincinnati Civil War Round Table, January 1965, www.cincinnaticwrt.org/data/ccwrt_history/talks_text /moffat_soldiers_pay.html; Edward Davis Townsend, *Anecdotes of the Civil War in the United States* (New York: D. Appleton, 1884), 103.

56. On the Foreign Enlistment Act, see Tyler Wentzell, "Mercenaries and Adventurers: Canada and the Foreign Enlistment Act in the Nineteenth Century," *Canadian Military History* 23, no. 2 (2015), http://scholars.wlu.ca/cgi/viewcontent .cgi?article=1736&context=cmh; "The American Civil War Was an International Affair," The Colonel and the Vicar, July 16, 2016, https://thecolonelandthevicar .wordpress.com/tag/foreign-enlistment-act-of-1819; Gordon S. Barker, *"African Canadians in Union Blue: Volunteering for the Cause in the Civil War* by Richard M. Reid (review)," *Canadian Journal of History* 50, no. 3 (2015): 599–601, Project Muse, https://muse.jhu.edu/article/604700/summary; www.civilwarcollector.ca /canadas-connection.html.

57. The quotations in this section are from Henson, *"Uncle Tom's Story of His Life,"* 177–186.

58. Matt Boucher, "Lincoln and the Key to Uncle Tom's Cabin," *Connecticut Explored*, January 2, 2013, https://ctexplored.org/sample-article-lincoln-and-the-key -to-uncle-toms-cabin.

59. *The Liberator*, August 15, 1862, www.newspapers.com/newspage/35031641.

60. Conversation from Henson, *"Uncle Tom's Story of His Life,"* 169.

61. This incident is recounted in ibid., 175.

62. Frederick Douglass, *The Frederick Douglass Papers: Correspondence, 1842– 1852*, vol. 1 (New Haven, CT: Yale University Press, 2009), 135.

63. On Greeley, see "The Prayer of Twenty Millions," open letter to Lincoln from Horace Greeley, *New-York Tribune*, August 20, 1862, Library of Congress, http:// memory.loc.gov/mss/mal/mal2/423/4233500/001.jpg; "Horace Greeley's 'Prayer of Twenty Millions,' Front Page," NewseumED, https://newseumed.org/artifact /the-new-york-tribune-aug-20-1862-page-1-2; transcript at Northern Visions of Race, Region & Reform, American Antiquarian Society Online Resource, www .americanantiquarian.org/Freedmen/Manuscripts/greeley.html; "Horace Greeley's 'The Prayer of Twenty Millions' Is Published," History.com, This Day in History for August 20, www.history.com/this-day-in-history/horace-greeleys-the-prayer-of -twenty-millions-is-published; "A Letter from President Lincoln: Reply to Horace Greeley. Slavery and the Union; The Restoration of the Union the Paramount Object," *New York Times*, August 22, 1862, www.nytimes.com/1862/08/24/news /letter-president-lincoln-reply-horace-greeley-slavery-union-restoration-union .html; Joan D. Hedrick, *Harriet Beecher Stowe: A Life* (Oxford: Oxford University Press, 1994).

64. For Stowe's retort, see *Advocate and Family Guardian* 28 (1862): 303, available at https://books.google.ca/books?id=vnMXAAAAYAAJ; Hedrick, *Harriet Beecher Stowe: A Life*.

65. On Stowe and Lincoln, see also "Harriet Beecher Stowe Meets Lincoln," Kansas City Public Library, Civil War on the Western Border, http://civilwaron thewesternborder.org/timeline/harriet-beecher-stowe-meets-lincoln; Tevi Troy, *What Jefferson Read, Ike Watched, and Obama Tweeted: 200 Years of Popular Culture in the White House* (Washington, DC: Regnery, 2013), 43; Michael Hanne, *The Power of the Story: Fiction and Political Change* (Providence, RI: Berghahn, 1994), chap. 3; Fred R. Shapiro, *The Yale Book of Quotations* (New Haven, CT: Yale University Press, 2006), 465; Barbara A. White, *Visits with Lincoln: Abolitionists Meet the President at the White House* (Lanham, MD: Lexington Books, 2011), 59; *Littell's Living Age* 80 (1864): 284, available at https://books.google.ca/books?id=OqFJAQAAMAAJ; Francis Fisher Browne, *The Every-day Life of Abraham Lincoln* (New York: N. D. Thompson, 1887), 576.

66. Barbara A. White, *The Beecher Sisters* (New Haven, CT: Yale University Press, 2008), 90.

67. Charles Edward Stowe and Lyman Beecher Stowe, *Harriet Beecher Stowe: The Story of Her Life* (Boston: Houghton Mifflin, 1911), available at UTC/IATH, http:// utc.iath.virginia.edu/articles/n2escesb3t.html.

68. "Days with Mrs. Stowe," *Atlantic Monthly* 78 (1896): 148, available at https://books.google.ca/books?id=yj5PM9oSXdIC.

69. For Stowe's reply to the Stafford House petition, see "Harriet Beecher Stowe," Society for the Study of American Women Writers, Lehigh University, www.lehigh .edu/~dek7/SSAWW/writStoweReply.htm; Hedrick, *Harriet Beecher Stowe: A Life*.

70. Harriet Beecher Stowe, "A Reply: The Author of Uncle Tom's Cabin Urges the Women of England to Action Against Slavery," *The Atlantic*, January 1863, www .theatlantic.com/magazine/archive/1863/01/a-reply/308753.

71. "Union Blockade," Wikipedia, https://en.wikipedia.org/wiki/Union_blockade.

72. On the Emancipation Proclamation, see Louis P. Masur, "How the Emancipation Proclamation Came to Be Signed," Smithsonian, January 2013, www .smithsonianmag.com/history/how-the-emancipation-proclamation-came-to-be -signed-165533991; "Gold Pen Used by Lincoln to Sign the Emancipation Proclamation in the Executive Mansion," Yale University Library, Beinecke Rare Book and Manuscript Library, http://brbl-dl.library.yale.edu/vufind/Record/3521430; "Emancipation Proclamation: Information and Articles About the Emancipation Proclamation," History Net, www.historynet.com/emancipation-proclamation; "Original Emancipation Proclamation Signed by Lincoln Going on View at National Archives," *Huffington Post*, December 19, 2012, www.huffingtonpost.com/2012/12/19 /emancipation-proclamation-lincoln_n_2323943.html; "Emancipation Proclamation," Abraham Lincoln Online, Speeches and Writings, www.abrahamlincolnonline.org /lincoln/speeches/emancipate.htm; Daniel J. Vermilya, "Antietam National Battlefield: The Emancipation Proclamation," National Park Service, www.nps.gov /resources/story.htm%3Fid%3D235; "Andrew Johnson and Emancipation in Tennessee," Andrew Johnson National Historic Site, Tennessee, National Park Service, www.nps.gov/anjo/learn/historyculture/johnson-and-tn-emancipation.htm.

73. Bobby Jindal, *American Will: The Forgotten Choices That Changed Our Republic* (New York: Simon and Schuster, 2015), 329.

74. On Emerson, see Arthur Hobson Quinn, *The Literature of the American People: An Historical and Critical Survey* (New York: Ardent Media, 1951), 439; Ralph Waldo Emerson, "Boston Hymn," *The Atlantic*, February 1863, www .theatlantic.com/magazine/archive/1863/02/boston-hymn/303953; John Hope Franklin, "The Emancipation Proclamation: An Act of Justice," *Prologue Magazine* 25, no. 2 (1993), www.archives.gov/publications/prologue/1993/summer/emanci pation-proclamation.html.

75. Quoted in Harriet Beecher Stowe, *The Writings of Harriet Beecher Stowe, with Biographical Introductions, Portraits, and Other Illustrations* (Boston: Houghton Mifflin, 1896), lxxv.

76. Frederick Douglass, *The Essential Writings* (Loschberg, Germany: Jazzybee, 2017), 399.

77. For Maryland statistics, see Miranda S. Spivack, "The Not-Quite-Free State: Maryland Dragged Its Feet on Emancipation During Civil War," *Washington Post*, September 13, 2013, www.washingtonpost.com/local/md-politics/the-not -quite-free-state-maryland-dragged-its-feet-on-emancipation-during-civil-war /2013/09/13/a34d35de-fec7-11e2-bd97-676ec24f1f3f_story.html; Kevin Dayhoff,

"Eagle Archive: Here's a Toast to Maryland's Origins as 'The Free State,'" *Baltimore Sun*, October 7, 2012, www.baltimoresun.com/ph-ce-eagle-archive-1008-20121003 -story.html; "Maryland at a Glance: Name," Maryland Manual On-Line, http://msa .maryland.gov/msa/mdmanual/01glance/html/nickname.html.

78. On Davis, see James L. Swanson, "Was Jefferson Davis Captured in a Dress?," *American Heritage* 60, no. 3 (2010), www.americanheritage.com/content/was -jefferson-davis-captured-dress; Katelyn Fossett, "Pictures of Jefferson Davis Dressed Like a Woman," *Politico*, April 8, 2015, www.politico.com/magazine/gallery/2015 /04/pictures-of-jefferson-davis-dressed-like-a-woman-000141?slide=0; "On This Day [May 27, 1865]," *New York Times*, www.nytimes.com/learning/general/onthisday/harp /0527.html.

79. Matthew Karp, "In the 1850s, the Future of American Slavery Seemed Bright," *Aeon*, November 1, 2016, https://aeon.co/ideas/in-the-1850s-the-future-of -american-slavery-seemed-bright.

80. Matthew Karp, *The Vast Southern Empire* (Cambridge, MA: Harvard University Press, 2016), 170.

81. James Henry Hammond, *Selections from the Letters and Speeches of the Hon. James H. Hammond of South Carolina* (New York: John F. Trow and Company, 1866), 347.

82. Henson, *"Uncle Tom's Story of His Life,"* 170.

83. 1888 Kent County Almanac.

84. On the Wilberforce Institute, see *Statutes of the Province of Ontario* (Toronto: Queen's Printer, 1873), 774; "Documentary History of Education in Upper Canada from the Passing of the Constitutional Act of 1791 to the Close of Rev. Dr. Ryerson's Administration of the Education Department in 1876," https://archive.org/stream /documentaryhisto25hodguoft/documentaryhisto25hodguoft_djvu.txt; Catherine Slaney, *Family Secrets: Crossing the Colour Line* (Toronto: Natural Heritage Books, 2003), 109.

85. Robin W. Winks, *Blacks in Canada: A History*, 2nd ed. (Montreal: McGill-Queen's University Press, 1997), 196–197.

86. *Anti-Slavery Reporter*, May 1, 1856.

87. Henson, *"Uncle Tom's Story of His Life,"* 204.

CHAPTER 10. HOMECOMING

1. Josiah Henson, *"Uncle Tom's Story of His Life": An Autobiography of the Rev. Josiah Henson*, edited by John Lobb (London: Christian Age Office, 1876), 201.

2. On phrenology, see "Victorian Era Phrenology," The Victorian Era England, www.victorian-era.org/victorian-era-phrenology.html; John van Wyhe, "The His-

tory of Phrenology," The Victorian Web, www.victorianweb.org/science/phrenology
/intro.html; "Henry Ward Beecher," Wikivisually, https://wikivisually.com/wiki
/Henry_Ward_Beecher.

3. Henson, *"Uncle Tom's Story of His Life,"* 205.

4. See the title page of this edition at North American Slave Narratives, Documenting the American South, a webpage of the University Library of the University of North Carolina at Chapel Hill, http://docsouth.unc.edu/neh/henson/hensotp.jpg.

5. I have a copy of a letter sent from the Royal Archives to a researcher named Professor D. Smith at the University of Calgary. It was sent by Miss Pamela Clark (deputy registrar) on November 22, 1996, and contains the typed-out contents of the diary.

6. Josiah Henson, *An Autobiography of the Rev. Josiah Henson (Mrs. Harriet Beecher Stowe's "Uncle Tom") from 1789 to 1877*, with a preface by Harriet Beecher Stowe, edited by John Lobb, revised and enlarged (London: Christian Age Office, 1878), 266.

7. Ibid., 228.

8. Letter from Royal Archives.

9. Brion Gysin, *To Master, a Long Goodnight: The Story of the Real-Life "Uncle Tom"* (New York: Creative Age Press, 1946).

10. "John Lobb," London Wiki, Wikia, http://london.wikia.com/wiki/John_Lobb; John Lobb, *Talks with the Dead: Luminous Rays from the Unseen World, Illustrated with Spirit Photographs* (J. Lobb, 1907), at Internet Archive, https://archive.org/details/talkswithdeadlu00lobbgoog; *The Literary World* 20 (1879): 63, available at https://books.google.ca/books?id=ozcZAAAAYAAJ.

11. Conversation from Josiah Henson, *An Autobiography of the Rev. Josiah Henson ("Uncle Tom") from 1789 to 1881* (London, Ontario: Schuyler, Smith, and Company, 1881), 221–223.

12. Ibid.

13. 1880 Kent County Directory, 106–118, available at http://vitacollections.ca/ckpl/2818380/data?dy=1880&fz=0&grd=2372&rows=20&sort=groupid_2372+asc&v=t.

14. For the newspaper report, see *Hamilton Evening Times*, January 13, 1882.

15. Robin W. Winks, "The Making of a Fugitive Slave Narrative: Josiah Henson and Uncle Tom—A Case Study," in Charles T. Davis and Henry Louis Gates Jr., eds., *The Slave's Narrative* (Oxford: Oxford University Press, 1985), 143.

16. I have a typed copy of the will supplied by Henson's family.

17. On Josiah's funeral, see *Hamilton Times*, January 13, 1882; "Dawn Settlement Tour," Explore Dresden, http://dresden.ca/wp-content/uploads/2015/01/DawnI-WebTour.pdf.

EPILOGUE

1. *Proceedings of the 22nd Annual Communication of Eureka Grand Lodge of Louisiana (PHA)*, 1885, 53.

2. *Washington Post*, January 23, 1891, UTC/IATH, http://utc.iath.virginia.edu/articles/n2ar19cxt.html.

3. See "Henson House," Historical Marker Database, www.hmdb.org/marker.asp?marker=78387.

4. *Dresden Story*, 1954, National Film Board, www.nfb.ca/film/dresden_story.

5. "Josiah Henson, 1789–1883," Canadian Postage Stamps, www.canadianpostagestamps.ca/stamps/16260/josiah-henson-1789-1883.

6. See "Henson, Jehu William Josiah," Gathering Our Heroes: Chatham Kent WWI & WWII Enlistments, n.d., www.gatheringourheroes.ca/hero/henson-j-william, for information about a descendant of Josiah's who fought for Canada in four countries. He was taken prisoner and sent to Stalag 11-B in Poland during World War II, but survived. On the same website, see "Henson, Cleland Peter," www.gatheringourheroes.ca/hero/henson-cleland-peter-tex, for information on another descendant who served as "one of the first three blacks" in his parachute unit in World War II; and "Henson, William Isaac Jacob Beecher Stowe," www.gatheringourheroes.ca/hero/henson-beecher, for a descendant who served on a construction battalion in World War I.

7. W. E. B. Du Bois, *W. E. B. Du Bois: Selections from His Writings* (New York: Dover, 2013), 22.

8. W. E. B. Du Bois, *Darkwater: Voices from Within the Veil* (New York: Dover, 1999), 121.

9. Dickson D. Bruce Jr., *The Origins of African American Literature, 1680–1865* (Charlottesville: University of Virginia Press, 2001), 259.

10. *Anti-Slavery Reporter*, May 1, 1856.

A CLARION CALL

1. On the Black House, see "Q&A: Did Slaves Build the White House?," White House Historical Association, www.whitehousehistory.org/questions/did-slaves-build-the-white-house; Julie Hirschfeld Davis, "Yes, Slaves Did Help Build the White House," July 26, 2016, *New York Times*, www.nytimes.com/2016/07/27/us/politics/michelle-obama-white-house-slavery.html; David Johnson, "Slaves at the White House Did More Than Just Build It," *Time*, July 28, 2016, http://time.com/4428368/white-house-slaves-history; www.aoc.gov/art/other/slave-labor-commemorative-marker.

2. See *Harper's*, November 2000.

3. On modern slavery and human trafficking, see "Worst Child Labor Products," *Huffington Post*, www.huffingtonpost.ca/entry/child-labor-products_n_798601 #gallery/15077/13; Alexander E. M. Hess and Thomas C. Frohlich, "Countries with the Most Enslaved People," *USA Today*, November 23, 2014, www.usatoday .com/story/money/2014/11/23/247-wall-st-countries-most-slaves/70033422; "Countries That Still Have Slavery," The Blog, The Borgen Project, July 4, 2017, https://borgenproject.org/countries-that-still-have-slavery. See also Matthew Karp, "In the 1850s, the Future of American Slavery Seemed Bright," *Aeon*, November 2016, https://aeon.co/ideas/in-the-1850s-the-future-of-american-slavery-seemed-bright.

4. Nicholas Shaxson, *Treasure Islands: Tax Havens and the Men Who Stole the World* (New York: Random House, 2011), 157.

JARED A. BROCK is a film producer and the director of *Josiah,* a documentary about Josiah Henson. He is the author of two previous books, *A Year of Living Prayerfully* and *Bearded Gospel Men*, and his writing has appeared in *Esquire, Huffington Post*, and *Writer's Digest*.

Photo credit: Michelle Amy

PublicAffairs is a publishing house founded in 1997. It is a tribute to the standards, values, and flair of three persons who have served as mentors to countless reporters, writers, editors, and book people of all kinds, including me.

I. F. STONE, proprietor of *I. F. Stone's Weekly*, combined a commitment to the First Amendment with entrepreneurial zeal and reporting skill and became one of the great independent journalists in American history. At the age of eighty, Izzy published *The Trial of Socrates*, which was a national bestseller. He wrote the book after he taught himself ancient Greek.

BENJAMIN C. BRADLEE was for nearly thirty years the charismatic editorial leader of *The Washington Post*. It was Ben who gave the *Post* the range and courage to pursue such historic issues as Watergate. He supported his reporters with a tenacity that made them fearless and it is no accident that so many became authors of influential, best-selling books.

ROBERT L. BERNSTEIN, the chief executive of Random House for more than a quarter century, guided one of the nation's premier publishing houses. Bob was personally responsible for many books of political dissent and argument that challenged tyranny around the globe. He is also the founder and longtime chair of Human Rights Watch, one of the most respected human rights organizations in the world.

•　　•　　•

For fifty years, the banner of Public Affairs Press was carried by its owner Morris B. Schnapper, who published Gandhi, Nasser, Toynbee, Truman, and about 1,500 other authors. In 1983, Schnapper was described by *The Washington Post* as "a redoubtable gadfly." His legacy will endure in the books to come.

Peter Osnos, *Founder*